From Coppenthorpe to Copmanthorpe

Aspects of life in an Ainsty village

From Coppenthorpe to Copmanthorpe

Aspects of life in an Ainsty village

South Ainsty Archaeological Society
2010

First published in 2010 by South Ainsty Archaeological Society
c/o St Mary's House
66 Bootham
York
YO30 7BZ
Copyright © 2010 Individual authors and South Ainsty Archaeological Society
The moral right of the authors has been asserted.
British Library Cataloguing in Publication Data
A catalogue card for this book is available from the British Library
Page design and typesetting by Carnegie Publishing Ltd
Printed and bound by: Information Press, Oxford
Softback ISBN: 978-0-9567168-0-4
Hardback ISBN: 978-0-9567168-1-1

Front cover: Copmanthorpe village from Temple Lane, 1972 (from an oil painting by Betty Wood)

Contents

List of figures

Abbreviations

BI	Borthwick Institute, University of York
CL	Copmanthorpe Library, York Library Services
EYCRO	East Yorkshire County Record Office
NA	National Archives, Kew
NYCRO	North Yorkshire County Record Office
PRO	Public Record Office
SS	Surtees Society
VCH	Victoria County History
WYL	West Yorkshire Library (now part of WYJAS)
WYJAS	West Yorkshire Joint Archive Services (Leeds)
WYDR	West Yorkshire Deeds Registry (Wakefield)
YAJ	Yorkshire Archaeological Journal
YAS	Yorkshire Archaeological Society
YASRS	Yorkshire Archaeological Society Record Series
YCA	York City Archives
YCRL	York City Reference Library
YFHS/YFS	York Family History Society
nd	No date

Preface and Acknowledgements

COPMANTHORPE TODAY IS A 'COMMUTER' village, hardly separated from the City of York. Much of its population leaves each morning for York and other towns and cities across West Yorkshire and returns each evening. You can stand in the compact centre of the village by St Giles church, the Royal Oak and the green, and survey the new and what is left of the old. The Indian restaurant and the Co-op store stand cheek by jowl with the Victorian farmhouses and the war memorial. This book sprang from a desire by members of this village community, along with a few 'outsiders', to record how the village became what it is today.

From Coppenthorpe to Copmanthorpe grew out of *The Copmanthorpe Story*, written by a former villager, Jean Johnson, in 1983 at a time when the village was undergoing immense change. *The Copmanthorpe Story* was an attempt to compile a brief history before memories of 'how it was' were lost. The present authors were lucky to have not only Jean Johnson's work, but also two other important sources. In the 1970s, an oral history project had recorded many of the older villagers' recollections of life in the early 20th century and these have proved a rich seam of information. Meanwhile, throughout the 1960s and 70s, long-time resident Ernest Sanderson was busy with his camera, photographing life in the village. As can be seen from the picture credits, this book would have been much the poorer without his pictures.

The present book is the work of no fewer than sixteen people under the auspices of the South Ainsty Archaeological Society, a small group formed in 2004 to investigate the history of the area known as the South Ainsty. This area is defined by the Ouse to the east, the Wharfe to the south and the present A64 road to the west. Within this triangle lie several historic villages, including Copmanthorpe, Bolton Percy, Appleton Roebuck and Acaster Malbis, as well as several smaller settlements. All appear in Domesday Book. The history of several of the villages had already been explored by individuals who became members of the Society,[1] but there was no published history of Copmanthorpe. The Society's initial focus of interest was on the supposed-site of the Knights Templar preceptory at Copmanthorpe, culminating in an exploratory excavation in 2006 (see chapter 2), but members were keen to see this work incorporated into the wider history of the village.

The present book is not a definitive history – authors have written on subjects that interest them and individual voices can be clearly heard – but we have tried to give a feel for the development of the village since the Norman Conquest. There are inevitably gaps, such as the Reformation and the chaotic Civil War period, when few records survive, but we believe the result is a far wider and deeper knowledge of the history of the village than before. Writing it has been a pleasure: over numerous meetings in the St Giles Centre and around various dining tables, new skills have been learnt, much knowledge has been passed on, and new friendships have been formed. We hope that the book offers 'something for everyone'.

The authors: Catrina Appleby, Phil Batman, David Brewer, Graham Collett, Doreen Felton, Ruby Foster, Marjorie Harrison, Martin Higginson, Lenore Hill, Ron Hill, Elaine Marshall, John Meredith, Martin Murphy, Mike Rogers, Patrick Solich, Wendy Wright. (We are grateful for the contributions from Alison Sinclair, Martin Pickard and Nigel White.)

The book was edited by Catrina Appleby, Phil Batman, Marjorie Harrison and Mike Rogers. Mike Rogers also undertook the picture editing and has done much to enhance the archive maps and photographs. We are grateful to Frank Grace for many of the modern photographs, and to Catherine Pemberton who undertook the transcription of the Oral History tapes.

Books such as this cannot be written without the help of an enormous number of people. Firstly, thanks are due to the staff at Askham Bryan College; the Borthwick Institute for Archives, University of York; the East Yorkshire Archive Service, Beverley; Hull City Archives; the West Yorkshire Joint Archive Service at both Leeds and Wakefield; John Rylands University Library, Manchester; North Yorkshire County Record Office; York City Archives; York Minster Library Archives; York City Reference Library and the Library Service (particularly the staff at Copmanthorpe Library who have been unfailingly helpful, and David Main, formerly Family and Local History Librarian at City of York Libraries); and the Yorkshire Archaeological Society.

We would like to offer our warmest thanks to all those we have spoken to while carrying out the research for this book, and have especially appreciated the willingness of local people to give access to their photographs, memorabilia, title deeds and other records and to share their memories and their time. We are grateful to: E Allan, N Anderson, A & M Ansell, S & C Arnott, P Barraclough, P Bristowe, C & S Burton, J Burton, D Caunt, P Cavill, A & S Conyers, P Daniels, M Driver, P Eady, A Fowles, R Freedman, D Forth, J Fowler, F Frost, C Godber, E Grossett, R Hall, L Haywood, F Horsley, J & E Howell, J Hudson, T Hudson, W Kendall, J Kenny, C Mace, J Miller, A & J Milner, S Oates, M Pawsey, J Payne, M Pickard, R Piercy, H Schofield, H & M Smith, F Snowden, K Stead, E Steele, L Stone, D Thompson, G Thompson, H Thomlinson, K Thomlinson, M & D Unwin, N White, M Whyman, H & B Wood, J Wright, Revd P Worth and members of the Good Companions Club.

Finally, we would like to thank Copmanthorpe Parish Council, the Marc Fitch Fund and the Yorkshire Architectural and York Archaeological Society for their generous financial support towards the publication of this book.

Copyright

The illustrations have been chosen from a wide range of available material, and those not published here will be retained as an archive of our research.

Picture editing

Where appropriate, some images have been edited digitally to improve clarity and minimise the effects of age and damage on the original.

Notes

1   Appleby C & Smith D *Of Malet, Malbis and Fairfax A History of Acaster Malbis* 2000; Harrison, M J *Four Ainsty Townships The history of Bolton Percy, Appleton Roebuck, Colton and Steeton 1066–1875* 2000; Harrison, M J *The History of Acaster Selby in the parish of Stillingfleet 1066–1875* 2003; Harrison, M J (ed) *Living history in the Ainsty: memories of Appleton Roebuck, Bolton Percy, Colton and Acaster Selby* 2010

CHAPTER ONE

Introduction

CATRINA APPLEBY

T HE VILLAGE OF COPMANTHORPE LIES some 3 miles (5km) south-south-west of the centre of the historic city of York. The history of Copmanthorpe, in common with many other villages around the perimeter of the city, is in some respects closely linked to the fortunes of York while at the same time having its own unique history. For Copmanthorpe that individual history is marked by such factors as its proximity to a Roman road, and the presence of a medieval preceptory of the Knights Templar. The name itself is interesting: in Domesday Book of 1086 it appears as Copeman Torp, derived from the Old Norse kaup-manna, 'of the merchant', and the Old Scandanavian thorp, an outlying farmstead or hamlet, hence 'the outlying farmstead of the merchant' (presumably one resident in York).[1]

Topographically, Copmanthorpe sits to the south of the terminal moraine which runs south from the centre of the city, on the line of Tadcaster Road. We know this ridge of higher ground, left behind as the glaciers retreated at the end of the last Ice Age some 10,000 years ago, was utilised by the Romans for their main road south, but it is highly likely that it has formed a routeway through the low-lying damp ground since prehistoric times. This ridge, which is clearly visible as one approaches from the north, reaches a height of *c* 25m OD on Top Lane. In contrast, much of the rest of the parish consists of low-lying arable land, prone to flooding, dipping to only *c* 10m OD near the Foss. The soils in themselves are quite rich, consisting of layers of alluvium, the fine sediments deposited by the rivers, but the ever-present risk of flooding can make farming quite challenging. Beneath the alluvium lies a heavy layer of clay, frequently brought to the surface by modern deep ploughing. The farms of the area are generally mixed, with both sheep and cattle kept and a variety of crops grown. Until recently, sugarbeet was one of the principal

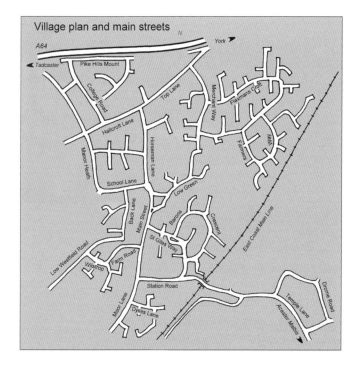

Village plan and main streets

A64
Tadcaster
Pike Hills Mount
York
College Road
Top Lane
Merchant Way
Flaxmans Croft
Hallcroft Lane
Manor Heath
Horseman Lane
Farmers Way
School Lane
Low Green
Back Lane
Main Street
Barons
Crescent
East Coast Main Line
Low Westfield Road
Wilstrop
Farm Road
St Giles Way
Moor Lane
Dykes Lane
Station Road
Temple Lane
Drome Road
Acaster Malbis

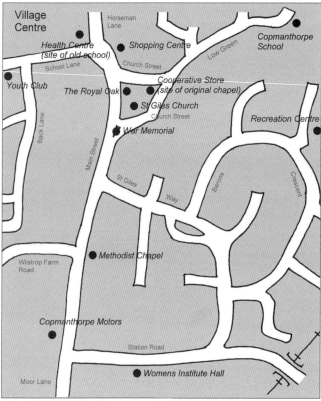

Village Centre
Horseman Lane
Copmanthorpe School
Health Centre (site of old school)
Shopping Centre
Low Green
School Lane
Church Street
Youth Club
Cooperative Store (site of original chapel)
The Royal Oak
St Giles Church
Church Street
Recreation Centre
Back Lane
War Memorial
Main Street
St Giles
Way
Barons
Crescent
Methodist Chapel
Wilstrop Farm Road
Copmanthorpe Motors
Station Road
Moor Lane
Womens Institute Hall

crops, but the demise of the nearby sugarbeet factory has forced a shift to alternatives. Root vegetables in general grow well, with a large acreage given over to potatoes.

Administratively, the villages around York have been shuffled according to the political whim of the day: Copmanthorpe has been variously in the West Riding of Yorkshire, North Yorkshire, and since 1996, the City of York, but historically it belongs in the administrative unit known as the Ainsty, and more specifically, the South Ainsty.

Our knowledge of Copmanthorpe before Domesday is necessarily very limited, but a walk around the village today reveals the survival of key elements in its history and an interesting mix of housing from the last three hundred years. There may well have been a small settlement adjacent to the Roman road during the period of the Roman occupation, but we do not know whether this settlement continued after the departure of the Roman military in the early 5th century. However, the village was clearly well-established by the late 11th century, and by then the focus of settlement lay a few hundred metres south of the line of the road, around the present church. The village is located close enough to the city of York to have fallen within its orbit at various times during its history, and indeed the church of St Giles was a satellite of St Mary Bishophill Junior until 1844.

In essence, Copmanthorpe is a nucleated village centred around Low Green and the twelfth-century church of St Giles, with settlement spreading south along Main Street (**fig 1.1**). Sadly, the medieval core of the village was destroyed in the 1960s to make way for the modern shopping centre.

To the west of Main Street, Back Lane provides the best example of the limit of the original tofts (or plots), although the majority of these now have modern buildings on their western ends. Elsewhere, only vestiges of the crofts and tofts can be identified. To the north, Horseman Lane gives access to the Roman road. The OS maps illustrate graphically how much the village has altered over the course of the twentieth century, most noticeably since the 1970s.

Prehistory

The city of York lies at the centre of the largest river valley in England, some 25 miles (40km) wide at its greatest extent. To understand how this valley formed one must go back over 10,000 years to the end of the last Ice Age, known to geologists as the Devensian, which, from about 20,000 years ago, buried the ground surface of what would become the Vale of York beneath a layer of ice tens of metres thick. This ice sheet originally extended southwards beyond the Humber, but as average temperatures increased the front edge of the glacier retreated, first to the vicinity of Escrick and then to the vicinity of York. At both locations it left behind 'moraines', ridges of clay and rock deposited by the glacier, extending from west to east across the Vale. A second mass of Devensian ice, moving south down the line of the modern North Sea coast, had deposited a further moraine which blocked the drainage of water from in front of the melting ice sheet. This led to the creation of a large lake, known as Lake Humber, about 14,000 years ago. The lake gradually silted up and by about 11,000 years ago – 11,000 years Before Present, or 'BP' – was probably almost dry. Rising temperatures and continuing melting of the ice created rivers which flowed across this silted-up lake bed towards the sea, depositing layers of sand as they went. These were the predecessors of the present rivers of the Vale, the Swale, Ure, Nidd and Wharfe. Between about 11,000 and 10,000 years ago, temperatures once again fell. Although not enough to cause another Ice Age, this did result in a significant lowering of sea level. Consequently, in order to reach this lower sea level, the rivers carved out channels up to 20m deep through the dried-up lake-bed of Lake Humber. As temperatures increased again from *c* 10,000 years ago, these channels became filled with alluvium, river-deposited sediment, until the level of the rivers was close to that of the surrounding land surface, as it is today.[2]

The British Isles were first settled during warm episodes in the period known to archaeologists as the Lower Palaeolithic (Old Stone Age), some 500,000 years ago, but most of the evidence for this settlement, particularly in northern Britain, has been eroded by the subsequent glaciations referred to in the previous section. The earliest settlement remains in east Yorkshire come from sites such as Star Carr in the Vale of Pickering, which dates back some 9500 years. Here, the camp of a group of hunter-gatherers has been excavated, revealing stone tools and butchered animal bones. The settlement at Star Carr was on the shore of a lake and there is evidence that it was reoccupied several times during the period known as

Askham Bog

Just to the north of Copmanthorpe, on the other side of the A64, lies the Yorkshire Wildlife Trust's oldest nature reserve, Askham Bog (**fig 1.2**). In part gifted by Sir Francis Terry and Arnold Rowntree in 1946, the reserve covers an area of *c* 45ha (110 acres) and is the remains of a small valley mire formed between ridges of glacial moraine. The site, originally a fen, then developed as a raised bog but was reduced back to a fen by peat cutting in the Middle Ages. Today it supports an unusual range of both bog and fen flora and fauna and is particularly renowned for its insect life.

1.2 View across Askham Bog
(© Frank Grace)

1.3 Neolithic axes
found at Acaster
Malbis
(© Catrina Appleby)

the Mesolithic or 'Middle Stone Age' (c 10–6000 BP, or 8–4000 BC).

Unlike many other areas of lowland England, finds from the Mesolithic, and indeed the later prehistoric periods, are rare in the Vale of York. We know people were living in northern England at this time because in contrast to the Vale, numerous Mesolithic flint artefacts have been found in the surrounding uplands, to both east and west. It seems that at this time the Vale would have provided rich hunting grounds, particularly around the wetlands left by Lake Humber, but the bands of hunter-gatherers chose to place their transient settlements on higher ground. Perhaps the valley was deemed too dangerous, with extensive areas of woodland where large game roamed. However, it may be that the apparent lack of evidence for Mesolithic activity and settlement in the Vale reflects the comparatively limited amount of archaeological field-work which has been undertaken there, and the particular difficulties of recognising archaeological sites on the surface of this extensive lowland plain. Sites of Mesolithic occupation comparable to Star Carr may there-fore remain to be discovered in the Vale of York, especially around its margins.

When discussing the prehistoric landscape, it is necessary to consider a much wider area than the particular parish or area that is the principal focus of research. This is partly because populations were so much sparser in prehistory, at least until the Iron Age, and hence the chances of finding artefacts and evidence for settlement much lower than is the case for more

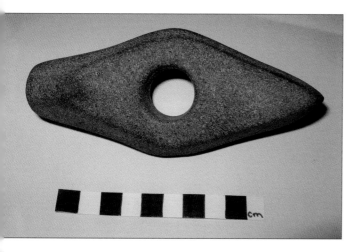

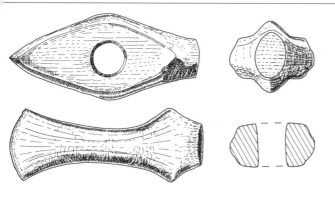

1.4 An Early Bronze Age stone axe hammer found near Appleton Roebuck; length 144mm (Drawing by Helen Gardiner; reproduced by permission of Harold Mytum & Yorkshire Archaeological Society)

recent archaeological periods, but also because patterns of ancient settlement cannot be understood from the study of only a few square kilometres in isolation.

Around 6000 years ago (*c* 4000 BC), there was a major change in the settlement pattern over the British Isles, as communities which had formerly been nomadic hunter-gatherers began to settle in one place and build permanent homes. At the same time, they began to clear the land of trees, plant crops, and keep animals such as sheep and cattle. This period is known as the Neolithic or 'New Stone Age' and lasted for *c* 2000 years. Evidence for clearance includes beautiful stone axes which were traded over long distances. Examples include these (**fig 1.3**) recovered from a field at Acaster Malbis. The Neolithic saw major changes in the way society was organised and operated – this is the period of the earliest phases of Stonehenge, and the construction of monuments such as the massive Thornborough henges near Ripon. However, as with the Mesolithic, there is little evidence for settlement within the Vale of York itself during this period.

A similar pattern prevails in the Bronze Age, which saw the introduction of metal-working to the British Isles. The most prominent archaeological monuments of this period, from *c* 2000 to 800 BC, are the numerous burial mounds or 'barrows'. Once again, the densest concentration of these monuments lies on the surrounding uplands, although archaeologists are beginning to identify such sites in the lowlands through excavation, and some up-standing examples at places such as Skipwith Common.

The introduction of metalworking did not mean that stone tools were abandoned, indeed in the early Bronze Age, metal tools would have been only for the elite. An early Bronze Age stone axe hammer, found some years ago at Woolas Hall, in the neighbouring parish of Appleton Roebuck, illustrates beautifully the skill of the stone worker (**fig 1.4**).[3] The fine-grained dolerite from which it is made is not local, originating probably in County Durham or Northumberland, and demonstrates the trading networks that were operating at this time. Bronze Age palstaves, flat, axe-shaped tools made from bronze, are recorded from both Bishopthorpe and Bolton Percy, these finds confirming at least a limited presence in the Copmanthorpe area during the Bronze Age.[4]

In an article in the *Yorkshire Archaeological Journal* for 1974 entitled 'The Prehistory of the Vale of York', Jeffrey Radley noted the paucity of prehistoric finds from the Vale of York in general, a situation that has not altered dramatically over the last 30 years. More extensive archaeological fieldwork undertaken since the mid-1990s has, however, begun to increase the amount of evidence available, and it seems likely that the apparent paucity of material is largely the result of the problem of visibility of archaeological sites on the sand, silt and clay soils of the Vale. Some sites may indeed be buried and concealed deep beneath alluvium, deposited by repeated flooding of areas of the Vale by its rivers over many centuries.

York, at the centre of the Vale and at the point where the river Ouse, fed further upstream by the Pennine rivers Swale, Ure and Nidd, breaches the raised east–west ridge of glacial moraine, would have been a nodal point for transport throughout prehistory. The earliest boats from the region date to the Bronze Age, and although these were recovered from a site at North Ferriby, on the north bank of the Humber and some distance downstream, their flat bottoms and shallow draft would allowed them easily to navigate the tidal waters further inland. From the site where York now stands, people and materials could have moved both inland and downstream.

As we move into the later prehistoric period – the Iron Age – the number of known sites and finds increases. Several defended settlements of this period have been identified around the edges of the Wolds and North York Moors, but aerial photography is now revealing areas of fields and trackways, often with associated settlements of round houses, in the lowlands. One of the best examples is located only a short distance east of Copmanthorpe, on the east bank of the Ouse at Naburn. These sites are usually situated on slightly higher ground, above normal flood levels, although such sites may still have only been occupied seasonally. Even more exciting are the square-ditched barrows found in a number of places in East Yorkshire, including the Danes' Graves at Skipwith in the Vale of York. These graves date not, as their name might seem to imply, from the Viking period but from the middle to late Iron Age (c 500 BC–AD 71). Some of the excavated examples from the Yorkshire Wolds to the east of the Vale have included rich grave goods such as swords and shields, and even carts (or chariots as they have sometimes been called). A spectacular example, dated to *c* 300 BC, was found in 2003 near Ferrybridge,[5] during the widening of the A1 to the *west* of the Vale. Clearly the Vale was becoming a much busier place in the years before the arrival of the Romans.

The Roman period

The arrival of the Roman Ninth Legion in AD 71 must have made a dramatic impact on the lives of those living in the central area of the Vale. The legion swiftly established its headquarters on land around where York Minster now stands, and built a bridge over the Ouse there. The legionary fortress and its adjacent settlement, named *Eboracum* by the Romans, would have been home to several thousand men, with a huge appetite for foodstuffs of all kinds. There would have been a steady market for cattle in particular, which could be raised locally. The demand for corn would have encouraged the clearance of woodland to create arable fields. The tidal river Ouse became a major routeway, bringing not only foodstuffs but also building materials to the rapidly expanding settlement.

At the same time, the Romans began the construction of a network of roads radiating out from the fortress to control the surrounding area and aid the movement of men and supplies. The principal route south took the line of slightly higher ground left by the retreating glacier, running south-south-west along The Mount and what is now Tadcaster Road. It skirted Askham Bogs to the south on the line of Top Lane, then ran south-west towards Tadcaster along Colton Lane. Where Colton Lane now turns south, the road continued west-southwest, crossing the line of the present A64 in the vicinity of McDonalds and continuing to Tadcaster, Roman *Calcaria*. Here there may have been a fort, controlling the crossing of the Wharfe and the valuable stone quarries which provided much of the stone for the building of *Eboracum*. Excavation in the 1980s revealed definite evidence of Roman settlement in the vicinity of Tadcaster parish church, although it is not clear whether this was military or civilian in character.

At Copmanthorpe, the discovery of Roman pottery and an area of paving adjacent to the line of the road has led archaeologists to suggest that there may have been a settlement somewhere along Colton Lane. Elsewhere in what is now Copmanthorpe parish, any farmsteads would probably have been under the control of the military. Historians have tended to regard Copmanthorpe as a settlement of medieval origin, but its close proximity to both the fortress and the road make it entirely possible that there could have been an agricultural settlement of some kind here, although it may not have looked any different from a late Iron Age one.

The departure of the Roman legions in AD 410 would have had a similarly dramatic impact on the local inhabitants to their arrival almost 350 years previously. Overnight, the market for cattle and foodstuffs would have collapsed, but the local population probably adjusted back to a subsistence economy fairly quickly.

The Early Medieval period

The years after the departure of the Roman legions in AD 410 are traditionally referred to as the Anglo-Saxon period. In Yorkshire, the incomers were principally Angles, and they brought with them distinctive burial practices – primarily cremation in heavily decorated pottery vessels, but also inhumations accompanied by rich artefacts. Early Anglo-Saxon (5th–early 6th century AD) settlements and artefacts are largely confined to the area to the east of the Wolds and Howardian Hills, suggesting control of the area around York may have been in the hands of a group of native Britons until the later 5th or early 6th century.

By the 7th century York was firmly in the control of the Anglian aristocracy and formed part of the Kingdom of Deira. Deira, along with the Kingdom of Bernicia and later Northumbria, came under the rule of Edwin. Edwin, a convert to Christianity, was responsible for the first church dedicated to St Peter at York – the predecessor to the present minster. By the early 8th century York was an important royal and ecclesiastical centre and a well-established European trading settlement. Around the fringes of the Vale of York, a number of important monastic centres had been created, several of which were producing high-quality ecclesiastical sculpture.

All this was to change in the mid-9th century with the arrival of the Viking armies. In AD 866 they captured York, and in AD 876 they settled in Yorkshire, York becoming the Viking capital, Jorvik. By the 10th century a pattern of nucleated villages had developed across Yorkshire, and it is likely that Copmanthorpe, and neighbouring villages such as Acaster Malbis, date from this time. The evidence from Domesday Book (1086) shows that there was already a complex pattern of pre-Norman landowners in the area south of York.

A walk around Copmanthorpe

A walk through the village reveals the survival of an eclectic mix of buildings from the late seventeenth century onwards. Approaching from the south, it is easy to ignore the buildings occupied by Copmanthorpe Motors, but in fact this is housed in old livery stables, with the cart shed at the right-hand end. The chimney at the left-hand end may indicate the location of a forge. Meanwhile Copmanthorpe MoTs, the repair garage, is housed in an agricultural building of a style that is typical of the late eighteenth century in the Vale of York.

Proceeding north along Main Street towards the church, one passes a variety of late nineteenth- and early twentieth-century houses, including some constructed in a type of white brick that was brought in by rail from Scarborough. The majority of these face on to the street, but Beechwood, on the east side, lies gable end on to the road, enabling the main front and garden to face south. Such an arrangement suggests a relatively undeveloped landscape at the time of construction. The garden of this house also includes a mini 'ha-ha', in the style of much grander properties such as Beningbrough Hall.

As one approaches the centre of the village there are several significant buildings, including the old post office (**fig 1.5**), Ivy House Farm, Manor Farm (**fig 1.6**) and Trowel House Farm (see **fig 8.9**). The earliest of these may well be the old post office, which was once a farmhouse dating to the late seventeenth or early eighteenth century. The building, built of brick and rendered, is tall and thin with a steeply pitched roof that could once have been thatched. The neighbouring Manor Farm is of a similar, but probably slightly later date, with more decorative features, including pilaster strips of a kind also seen on the Red House in Duncombe Place, York. To the left of the building lies a wall built of massive limestone blocks, which local tradition says may have been reclaimed from the Knights Templar preceptory. To the rear lies a fascinating complex of brick barns and associated agricultural buildings. Features include a high cart arch, designed to accommodate a loaded hay wagon, and what was probably a threshing barn. The primary access to these is off Back Lane where it is possible to appreciate the full length of the original tofts. The neighbouring Trowel House Farm is perhaps a century later than Manor Farm, dating to the 1830s. Here the slate roof has been added later, and the gable has clearly been raised at some time. Once again the architectural details are typical of the Vale of York.

1.5 The Old Post Office, showing the architectural detail on the gable end
(© Frank Grace)

1.6 The imposing bulk of Manor Farm
(© Frank Grace)

The building which now houses the Royal Oak public house (**fig 1.7**) is recorded as a dwelling in 1793, although its present appearance is very much nineteenth century. At that time it had a blacksmith's attached as well as its own brewhouse; this may have been housed in the low building at the southern end. The pub was probably the final element in the early group of buildings surrounding the twelfth-century church of St Giles.

1.7 The Royal Oak public house (© Frank Grace)

1.8 Swain's Butchers Shop, Church Street. Originally a pair of brick cottages, now knocked into one but retaining the through passage at the left-hand end (© Frank Grace)

The present complex of buildings to the north of the church, which houses the Co-op, at first glance appears to be devoid of architectural merit, but in fact the Co-op's store room on the east side once housed an early Methodist chapel (see **chapter 5**).

To the east of the triangle of land occupied by the church lie a number of interesting buildings, including Ivy House Farm, of which more later (see **fig 3.7**). Next door is the imposing bulk of the old vicarage (No. 3 Main Street), built of red brick in 1866 and standing in extensive grounds (see **fig 5.3**). Moving north, hidden away off Stakers Orchard, lies what may be the earliest surviving cottage in the village, dating to the 1600s. Once gain the steep pitch of the roof suggests it would originally have been thatched. Meanwhile the butcher's shop is a typical late Victorian pair of utilitarian brick cottages, now knocked into one but preserving the through passage at the north end (**fig 1.8**).

To the north of the church, the recently restored Blow's Cottages (**fig 1.9**) are a pleasing survival in an area blighted by development in the 1960s. This terrace of four cottages dating to 1826 once stood adjacent

1.9   The newly restored Blow's Cottages (© Frank Grace)

to the timber-framed 'manor house' (see chapter 3), although research for this book suggests it may not have been one of the original manors, merely a late survival from the medieval period.

Clustered around Low Green are a number of farmhouses, including Croft Farmhouse, an excellent example of a solid Georgian house from the early eighteenth century. At this end of the village, several properties are built to face south, taking advantage of the more irregular layout. Tucked in between modern infill are a few barns and cottages, reminders of the fact that until very recently this was primarily an agricultural community. The farmhouses are the principal survivors, providing some excellent examples of Yorkshire vernacular architecture of the eighteenth and nineteenth centuries. Many of the labourers who worked on these farms would have occupied small, less substantial buildings which have been swept away, allowing more modern buildings to occupy their plots and create the varied pattern we see today.

Notes

1 Smith, A H *Place-names of the West Riding of Yorkshire Pt 4 Wapentakes of Barkston Ash, Skyrack and Ainsty* EPNS XXXIII 1961 p 227

2 For a good summary of the archaeology of the Vale of York, see M Whyman & A J Howard, *Archaeology and Landscape in the Vale of York* (YAT, 2005)

3 Mytum, H 'A Battle-axe from Appleton Roebuck', *Yorks Arch J* 60, 1988 pp 175–6

4 Radley, J 'The prehistory of the Vale of York', *Yorks Arch J* 46, 1974 pp 10–22

5 'The Ferrybridge chariot burial', *Current Archaeology* 191, 2004, pp 481–5

CHAPTER TWO

Copmanthorpe in the Middle Ages

MARJORIE HARRISON

S OURCES FOR THE MEDIEVAL HISTORY of Copmanthorpe are
sparse and fragmented but we can begin with the Domesday
survey of 1086 which gives the first description of the village and
its environs. In 1086 Copmanthorpe was in two parts; one contained
about 270 acres (109 ha) of arable land and was held by Erneis de Burun
(a founder of Selby Abbey). Three villagers and two smallholders were
recorded there with one plough between them. The other estate, a larger
share with about 450 acres (182 ha) of arable land, was held by a Count
W, sometimes thought to be William Rufus, the son of the Conqueror.[1]
There is no real evidence to confirm this so the ownership of this portion
of the vill remains shadowy. Copmanthorpe was then worth 40s, twice as
much as its pre-Conquest valuation.[2]

There were five households in Erneis de Burun's portion of
Copmanthorpe with enough status to be noted in Domesday. This
seems a very small population for a village which had doubled in value
since 1066 and there would certainly be others less worthy of note living
there. For some reason Copmanthorpe had bucked the trend; most
other townships in the Ainsty were reduced in value through the vicious
retaliation in 1069 by William I after rebellion in the North. This
was a time when houses and crops were burned, cattle killed and the
local population displaced. Copmanthorpe could perhaps have escaped
serious destruction if it did indeed had a royal connection through
Count W; a similar situation occurred at neighbouring Acaster Malbis
which was held by William Malet, the king's commander in the north,
or his son Robert. If devastation had occurred, a quick recovery may
have taken place, helped by its location close to the old Roman road
(known as the Streete) in a place where routes crossed near to the city of
York. The trading or market function thought to have been long estab-

lished in the village may have been disrupted for a time but, as the rural economy began to recover, many small transactions made by people bringing goods and stock from a wider area may gradually have brought prosperity back to the village.

The central focus of Copmanthorpe is unchanged and although no church was recorded at the time of the Domesday survey, the area now occupied by the row of shops, the church and the Royal Oak was the nucleus of the village in 1086. Things would have looked very different then; small timber and thatched houses would have clustered around a manor house – not a substantial affair – where the manor courts were held and villagers came to pay rents and do other business with the lord's bailiff or steward. The blacksmith's shop, traditionally sited in the centre of a village, probably also stood there and the surrounding greens were much bigger (or at least were not covered in tarmac). St Giles' well on Low Green may have helped to determine this early settlement pattern, since its water source may once have been a spring that was regarded as holy.

The villagers had a substantial amount of land already cleared and cultivated and the open fields (York Field and High and Low West Field) were well established, along with another which later came to be known as Temple Field (see **fig 8.5**). However, the villagers, with their single plough, would have been hard pressed to cultivate even a quarter of this. Trade, rather than the internal rural economy, is more likely to have brought increased wealth as the village attempted to regain its previous agricultural state. Domesday does not mention any woodland in the township although there would undoubtedly have been some there, as well as areas of common grazing; even so, a substantial part must have remained uncultivated. The whole area of Copmanthorpe consisted of about 1600 acres (647 ha); it was a tiny part of the estates of great men whose stewards were sent to collect rents and hold manor courts at regular intervals.

Copmanthorpe contained two estates within the single township. Erneis de Burun's portion was recorded as the manor, and those men holding land belonging to Count W would have to attend Erneis' manor court (or some other) and pay their manorial dues there. There are many questions left unanswered by the Domesday survey regarding the pattern of landholding in the village at this time.

Land holding

The Ros family

The portion held by Erneis quickly came into the hands of the Trussebut family and can be reasonably well traced down to its eventual ownership by the Knights Templar. The Trussebut Fee had been divided in 1193 between three sisters: Roese, Hillary and Agatha. Roese became the wife of Everard Ros II and their son, Robert Ros, clearly had an interest in the lands belonging to his mother and aunts as during his lifetime he was able to give the part of Copmanthorpe belonging to Hillary to the Knights Templar, along with his mother's lands in Ribston and Hunsingore. Robert is thought to have died in 1227; the date of his mother's death is uncertain, but his aunts survived him and the remainder of the fee did not become re-united until their respective deaths in 1241 and 1245 when Robert's son William inherited.[3]

The Malbis family

Count W's estate in Copmanthorpe however is more complicated. To sum up briefly, it was held by Hugh Malbis in the mid-12th century. (Hugh's grandson, Richard, was named as 'Mala-bestia' or evil beast after his involvement with the massacre of the Jews in 1190.[4]) Count W's holding was still intact and in Malbis hands in 1284/5,[5] running alongside the Knights Templar estate. The Templars had been lords of the manor of Copmanthorpe but in 1316, some time after the Order had been dissolved, William Malbis was named as sole lord of Copmanthorpe[6] showing that a single manor was still in place in the township and the family must have somehow acquired the manorial rights either from the king or the Knights Hospitallers, who were eventually granted the Templar estates after the suppression.

The Fairfax connection

In the mid-14th century, to raise funds before going on pilgrimage, Walter Malbis pledged his property to members of the Fairfax family and made Richard Fairfax his heir with one essential condition that he changed his name to Malbis. A journey to the Holy Land was fraught with hazards and Walter was not only raising money for his trip but acknowledging that he may not return. He did survive and came home to find that his lands were in possession of his niece, whose husband was Sir William St Quintin. A court case ensued with no clear outcome but in 1368 St Quintin granted the lands to William Fairfax. Walter had disappeared from the scene, the date of his death is unknown, and eventually, after the death of his father, and uncle (John of Gilling), Richard Fairfax re-gained Walter's lands and adopted the Malbis name.

After Richard's death in 1401, infighting broke out in the family. Isabella, his widow, petitioned Parliament in 1402 saying she had been peacefully seized [put in legal possession of] of the manors 'then one Richard Fairfax, with a great number of armed persons, ejected her'. She was told to resort to common law and so sued the mob. By now, Isabella had remarried; her new husband was Nicholas Saxton. Sixteen of her aggressors were named in court: five of them were Fairfaxes, and there were others all armed with swords and bows and arrows. She claimed that they had forcibly broken into her houses and closes in Acaster Malbis, Copmanthorpe and Scawton, killed livestock worth ten marks, taken away oxen and bullocks worth £30 and trampled and consumed her corn and grass valued at 100s. Tenants had been beaten and threatened with death or mutilation so that they dare not work the land or do any other business for her, and she lost the rents and services of her tenants.

Arguments and wrangling went on in the courts with accusations of fraud and collusion on both sides, and disagreements continued about the wardship of Richard Fairfax/Malbis' heir, William. According to Isabella, at that time the manor of Copmanthorpe was worth 10 marks – £6 13s 4d.[7] The case dragged on until 1407, when Isabella was forced to concede defeat.

Copmanthorpe continued in Fairfax ownership in a more peaceable fashion and was eventually granted or sold to the Vavasour family at a date unknown although they were said to be lords of the manor in 1521.[8] Thomas Vavasour died seized of the manor in 1558 and it continued in Vavasour hands, occasionally being leased to others, until the end of the 16th century.

The village

Domesday shows us that by 1086 the village was prospering and during the next 50 years, the layout changed as the population grew. Part of High West Field, adjoining what was then the green, was taken in to provide a planned development of houses with attached land, often known as tofts and crofts (although in Copmanthorpe the term garth frequently replaces

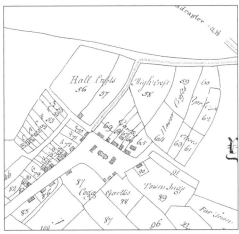

the word croft). These properties utilised furlongs already cultivated; some of their boundaries today still show a characteristic reverse-S swing created by the team of oxen swinging round at the end of a furrow to plough the next (**fig 2.1**). (The reversible plough had yet to be invented.) The church of St Giles was established in the middle of the green and a map first drawn in 1722 and copied in 1779 gives a good indication of the medieval layout of the village (**fig 2.2**).[9]

By 1200 Copmanthorpe may have expanded its cultivated land by clearing woodland and waste ground as more food was needed for the growing population in and around York. Once the Knights Templars had established their preceptory, more clearance took place on the marginal land they had been given lying near to the parish boundary. The larger village houses – timber-framed thatched structures – spread down Main Street from the central nucleus of the church and the greens.

Each house stood in a yard with barns and other buildings – the toft – and beyond was the garth or small field which had many purposes: bee hives, calves, orchards, wood piles, chickens, all would be found there. Today there are still two examples of tofts on Main Street: Manor Farm and Trowell House both stand in long yards with their farm buildings separated by Back Lane from their long-gone garths beyond. (Back Lane clearly arose from a need for the farmers to access High West Field, thus dividing their properties.) Smaller cottages with little or no land appeared as the population grew; these were sometimes built on the waste land which although owned by the lord of the manor was regarded as common within the village. This kind of land comprised the greens and also wide grass verges alongside the village street, so the cottages squeezed on to them had no attached garths.

Evidence from the Knights Templar valuations (made in 1308 after the

2.1 The curving medieval boundary is clearly visible to the rear of Manor Farm (Sanderson Collection, Copmanthorpe Library; York Library Service)

2.2 Extract from the 1722/79 estate plan by Edward Watterson, showing the centre of the village (Reproduced by permission of the Borthwick Institute, University of York; CC D/C 11/21)

preceptory in Copmanthorpe was dissolved) show that there was a wind-mill on the Templar lands near the township boundary. There was also a manor house with a dovecot, four larger farms and 21 cottages. The situation of the latter are not described but we can assume that these were the village houses along the west side of Main Street and on Low Green, to the north of the church. The population can be estimated at about 120 from this evidence.

The suppression of the Knights Templar in 1308 would undoubtedly have had an impact on the village, bringing uncertainty about the future. The preceptory lands continued to be farmed, initially for the king and then, after being given to the Knights Hospitallers, they were leased to Walter Fauconberg and run as an estate.

The Black Death overtook the country in the middle of the 14th century and Copmanthorpe would have been just as badly affected as all the other surrounding villages, although the poll tax return of 1379, nearly 30 years after the plague, shows that the township had a healthy population.[10] Fifty-one people are listed and of these, fifteen had family or servants living in the same house who were liable for tax, indicating that there were about 36 households and a possible population of 170. (Neighbouring villages seem to have been equally populous.) Villagers had recovered very quickly from those terrible years when a large part of the population died and there was no one to bring in the harvest or plough and sow the fields, or to tend the stock which died in the barns and fields due to lack of feed and care. Perhaps Copmanthorpe's location so close to York, one of the principal cities of the north of England, made it easy to re-establish a market for the villagers' produce.

The land which comprised the 'Templar' estate would also have suffered during the plague years. There is no clear evidence of how it fared after Walter Fauconberg's time, although the Malbis/Fairfax documents suggest they held it until the mid-16th century, when it again reverted to the Crown after the dissolution of the monasteries (the Order of Knights Hospitallers was dissolved at this time) and was then leased to Thomas Vavasour who already held the manor.

The 1379 tax return shows the trades being carried on in the village: a weaver, tailor, carpenter and blacksmith are all listed, along with the 'firmarius', Thomas Multon, who was a kind of bailiff, running the lands belonging to the lord of the manor and dealing with the day-to-day business. Most people paid a tax of 4d (2p), the tradesmen 6d (2½p) and Thomas Multon a shilling (5p). No merchant is listed, suggesting that by this time Copmanthorpe was no longer functioning as a market place, although goods would no doubt be sold in the city. The township was on a par with neighbouring villages such as Acaster Selby and Appleton Roebuck in terms of its size and occupations.[11]

This picture of medieval Copmanthorpe is based on fragments of evidence; what is clear is that its geographical position on the Streete provided good access to the city of York and beyond. This, along with the short distance to the river Ouse at Acaster Malbis, gives credibility to the idea that it had standing as some kind of market place for at least part of this period. It later became a rich agricultural community as the wills and inventories of the 16th and 17th centuries show (see chapter 4).

The Knights Templar in Copmanthorpe

Documentary evidence tells us there was a small preceptory of the Knights Templar at Copmanthorpe, a basic farming operation with agricultural buildings and a complex of hall, kitchen and church occupied by the Knights and their servants. It probably existed for about 100 years from *c* 1210 until 1308.

The Knights Templar

In the early 12th century, two orders with similar aims were established. The First Crusade had identified a need for safe houses for pilgrims en-route to the Holy City and also during their stay in Jerusalem. The Knights of St John, based at their church of St John in Jerusalem, were established by 1113 for that purpose and became known as the Knights Hospitallers. The Knights of the Temple had different aims: they pledged to provide protection for pilgrims on their journey and sought recognition in 1127. Their headquarters were at the Temple of Solomon in Jerusalem. Both were religious orders and attracted many donations of land and money in England and abroad.

The Knights Templar founded preceptories to farm and manage their land, either donated or purchased. These were viable, well-managed economic holdings, generating wealth which supported the work of the order in the Holy Land. By the end of the 12th century there were about 34 in total of both Templar and Hospitaller foundations in England and Wales, some coinciding with the preaching [launching] of the Second and Third crusades in the 1140s and 1190s. Almost 50 more of both orders were established during the 13th century. The Templars had a strong base in the north of England, their Yorkshire estates being valued at a quarter of their total possessions in England at the beginning of the 14th century when the order was threatened.[12] Preceptors and a small number of knights, along with others of a lower social status, managed these estates and outlying land. They lived in common and observed vows of poverty, chastity and obedience as in any other monastic order, but were not enclosed.

The Order of the Knights Templar benefited from the generosity of both the Ros and Malbis families in the 13th century and it was their gifts of land, along with other small donations, which allowed the preceptory to be established on the outskirts of the village.

Documentary evidence

In a charter dated between 1206 and 1212, Robert Ros gave to the Knights land at Hunsingore and Cattal belonging to his mother, Roese, although she may have been dead by then.[13] In 1227, on his deathbed, he gave Great Ribston – again his mother's land.[14] Copmanthorpe is not mentioned in that charter but is included in a later document, dated 1258, in which his son, William, confirmed 'his father's gifts' to the Knights.[15] Robert's earlier gifts to the Order allow us to guess that the foundation of the preceptory at Copmanthorpe was in the first quarter of the 13th century. William de Malbis was also mentioned as a founder in later evidence, given at the suppression (see below). Both William and Robert were strongly associated with the crusades.

Apart from a single court case of 1252,[16] an entry in Kirkby's Inquest (1284/5),[17] and a reference to Robert Reygate as preceptor of Copmanthorpe in 1292,[18] no other evidence has been found for the preceptory itself until the suppression of the Order by the king in 1308. Several documents survive relating to the suppression which really begin to put flesh on the bones of the story but they also pose questions about the donors and their gifts. An inquiry into the lands held by the Knights showed that they held a manor in Copmanthorpe and property there consisting of the manor house and dovecot, the rents from 4 messuages (larger houses) and 21 cottages in the township, about 300 acres (122 ha) of land, and a windmill. The documents include an inventory of the chapel, which was well but not richly furnished, and the kitchen containing cauldrons, pitchers and equipment for brewing and baking. The grange and granary held grain and there were sheep and other livestock. A later inventory of 1311 listed the goods in the hall: a board with trestles, two tables and two forms. Some time had elapsed since the property was seized and it is quite possible that other furniture and goods had been appropriated, either by the administrators or others, but the evidence is telling for a very basic, plainly furnished property, the preceptor and any other knights and servants living in a small complex with a hall, chapel, and kitchen. Although not described, this must have been in the inner court designed to separate the religious life from the world outside. The outer court held a large granary and barn. Other housing for the animals (eleven plough oxen, six plough horses, three ploughs, and four cart horses and more) is not described in the inventory but must have been there. Also included were ten oxen belonging to the king en-route for Scotland – this preceptory, like others, was being used as a staging post during the time of wars against the Scots.

The estate at Copmanthorpe was linked to Templar land holdings at Naburn, Stamford Bridge and the Castle Mills in York. The outlying land may have been managed from Copmanthorpe but the extent of the preceptor's involvement in the administration of the Castle Mills is unclear.

On the continent, the suppression of the Order began in October 1307 but in England, it was not until 15 December that the king, Edward II, began the process of closure in Yorkshire when he issued a writ to the sheriff of York to assemble 24 men on 7 January 1308. Meantime, a writ of arrest had been issued on 20 December and was executed on 8 January. The inquisitions and inventories were taken very quickly after this once the knights and their sergeants were in custody and the king's men were instructed to take over the properties, continuing to run them on behalf of the crown.

It is at this point that confusion arises over the founder. Looking back, Kirkby's Inquest held in 1284/5 showed that of the five and a half carucates of land in Copmanthorpe, two and a half were held by the Knights Templar of the gift of Robert de Ros and the other portion of the vill was held by Richard Malbis[19] which seems to be a very clear statement, but later evidence confuses the issue.

An inquisition was held on 10 June 1308 before the sheriff of York when the jury gave an account of the Copmanthorpe lands and the various donors,[20] naming Sir William Malbis and John of Garton. No direct reference is made to Robert de Ros and in September of that year William Malbis was named specifically as the donor of the manor of Copmanthorpe 'for the maintenance of a certain chapel to celebrate [masses in] for the souls of his ancestors and their heirs and that chantry is worth 5 marks annually'.[21] This could be a complete red herring, William de Malbis being confused with William de Ros, who, although one step removed, would undoubtedly have been involved on behalf of his father. The extent also names William de Malbis as the donor of 180 acres of arable land – one and a half carucates – given in two blocks, one of which held the sheep-fold. All the rest of the land described was said to have been 'acquired' by the knights and may indicate purchase rather than gifts.

Given the confusion over founders and dates it may be safer just to assume that the preceptory in Copmanthorpe was in existence by 1220 or thereabouts and that the main donors were the Ros family with additional gifts (or purchases) of land in Copmanthorpe from William de Malbis, Robert or John of Garton, and an unidentifed member of the Fauconberg family along with just two acres from Isote Osbertson.

After the suppression of the Order the pope decreed that the Templar estates should be taken over by the Knights Hospitallers but the king had other thoughts; he kept some in hand and granted others to courtiers and it was several years before the situation was resolved. An Act of Parliament in 1324, putting the Hospitallers in legal possession of Templar estates, confirmed the pope's decree. At that time Thomas Larcher was the prior of the order but he had been superceded by 1328 and the Hospitallers' finances were in chaos. By 1338 order had once again been imposed and we can see what had happened to individual estates in the accounts of all their properties. Sometime before 1328, the Templar estate in Copmanthorpe was leased to Sir Walter Fauconberg for life by Thomas Larcher (this arrangement may have been made in 1324). It was described as: 'One messuage, 3 carucates of land, 70s annual rents, 10 acres of pasture' for which Sir Walter paid £10 per year.[22] The lease did not include the manor of which there was no mention.

This would be a convenient holding for Sir Walter, who held land in the adjacent township of Appleton Roebuck. The hall and farm buildings may have been retained and evidence from a visitation in 1411 shows that the chapel was still in use at that time. The vicar and parishioners of St Mary Bishophill Junior, York, of which parish Copmanthorpe was a detached portion, reported that there was a chapel called 'le Tempyll juxta Copmanthorpe' in which a priest called Andreas Payntor had celebrated masses for many years dishonestly. They also said that the stone walls of the chapel, the bell tower and also the roof were in need of repair.[23]

The property was kept as a compact holding and seems to have been associated with the preceptory at Ribston until the Reformation, when the Hospitallers' property was taken in hand by the king in 1540 after the order was dissolved. In 1541 Thomas Vavasour was the collector of rents for Copmanthorpe on behalf of the crown, a convenient arrangement since he was also the farmer or lessee of the manor and demesne of Templecopmanthorpe, as the village had become known by this time.[24]

Map evidence

The earliest map of Copmanthorpe is an estate plan of 1779 based on an earlier survey of 1722 (see chapter 7).[25] This shows a profusion of small enclosures called Temple Garths and Temple Lees, in addition to Temple

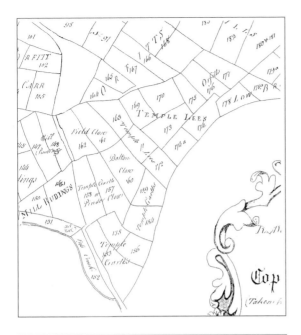

2.3 Extract from 1722/79 estate plan by Edward Watterson, showing the area of the Knights Templar preceptory
(Reproduced by permission the Borthwick Institute, University of York; CC D/C 11/21)

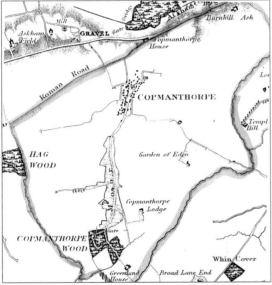

2.4 Robert Cooper's 1832 Map of *York and the Ainsty*, showing the area of the preceptory
(Reproduced by permission of York Library Service)

2.5 Detail from OS 1st edition 6" map showing site of preceptory
(Reproduced by permission of York Library Service)

Field, one of the large open fields of Copmanthorpe (**fig 2.3**). The 'garth' place name is indicative of land attached to a dwelling such as a garden or close; this might suggest the position of the Knights' hall.

Although Robert Cooper's map of York & the Ainsty, published in 1832,[26] does not identify the site, it shows how the small enclosures seen on the 1779 plan relate to the village – they lie well away, near a stream which defines both parish and township boundary (**fig 2.4**). This kind of marginal land on the outside edge is very typical of donations to religious houses; land not yet cleared or cultivated, or underused, was worth little to the donor but could be transformed by the will and energy of a religious house to create wealth for a greater cause.

The 1st edition OS map (1851) actually identifies the preceptory in the area of the small enclosures and shows a pond and a small rectangular feature (**fig 2.5**). This area was the subject of an archaeological dig in 2006 (see below) and has now been eliminated as the site.[27]

Two 19th-century sources talk of landscape evidence but do not clearly identify where the features lay – James Raine writing in 1858[28] said 'some traces of their mansion may still be seen', and Bulmer's Directory for 1890[29] says of Temple Field 'mounds which may still be seen in the field, probably mark the site' – although this conflicts with the OS evidence.

Excavations at the Knights Templar Site

Catrina Appleby

Soon after the SAAS was formed in 2004, attention was focused on the supposed site of a Knights Templar preceptory situated on the eastern edge of the parish. As explained above, there was sound documentary evidence for the presence of a preceptory, but no firm physical evidence. Aerial photography had, however, revealed so-called 'soil marks' at the location marked by the Ordnance Survey as the site of the preceptory (see **fig 2.5**). Fieldwalking revealed large quantities of medieval tile on the field, and a small amount of medieval pottery (**fig 2.6**). There were also reports of dressed limestone blocks being turned up by the plough, while an appeal to local villagers revealed several significant medieval artefacts had been found on the field. It was agreed that there was sufficient evidence to warrant an exploratory excavation of the site and a successful bid was made to the National Lottery's *Awards for All* scheme for money to fund this.

The excavation took place over four days in September

2.6   Medieval tile recovered from the Knights Templar site
(© Catrina Appleby)

2.7 Excavations in progress at the Knights Templar site, 2006 (© Catrina Appleby)

2006, when two trenches were opened over features visible on the aerial photographs. This was a community excavation, with labour provided by members of the Society and interested local people (**fig 2.7**). Sadly, none of the features revealed in the trenches could be attributed to the medieval period; they consisted of field drains, the remains of post-medieval and modern field boundaries, and a back-filled pond. This pond features on the 1st edition OS map and it had been thought that it might be a medieval fishpond, but although thick layers of silt were encountered in the bottom, below the rubbish tipped in by the farmer thirty years ago, no dating evidence was recovered.

We now believe that many of the soil marks visible on the aerial photographs are damp patches left by seasonal flooding of the field. However, the quantity of medieval tile and pottery that continues to be found on the field suggests the preceptory *did* lie in this general location; the challenge is to locate it precisely. It is hoped that further work, particularly geophysical survey, will help us to do this.

The excavation itself was hugely enjoyable, helped by the fact that we had fantastic weather all weekend, and it allowed many people to experience an archaeological excavation for the first time.

Notes

1   Faull, M & Stinson, M *Domesday Yorkshire* pt 2 Chichester 1986 *n* SW, AN2

2   Faull, M & Stinson, M op cit f 328c & f 379d

3   Clay, C T (ed) *Early Yorkshire Charters* vol 10 Trussebut Fee YASRS extra series vol 8 1955 p 25

4   Dobson, R B *The Jews of Medieval York and the Massacre of March 1190* Borthwick paper no 45 (1974) p 33

5   Skaife, R H (ed) *Kirkby's Inquest, Knights Fees & the Nomina Villarum for Yorkshire* SS vol 49 1866 p 2

6   Ibid p 343

7   Baildon, W P Acaster Malbis and the Fairfax family in *YAJ* vol 19 1907 passim; Brown, W (ed) *Cartulary of Guisbrough Priory* vol 2 SS vol 89 1891 p 61*n* & Appleby, C A & Smith, D B *Of Malet, Malbis and Fairfax: a history of Acaster Malbis* Acaster Malbis 2000 p 15

8   Johnson, J *The Copmanthorpe Story* Copmanthorpe 1995 p 9

9   BI CC D/C 11/21 1772/1779 map

10 Clark G (ed) West Riding Poll Tax and Lay Subsidy Rolls 2 Ric II in *YAJ* vol 7 1882 p 178

11 Clark, G (ed) op cit

12 Burton, J E The Knights Templar in Yorkshire in the twelfth century: a reassessment in *Northern History* vol 27 1991 p 27

13 Clay, C T (ed) Early Yorkshire Charters vol 10 *Trussebut Fee* YASRS extra series vol 8 1955 p 25

14 Ibid

15 Ibid

16 Clay, C T (ed) *Yorkshire Assize Rolls* YASRS vol 44 1910 p 46

17 Skaife, R (ed) *Kirkby's Inquest* SS vol 49 1866 p 24

18 VCH *Yorkshire* vol 3 p 257*b* – he was keeper of the Castle Mills in York

19 Skaife, R (ed) *Kirkby's Inquest etc* SS vol 49 1866 p 24

20 PRO E142/17

21 PRO E142/18

22 Larking, L B *The Knights Hospitallers in England* Camden Society Original Series 1855 p 143

23 Raine, J (ed) *The fabric rolls of York Minster* SS vol 35 1858 p 250

24 Crossley, E W Documents relating to the lands of the preceptories of the Knights Hospitallers in *Miscellanea* vol 4 YASRS vol 94 1936 p 133

25 BI CC D/C 11/21 Plan of Copmanthorpe 1772/799

26 YCRL *Map of York & the Ainsty* by Robert Cooper 1832

27 Appleby, C A & Harrison, M J Searching for the Knights Templar at Copmanthorpe Unpublished report by South Ainsty Archaeological Society 2007

28 Raine, A J (ed) *The fabric rolls of York Minster* SS vol 35 1858 p 250

29 Bulmer, T *History & Directory of North Yorkshire* 1890

Chapter Three

The Manor of Copmanthorpe 1600–1800

Marjorie Harrison

The period of the Vavasour lordship of the manor was over by 1599 when Thomas Vavasour and his wife Mary sold it to Richard Swale, a London lawyer. He was a Doctor of Law and a Master in the court of Chancery.[1] So, the ownership was now more distant and the manor had been reduced to a revenue-producing property. In 1610 the manor came into the hands of another Londoner, Robert Sprignell, a gentleman, who that year bought it from Sir Edmund Hildesley, the sheriff of Yorkshire.[2] (After the death of Dr Swale, Sir Edmund had married Dame Susan Swale, his widow, and so acquired her property.) Robert's father, Richard, also had an interest in the manor; he was created a baronet in 1641 becoming Baron Sprignell of Copmanthorpe before dying in 1659. Robert himself was married to Ann Livesey, the daughter of Sir Michael Livesey, one of the signatories of the death warrant of King Charles I. Ann Sprignell, Robert's sister, had married Sir Robert Harding, a London lawyer. All these characters played a part in the history of Copmanthorpe from afar. The family held the manor until 1651 when: 'Sir Michael Livesey Bt and Sir Richard Sprignell Bt and Dame Anne his wife, released the Manor of Copmanthorpe and estate there to the use of John Barnard and Mary his wife and their issue'.[3]

John Barnard was a merchant living in the city of Hull. After he and his wife died, the manor was split into three parts and a deed of 1678 describes the division between their two daughters, Elizabeth and Frances, and one of their granddaughters, Elizabeth Crofts.[4] One share went to Elizabeth Barnard who had married William Boynton, the first member of that family to live at Burton Agnes. Frances Barnard also had a portion: she was married first to Edward Crofts, a merchant of Hull and York,[5] and had two daughters (also named Frances and Elizabeth); after she was widowed she married Sir John Boynton, William's uncle.

Elizabeth Crofts was to receive a portion on her forthcoming marriage to Christopher Adams of Camblesforth and her sister, Frances, who later married Dr John Nicholson of York, eventually inherited her mother's share. Elizabeth Adams, Frances Nicholson and their children then benefited from Elizabeth Boynton's will as her descendants did not produce heirs. Confusingly, Frances Nicholson named her daughter Frances: this Frances firstly married Thomas Ingram and later, in 1706, became the wife of John Wood of York.

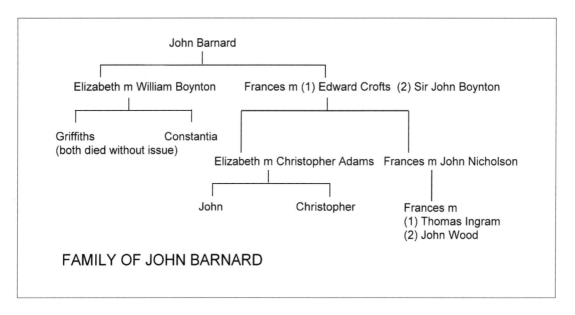

FAMILY OF JOHN BARNARD

John was already a Copmanthorpe landholder through his ancestor, Anthony Wood, so this marriage brought together in his ownership a large part of Copmanthorpe. During the 17th century, members of the Wood family were described as 'of Copmanthorpe' and their house was probably the 'mansion house' which stood on Low Green and is numbered 90 on the 1722/79 map.

Elizabeth Adams' share remained with the Adams family until her granddaughter, Clare, married the Reverend Francis Leighton.[6] The manor was thus divided, with the Wood family having the larger part, until 1800 when a private act was passed through Parliament enabling the Wood portion, which had been legally tied up, to be sold.[7] This began in 1813 when sale particulars show that 280 acres of land, 2 farmhouses, 2 cottages and the Oak Tree public house were put up for auction[8] and in 1840, Leighton's land was sold along with his share of the lordship of the manor.[9]

The manor house

The site of the manor house has been the subject of great debate whilst this history has been in preparation; there are several sites within the village that have been, or are still, occupied by important houses. Two of these have no real claim to manorial status but may have been places where tenants paid rents to the Wood estate. In undated papers (assumed to be between 1747–57 but in fact pre-1735), a rental outlines John Wood's own inheritance from his grandfather, John, describing the mansion house with its garden, croft, summerhouse, kitchen garden, coach house, stables and dove house. This probably stood on Low Green where the school entrance is today and a greatly reduced portion of this house was still standing at the turn of the 20th century (**fig 3.1**). The site of the mansion house was not within the confines of the organic development of the village – it was built on the edge, and in 1722 was shown as an isolated development in the Town Ings, indicating a green-field site.[10]

Also listed was an 'ancient' house; this house could have been the original Wood family home, occupied by Anthony Wood in the 16th century and replaced by the 'mansion house' as the family gained in wealth. The Woods were not lords of the manor at this point in time, so the prop-

3.1 The remains of John Wood's 'mansion house', still standing to the east of Low Green in the early 20th century (Sanderson Collection, Copmanthorpe Library; York Library Service)

erty could not hold manorial status but nevertheless it was an important building in the village. The timber-framed house which once stood in the centre of the village, demolished to make way for the shops in the 1960s, is possibly the 'ancient' house (**figs 3.2** & **3.3**). It was a substantial property of at least two phases, as a photograph taken during demolition shows (**fig 3.4**). In more recent years it had been divided into two houses. During demolition an important carved stone depicting a head was found built into the fireplace, with the face turned inwards. It appears to be the head

of a soldier, since it has a helmet on (**figs 3.5** & **3.6**). Carved from local Calcarian limestone, the head has been very finely worked using a claw chisel. Such chisels were commonly used by the French masons working on the Minster in the 12th and early 13th century, and the forked beard is typical of 12th-century carvings. The head would originally have been painted, and slight traces can be seen down the left side. The head was almost certainly a corbel (a block of stone designed to support a roof timber). The age and style of this carving has led to it being linked to the nearby Knights Templar preceptory. (The amount of stone in and around the village of Copmanthorpe suggests that the preceptory proved to be a ready quarry for local people.)

The people of Copmanthorpe have long considered this building to be the 'manor house' but no direct evidence has been found until the 20th century when it became known as the 'manor house'. It may simply be that it was recognized for what it was – an important high-status late-medieval hall house – but there is no reason why another house of equally high status should not have existed elsewhere.

By 1840 the tithe redemption map shows that the ownership of this central plot was vested in two sisters, Elizabeth Barston and Anne Fawcett. They also owned two other near-by blocks of land and the owners of plots adjoining were John Hobson and Thomas Batman senior. Earlier, the 1779 manor court roll named Mr Thomas Fawcett as both a leaseholder and freeholder but does not describe his holdings. The Fawcetts and Hobsons were connected by marriage and much of this northern section

3.4   The Manor House during demolition in the 1960s (Sanderson Collection, Copmanthorpe Library; York Library Service)

3.4a   A timber post, rescued from the Manor House, now standing in the grounds of Copmanthorpe School (© Wendy Wright)

3.5 The stone head found in the Manor House, at the time of its discovery (© Patricia Daniels)

3.6 The stone head after conservation (© Catrina Appleby)

of the village apart from the glebe plot was in their hands. A manorial connection, if any, had been in the distant past.

Two other houses come into the 'manor house' frame. The first is Ivy House Farm and the earlier house on that site; secondly, Manor Farm and its predecessor. Seventeenth-century records refer to both *Copmanthorpe Hall* and the *Manor House* as places where rents were paid so there were within the Barnard estate two important houses. The earliest reference is in 1638 when a glebe rent was paid at Copmanthorpe Hall and in 1650 this Hall can be identified as being on the Ivy House Farm site by the description of the Intake *on the backside of Copmanthorpe Hall* (the Intake is shown on the 1722/79 plan). Despite this, the much later OS map of 1851 names Manor Farm as Copmanthorpe Hall.

In 1651 when the manor was sold to John Barnard a list of existing leases was made.

The annual rental (£150) of the Manor House itself, including associated land and tithes, was required to be paid at Copmanthorpe Hall but other rents had to be paid at the Manor House.[11] The lessees of the Manor House were Walter Laycock and William Beilby, and the Hearth Tax return for 1665 shows that Walter Laycock lived in a house with eleven hearths. (The 1671 return breaks this down to eight and three so it may have been divided at some point.) Walter clearly occupied a property of great status – the largest in the village and quite possibly the Vavasour 'manor house'. By contrast, Mr Wood had five hearths, presumably at his 'mansion house', and two at what may have been the 'ancient' house.[12]

In 1678, at the division of the Copmanthorpe manor following the death of John Barnard, the description of the 'manor house' matches that of Ivy House Farm found in many other rentals and surveys – *The Manor House of Copmanthorpe with the garden, orchard and outhouses, the Great Intake and the garths containing 54 acres*.[13] The land is the key factor: the Intake and 54 acres identify this property and can be seen behind the plot numbered 87 on the 1722/79 map.

An indenture dated 1709 relating to the *manor house or mansion house of Copmanthorpe* previously belonging to Sir John Boynton, shows it was then in the tenure of Alice Norfolk, widow of Christopher Norfolk, and her son Christopher.[14]

Just to confuse the reader a little more, a conveyance dated 1710 (not long after Wood had taken over his wife's portion of Copmanthorpe and become joint lord of the manor) records that Mr Wood purchased a half share of the Manor House from Elizabeth Adams (his wife's aunt), which he had already pulled down and rebuilt.[15] Had Wood suddenly realised that he was not in fact the sole owner of the property and hastily tried to cover himself?

On the 18th-century rental quoted earlier, describing Wood's 'mansion house', is listed a house matching the 1678 Boynton manor house (Ivy House Farm), with the Intake and 54 acres, simply termed 'a House'.[16] This he describes as his wife's property from the Boynton estate and so must be the same. The tenants are Christopher and Ann Norfolk.

The house re-built by Wood in 1710 has been thought to be Manor Farm but is more probably Ivy House Farm (**fig 3.7**). The stylish front of Manor Farm is decorated by pilasters (see **fig 1.6**); these were in vogue after the Civil War and could suggest that this new house was built earlier, after the Barnard purchase of Copmanthorpe, to provide somewhere comfortable for its new owners or administrators to stay when

3.7   Ivy House Farm
(© Frank Grace)

visiting their property. They re-used an important site and this would account for both Copmanthorpe Hall and the Manor House as two separate places for Barnard tenants to pay rent. The division of 1678 may have been another reason for the re-building of a high-status property on this site.

Three houses have claims to be the manor house. The demolished 'manor house' in the centre of the village, which if indeed the old Wood ancestral home, did not have manorial connections; Ivy House Farm, occupying the site of a manor or high-status house; and Manor Farm, associated with the manor and becoming known as Copmanthorpe Hall in the 19th century if not before.

It is not surprising that confusion arises when 17th-century documents seem to identify both Copmanthorpe Hall and the Manor House as being on the Ivy House Farm site at different times.

Another factor in this puzzle is that Copmanthorpe has been considered to have two manors by the 16th century, Copmanthorpe and Temple Copmanthorpe, even though originally there was only one. During the occupation of the Knights Templar, the village took on the 'Temple' prefix and after that time, lawyers, to cover every eventuality, frequently referred to 'the manor and manors of Temple Copmanthorpe and Copmanthorpe alias Coppenthorpe'. We have seen in the chapter on Medieval Copmanthorpe that there were two estates at Domesday, but only one (the later Templar estate) had manorial rights. The other estate was sold in 1545 by Sir Nicholas Fairfax to Thomas and Richard Vavasour as a manor[17] and so may in the intervening years have acquired that status but there is no real evidence for two manor courts. There would, however, be two important houses where rents were paid and other business would take place. A single manor remained but the lordship was divided according to the 1678 agreement and the manor court was held before representatives of the joint lords of the manor.

Manorial sites shift and change and the confusion seen in Copmanthorpe may not be so unusual, given the rapid changes in ownership of the manor in the 17th century and the divisions of the 18th century. There is a downgrading in the status of the manor house as the manorial system disintegrated, and by the 18th century the manor itself had become almost fossilized. Two surviving manor court rolls from 1779 and 1780 are a reflection of how the system worked in much earlier times when the profits of the manor came from the demesne lands (or home farm) attached to the manor house, and fines, rents and fees were paid in to the manor court. Day work, along with rents in kind such as hens and capons, had gone long ago, commuted into small rent payments, often fixed in the Middle Ages, and their value eroded by inflation.

Copmanthorpe Manor Court

Records for two courts, May 1779 and June 1780,[18] follow the same pattern as surviving bi-annual records for nearby Colton from 200 years earlier.[19] For Copmanthorpe, we are unable to say how often the court was originally held but by this time it was reduced to an annual event.

The court was held at the home of Thomas Batman, *being the Manor House*. As we have seen, the Norfolk family were consistently occupying Ivy House Farm during the 18th century with the Intakes and garths but by 1779, Thomas Batman had moved into the property which he seems to have acquired by marriage. He remained there until 1807 when *his wife being dead, the land he got with her is now descended to William Lamb and Christopher Norfolk*.[20]

The hall or a barn may have been commonly used. Seated before the tenants in 1780 was Timothy Mortimer, the steward of the court of Richard Wood and Jocelyn Price – the latter was looking after the interests of his brother–in–law, John Boynton Adams, described as a 'lunatick',[21] who was joint lord of the manor with Richard.

Everyone was required to attend; if not excuses had to be sent, and so in 1780 we can see exactly who was living in Copmanthorpe and paying suit to the manor. People who lived elsewhere but held land or a house in the village were still required to be there or to send their excuses. There were 15 leaseholders and 27 tenants but nothing to indicate what kind of tenancies the latter had. They may have been copyhold, a very secure form of tenancy disadvantageous to landlords as the rents, fixed often in the Middle Ages, brought in very little profit. At that time there were six cottages built on the waste, or common land, and their occupants were listed. Two were poor and their rents may have been paid by the parish. Another was the blacksmith's shop occupied by William Knight – this may be the site next to the Royal Oak which once operated as a smithy and would be in exactly the right place in the centre of the village.

THE MANOR COURT 16 JUNE 1780
Leaseholders and tenants of the manor

The Devisees of Mrs Catherine Swaile widow	excused	John Batman	present
Mr Thomas Fawcett Freeholder & Leaseholder	excused	Matt^w Bewlay (poor)	present
		John Harrison (labourer) Bailiff for Mr Adams	present
Leaseholders	present	John Dawson	present
Benj, Hobson	present	Francis Wade	present
John Hobson	present	John Daniel	present
Christ^r Norfolk	present	Wm Latham	excused
Richd Norfolk	excused	Richard Eshelby Bailiff for Mr Wood	present
Mr Mich. Eastburn	present		
William Batman	present	Wm Knight	present
Jonathan Hobson	excused	Thomas Knight	excused
John Swaile Junr	present	Thos Hullay	present
Joseph Hill	& (sic)	Thos Bell	present
Wm Watkinson	(blank)	Thos Kirby	(blank)
Richard Dawson	present	John Lee	present
Francis Campey	excused	Henry Loncaster	present
John Swaile Senr		Chas Sowden	excused
Tenants		John Harrison	excused
Thomas Batman	present	Wm Bewley	present
John Newham	present	Franc^s Fearby To Benjn Hobson Wm Pulleyn	present
Joseph Hobson	present		
Francis Scott	present	James Marsh to John Hobson	present
Christopher Doughty	present		

The jurymen, along with their foreman, William Batman, were sworn in together with the officials. John Batman and Francis Campey were affeerers (collectors of fines and fees), the bylawmen were John Hobson and Thomas Kirby (they regulated the communal open fields), and the constable was Francis Campey – he had the thankless task of maintaining law and order. The pinder, or 'common impounder' as he is more importantly called in the roll, was Thomas Bell (he collected stray animals who were released on payment of a fine). Two bailiffs were named, Richard Eshelby for Mr Wood and William Batman for Mr Adams.

The names of the Jury

William Batman **Foreman**

Thomas Batman
Johathan Hobson
Joseph Hill
Christopher Norfolk
Francis Wade
Richard Norfolk
John Hobson
Benjamin Hobson
Francis Scott
John Newham
Joseph Swift
John Dawson

Affeerers
John Batman
Francis Campey

Bylawmen
John Hobson
Thomas Kirkby

Constable
Francis Campey

Common Impounder
Thomas Bell

Bailiffs
Richd Eshelby for Mr Wood
Wm Batman for Mr Adams

The previous roll for May 1779 shows that the court had two functions, Court Baron, dealing with general business to do with land and rents, and the Court Leet which dealt with minor common law offences. 'Pains' were regulations laid down by the court, designed to ensure the smooth running of the community and consideration for neighbours: fences, hedges and ditches were to be maintained, pigs ringed to prevent them from doing too much damage when grubbing up soil, and geese were not allowed to go 'trispising'. Quite substantial fines of 5s (25p) and 3s 4d (17p) could be levied but only 6d (2½p) each was paid by the eight people before the court in 1779 for various offences. By now, the court had in effect been reduced to a formality – a court dinner was held for the officials and it may have been looked on as a social occasion for those with time to spare.

Notes

1 Collins, F ed *Feet of fines of the Tudor period* pt 4 YASRS 1890 vol 8 p 126
2 WYL 5013/249 Newby Hall Papers & Hull City Archives DDWB/18 Wickham Boynton papers
3 Johnson, J op cit p 11
4 NYCRO ZET/2092 Wood of Hollin Hall Draft & copy deeds & papers
5 WYL 5013/257 & 262 Newby Hall Papers
6 YAS MS 214 Skaife, R F Materials for a history of the Ainsty vol 5
7 Minster Library Y-Cop: GRE SC Pamphlets
8 WYL 5013/466/17 Newby Hall Papers
9 EYCRO DDGU/3/3 Sale particulars 1840
10 NYCRO ZET/2333 Wood of Hollin Hall Papers *c* 1747–57 (These accounts are earlier than the date indicated in the NYCRO catalogue as they show payments to John Wood's mother, Margaret who died in 1735.)
11 WYL 5013/256 Newby Hall papers
12 YCA M30:22/47 1665 Hearth Tax Return
13 NYCRO ZET/2092 op cit
14 NYCRO ZET Quit claim 1709
15 NYCRO ZET Copmanthorpe title deeds: Copmanthorpe: moiety of manor house purchased from Adams 1710
16 NYCRO ZET/2333 Wood of Hollin Hall Papers *c* 1747–57
17 Collins, F Yorkshire Fines vol 1 in *YASRS vol 2* 1887 p 113
18 NYCRO ZET/2581 Wood of Hollin Hall Copmanthorpe Manor Court Papers
19 Harrison, M J *Four Ainsty Townships The history of Bolton Percy, Appleton Roebuck, Colton and Steeton 1066–1785* 2000 p 232
20 NYCRO ZET/3025 Wood of Hollin Hall Papers 1796–97. A rental showing that Thomas Batman had replaced Christopher Norfolk & ZET/3279 1807–11 Wm Lamb and Christopher Norfolk (jnr) are charged for tithes instead of Thomas Batman, his wife having died
21 NYCRO ZET/2581 op cit

CHAPTER FOUR

Standards of living in Copmanthorpe 1528–1694

MARJORIE HARRISON AND ELAINE MARSHALL
WITH A CONTRIBUTION FROM ALISON SINCLAIR

THE BORTHWICK INSTITUTE FOR ARCHIVES at the University of York holds no fewer than 32 probate documents (8 wills and 24 inventories) for residents, both men and women, who lived in the village in the period 1528 to 1694.[1] These documents have been transcribed by members of the Society and they tell us much about the dwellings and lifestyles of the residents of Copmanthorpe in the sixteenth and seventeenth centuries. They are particularly informative as there are few other records for this period which illuminate the lives of ordinary citizens, and yet it was a time of immense upheaval and change in English society (**fig 4.1**).

The documents

An analysis was done of these wills and inventories after transcription in an attempt to illustrate the standard of living enjoyed by Copmanthorpe people from 1528 to 1694. The sample was too small to come to any hard and fast conclusions but the documents illustrate how people lived in this small rural community. At the beginning of the period, the population may be estimated at about 100. The data reveals a religious, rural and prosperous way of life for many testators in an area of arable and livestock farming; but it also shows that there was poverty in Copmanthorpe and its locality. Wills ranged from the very simple to detailed dispositions of land and property with many charitable bequests. All indicated the religious beliefs of the testators and there was a division between Catholic and Protestant preambles in tune with the changing times of the 16th century.[2] The testators were linked with the land in varying degrees, the majority having specific farming and rural commodities, utensils, implements and livestock in the valuations of their goods.

Timeline

Tudor

1524	**Nine Copmanthorpe men pay Lay Subsidy tax**
1529	Parliament acts to curb powers of Catholic church (Reformation begins)
1534	Act of Supremacy passed (Henry VIII declared Supreme Head of the Church)
1535	Pilgrimage of Grace
1536	Dissolution of smaller religious houses begins
1539	**Nunnery of Nun Appleton suppressed**
1546	Edward VI ascends throne – Protestant religion enforced
1553	Mary ascends throne, country reverts to Catholicism
1558	Queen Elizabeth I restores Protestant faith
1588	Spanish Armada defeated
1599	**Thomas Vavasour sells manor of Copmanthorpe to Dr Swale**

Stuart

1603	James I ascends throne
1610	**Robert Sprignell buys manor of Copmanthorpe**
1625	Charles I ascends throne
1638	Scots resist imposition of the Book of Common Prayer
1642	Civil War breaks out
1643	Battle of Marston Moor
1649	Charles I executed
1651	**John and Mary Barnard buy the manor of Copmanthorpe**
1653	Oliver Cromwell becomes Lord Protector
1660	Charles II ascends throne & Samuel Pepys starts his diary
1666	Great Fire of London
1678	**Manor of Copmanthorpe divided between heirs of John and Mary Barnard**
1685	James II ascends throne and abdicates in 1688
1688	William and Mary ascend the throne
1689	Declaration of rights limiting power of sovereign and excluding Catholics from the succession

4.1 A typical example of the inventories examined: the Inventory of Francis Fairfax, 1597 (Reproduced by permission of the Borthwick Institute, University of York)

Will-making in the past was frequently very last minute, when a literate member of the community, often a priest, was summoned to the bedside of a dying man or woman to record their last will and testament. After the testator's death, four men of good standing in the village would be asked to make an inventory of the goods and chattels in and around the house. This happened very quickly – although perhaps not always as fast as for Richard Hodgeson's possessions, which were valued 'at the hour of his death' in 1562. These appraisals were necessary to produce an accurate record of the value of an estate so that the executors could apply for a grant of probate from the church courts. In some cases there was no will but an inventory was still needed for probate purposes. Probate (the proving of wills) was administered by the church from the Middle Ages until 1858, when civil legislation established the Probate Registry.

Status and occupations were recorded in only seventeen of the 32 documents. There was one esquire, three gentlemen, two yeomen, four husbandmen, four widows and one bachelor. Trades were represented by a blacksmith and a wheelwright. Of the remainder it is fair to assume that they were not regarded by the writers of their wills and inventories as having a very high status.

How they lived

In the 16th and 17th centuries, even people of very modest means with few possessions made wills and their goods were valued. As the four men who had the task of valuing their deceased neighbour's goods and chattels walked through the house and then into the yard, a detailed view of life emerges as the value of everything is appraised. Thus these documents can tell us much about social habits and how people lived and worked.

The houses described in these documents would have been timber-framed with panels infilled with locally available materials. Thatched roofs were the norm and until the mid-17th century, most village houses were only one and a half storeys high. The inventories showed that houses in Copmanthorpe had rooms called variously, 'hall house', house, and 'fire house'. This was the principal living space in a dwelling and would contain the main fireplace, hence the vernacular term, fire house. By the 16th century, the hall no longer had a central fire on a stone or earthen base with smoke vents in the roof as, particularly in Yorkshire, the smoke hood (a canopy) had been developed to funnel the smoke up and out. In addition, the development of brick making had made stacks cheaper and safer. The space between the principal upright posts in a timber-framed house is known as a bay. In small houses this may have been the entire space in which the family lived and slept and where all the cooking was done. In larger houses, perhaps occupied by a yeoman and his family, the principal living space, containing the main fireplace, might occupy one or two bays with a parlour in a third bay beyond. At the other end of the house, on the other side of the main fireplace, would be a further one or two bay space, used for work and or storage. In this type of house plan, there would be a half bay between the 'hall' and the work or storage bay into which the front door opened and where the smoke hood or chimney stack to the main fireplace was located. Sometimes, these houses had a low 'outshut' built against the rear wall, to accommodate a dairy or, later, the staircase. This kind of vernacular house with the front door opening on to the side of the chimney or smoke stack is known as a 'lobby-entry' type and is common in the Vale of York until the 19th century.

Everyday living took place mainly on the ground floor in the houses described in the inventories. In the 'hall house' or 'fire house' a great hearth either with a canopy or within a brick stack would accommodate a spit for roasting with a dripping pan. Gallows balkes, a transverse bar in the chimney or above the fireplace from which the reckons (pothooks) were suspended, was in place to hang pans over the fire. Here also would be a trestle table, forms and buffet stools where the family and their servants sat to eat, a chair or two and there may have been a cupboard with a range of pewter vessels standing on top and a chest containing clothes or other items. Many of the 24 inventoried houses had parlours: not parlours as we understand them but rooms having a dual function, being used both for sleeping and living and often containing one or more beds, frequently with hangings. Some houses had more than one parlour. Where there were chambers above, they had a variety of uses, from the maids' sleeping quarters to storing saddles, hemp, woollen yarn, butter, sacks and a great deal else. Generally these would be accessed by ladder in these long, low houses and only in the homes of the gentry, like Henry Vavasour (1583), might a staircase be found. As time passed, comfort crept in as wealth grew and domestic innovations were introduced in the later 16th century. This is demonstrated by cushions, hangings and a greater variety of furniture even in modest households like that of Thomas Fenton in 1658.

Brick became more predominant from the end of the 17th century and during the course of the 18th century; houses became taller and bigger as building practices changed. Farm servants no longer dined with their masters, who now had their own dining room, and the mistress could retire to the parlour to receive guests as the beds had been banished to the upper floors.

Domestic and semi-industrial activities went on in additional rooms and outbuildings. Sometimes a kitchen is mentioned; this might be used for brewing or baking if there was no specific area for these purposes. A bolting house, used for sieving flour, a kiln house, usually for malt, bake house, brew house, buttery, milk house (dairy) – all these occur in the Copmanthorpe inventories. Pigs were killed, scalded and their flesh cured; a tub with 'flesh in it' and 'salt flesh' are listed in the inventories of William Winterburn (1595) and Thomas Swale (1619) respectively. Nine houses had spinning wheels; one had three, and wool and linen yarn and cloth was very evident although no looms were noted.

Pots, pans and dishes were commonly made of pewter and brass; one inventory listed over 100 pieces of pewter as well as eight pewter candlesticks. Silver spoons, a prized possession, featured in inventories between 1557 and 1626. More personal items were bequeathed in wills and listed in inventories. There was little jewellery but clothing was highly valued and passed on; Ellen Wood (1551), for example, had two gowns, two kirtles, eight kerchiefs with veils to cover her head and two smocks, while William Fenton in 1560 had a doublet and a blue jacket and John Fenton (1562) a leather doublet and a velvet jacket. Even Elizabeth Doughty, a widow probably living with one of her children, had a pair of stockings and four ruffs valued in 1623 and William Swale (1626) left his workaday clothes to John Mote.

Farming gear in the yards such as ploughs, wains (carts), ladders, tools and implements, and even manure, was valued. Crops and grain were itemised throughout with wheat, barley and rye found very frequently and occasionally oats, along with peas and beans, both in the barns and growing in the fields. Livestock included cattle, horses, swine and poultry; there were also sheep, but in fewer numbers.

The three largest dwellings were found in the third quarter of the sixteenth century when Henry Vavasour (1583) had a hall and eleven other rooms. Anne Thursby (1584), in addition to the hall house, had seven rooms; and William Rowlay's house (1581) had six rooms. Copmanthorpe's wealthiest resident, Thomas Swale, whose inventory is dated 1619, had a relatively small house comprising a hall house, parlour, outer parlour and a chamber but this house had a 'low end' and according to the inventory, sixteen sheep were housed there along with the kiln and three sacks of 'green malt' and other tools and implements. This house might be a medieval survival, built as a longhouse where animals and humans shared the same roof.

The citizens

Thomas Jeffreyson, a substantial yeoman, made his will in July 1558 when Queen Mary was still on the throne and the nation had reverted to Catholicism. He bequeathed his soul to Almighty God, asking for intercession from St Mary and all the saints in heaven. At his funeral mass and dirge at St Mary Bishophill Junior, each priest attending, along with the parish clerk and scholars, was to receive a sum of money and a penny dole was to be given to every poor person who attended his burial. He also left money for a dinner at 'Harysons' which may be interpreted as an inn owned by the Harrison family, merchants and innkeepers, living on Micklegate, who were important citizens of York. This was for 'every neighbour that does office with me', indicating that Thomas was active within the Ainsty, doing civic duties such as helping with the organisation of the musters and beacon watch in times of national emergency.

Thomas also left money for a dinner at his house in Copmanthorpe for his neighbours' wives and widows and every householder in the village was to receive four pence as well as specifically named poor people. He was concerned about the state of the roads in the parish, leaving money for Back Lane to be made up, along with the way from St Giles' well to the Hall gate in Copmanthorpe, while further afield the road at Dringhouses was to be mended. Perhaps that particular stretch had caused him inconvenience on his way into the city. Prisoners at York Castle and the lock-up on Ouse bridge were remembered, as well as the hospitals of St Katherine and St Thomas, which cared for the sick and poor. Many other bequests were made to his family and friends, some in Colton, Bilbrough and Askham Bryan. Thomas left the remainder of his estate to his servant, Anne Irish.

The earliest inventory is that of William Featherstone, dated 1528. William was one of the few Copmanthorpe men who paid a tax known as the Lay Subsidy in 1524, indicating he was one of the wealthier members of the community. He and two others paid 12d on goods worth £2; they were at the bottom end of a list of nine men who produced a total of 16s 2d. Other villages in the area appear to have been far more prosperous: neighbouring Colton had fifteen taxpayers yielding 31s 2d.[3]

William's inventory does not indicate how many rooms were in his house but he had very few possessions and his bed was not listed – either forgotten or of no value. The appraisers began outside before moving indoors:

[text has been modernised where possible]

The Inventory of William Featherstone of Copmanthorpe of the parish of our Lady of New Bishophill late deceased appraised by Thomas Vavasour John Morton Edward Hodgson & Richard Swale made the 15th day of November in the year of our Lord God a thousand 5 hundred 28th (1528)

Imprimis 3 quarters winter corn	27s	
Item 1 quarter of haver [oats]	2s	4d
Item 8 quarters peas and beans	53s	4d
Item 1 hog price	6s	
Item 4 mares & 2 foals & 1 filly	40s	
Item 4 oxen	42s	
Item 4 kye (cows)	32s	
Item 1 sow 6 pigs & 1 shotte [young weaned pig]	4s	
Item 1 wain unbound [cart without ironwork]	4s	
Item 3 yokes 3 teams 1 horse team 1 shackle 1 iron harrow	4s	
Item 1 grindstone		2d
Item 8 acres of winter corn [still in the ground]	42s	8d
Item 2 load of woad⁴	2s	
Item 4 geese		12d
Item 12 pullen [chickens]	2s	
Item 3 bedclothes		8d
Item 14 sheets	6s	
Item 3 codde warres [pillow cases]		4d
Item 2 coverlets 1 window cloth 1 mattress price	3s	

Item 1 ark [large wooden chest for flour or corn] 2 chests	12d	
Item 1 kimling [oval tub] a trough 1 bushel [measure]	10d	
Item 2 stands 2 tubs & 1 trough	12d	
Item 4 old pots 1 spinning wheel price	12d	
Item 1 certain broken iron	12d	
Item 2 forks	6d	
Item 1 scythe	4d	
Item 3 sickles	6d	
Item 1 brandreth 1 axe 1 gorget 1 bill 2 wedges	14d	
Item 1 almery [food cupboard] 1 dish bink [counter] 1 chair	12d	
Item 4 brass bottles	5s	4d
Item 1 little cauldron 2 kettles 2 poringers	5s	
Item 7 dublers [large plates] 7 dishes 1 salt 1 saucer	5s	
Item 1 counter 1 board 1 banker	2s	8d
Item 1 hanging	4d	
Item old husslement of houshold	10d	
	£15	12d

The inventory goes on to list the many debts owed by William amounting to nearly £12. In addition, the bequests he made were valued at 32s which left very little for his heirs when deducted from the sum of his assets shown above.

Henry Vavasour, the lord of the manor, died in 1583; his inventory describes a high-status house, perhaps on the site of Ivy House Farm. It comprised a hall, great parlour, buttery and kitchen, bake house, larder and brew house on the ground floor with a great chamber and three more chambers above. This was a substantial house, probably a hall and cross-wing house, and the accommodation reflected his standing. The hall contained two tables, an old trestle table with three old forms, six jointed stools, a little round table, a turned chair and a pair of playing tables (for cards or dice). There were two old carpets and six cushions, but no evidence of cooking or storage: this was a place for eating and entertaining. The parlour contained two more tables, one long and the other round, a carpet and three forms with two cushions, and there was a fire in this room.

The kitchen was reserved for serious cooking as the eight brass pots, six brass pans, two great rakes, five spits, two dripping pans and other utensils testify. Items of value were kept in the buttery – two silver salts, a small pot with a gilt cover and eight dozen pewter vessels of one kind or another and eight pewter candlesticks. Also, there were two basins and ewers and, amongst other things, two hogsheads (large barrels) which may have contained ale brewed on the premises. In the larder more pewter vessels and a salting tub were listed and the brew house and bake house contained the appropriate equipment.

Upstairs, the great chamber was a bedroom containing three bedsteads with feather beds and bedclothes, an 'old court cupboard', three coffers, an old table, two old turned chairs, a woman's saddle, an old linen spinning wheel and other pieces of furniture. The chamber over the parlour was most likely the room occupied by Henry; it would be warmed by the parlour chimney and contained a bedstead and tester (canopy) with curtains, two featherbeds and bedclothes, a trundle bedstead and one or two other pieces of furniture. His clothes were kept in the maid's chamber along with a close stool (commode) and a Flanders chest – bound with iron. The chamber over the kitchen housed his armour, two bills and a halberd. This house demonstrates very well his superior status – it was vastly different to other village houses where inventories show people were still using parlours for sleeping and the hall for cooking and eating along with storage.

When Anne Thursby's goods were valued after her death in 1584 her clothes were listed: a silk hat, a cap and a felt hat, two gowns, a worsted frock and three petticoats, two kirtles and a worsted apron. She also had three smocks, three partlets (a large collar), two veils, three kerchiefs and two linen aprons. Her house consisted of a hall house, parlour, maid's parlour, kitchen, brew house and four chambers. The goods were valued at nearly £120; compare this with William Foster, who died in 1589 leaving goods worth only £2 15s 8d.

William may have been related to Robert Foster, the blacksmith, who died in 1622. Robert was relatively prosperous, farming as well as working at his trade, and his goods were valued at about £120. He had £43 worth of debt which included £3 12s for his funeral, no doubt covering the cost of taking his body to be buried at St Mary Bishophill Junior in York and food and drink for his relatives and friends afterwards.

In the 'smiddy' or blacksmith's shop were listed the 'stiddy' (anvil) and bellows, four great hammers and five lesser. There were four pairs of tongs, a vice and files and a nailing stiddy, shoe irons, punches, pincers and shoeing hammers, along with unwrought iron for horse shoes, a grindstone and coals.

Robert Foster lived in a substantial house with a fire house, two parlours and two chambers along with another low chamber. Stored in the house was a gallon and a half of honey, new woollen cloth, hemp and harden (coarser hemp) cloth. There was coloured wool and woollen yarn, five stone of salt butter and 'all the cheese'. Even three loaves of rye bread were listed.

Thomas Fenton's inventory shows that his relatively modest house with five rooms was comfortably furnished in 1658 although his possessions only amounted to £46 16s 6d.

A true and Perfect Inventory of all the goods and chattels moveable and unmoveable of Thomas Fenton late of Coppenthorp, deceased, in the County of the City of York as they were priced and valued the 19th day of November in the year of our Lord 1658 by us whose names are subscribed

		£ s d
First	his purse and apparel	2 0 0
	In the fire house	
	one iron range with a gallow balke, crookes, tongs a pair of iron rakes and other iron stuff	1 0 0
Item	one great table with a bink, beyond it 2 forms	1 0 0
It	a little table 2 chairs and 2 buffet stools	0 7 0
It	Fifteen pewter dishes, 6 saucers, 3 pewter cans, 2 flaggons, 2 chamber pots, 3 pewter bowls and four pottingers	2 13 4
	In the kitchen	
It	one great pot and a posset, a kettle and a pan	1 0 0
It	one churn, 2 wood bottles, some dishes, trenchers, a cheese press with other wood huslements there	1 0 0

	In the great parlour	
	two stand beds, a livery cupboard and a settle	2 0 0
It	one draw table, 3 chests, 1 coffer and a form	1 5 4
It	one warming pan, 2 voiders and a little iron range	0 4 0
It	two rugs, 3 coverlets, 2 pair of blankets, 3 feather beds, 5 little beds and 2 bolsters	4 0 0
It	two suites of hangings & valances with iron rods	1 16 8
It	some new hemp and harden cloth	0 12 0
It	nine yards of woollen cloth	0 16 0
It	two pair of lin sheets and fine hemp sheets	1 7 0
It	Seven pillowbears [pillow cases] 3 table clothes and a lin sheet	0 17 0
It	Sixteen table napkins	0 5 0
It	three sewed cushions, 4 strip cushions & 2 set cushions	0 6 0
	In the bed chamber	
It	one standbed a chest 2 covered chairs 3 stools	1 6 0
It	one mattress, 2 coverlets & rug, 3 feather coddes [pillows]	0 10 4
It	a trundle bed, a cradle and 3 spinning wheels	0 10 0
	In the corn chamber	
It	some sacks & pokes, a bushel, a hopper with other huslements there	0 15 0
	In the little parlour	
It	one stock bed with the bedding and a winnowing cloth	0 10 0
	In the barn	
It	all the rye unthreshed	4 10 0
It	all the barley	4 10 0
It	all the beans	7 13 4
It	all the hay	0 10 0
It	one acre & half of rye sown	2 5 0
It	two kine and a calfe	5 0 0
It	a sow and a pig	1 0 0
It	dung in the garth and a ladder	1 4 0
		46 16 6d
	Debts owing to the deceased by Christo: Johnson	0 18 6
	Appraisers	
	Edward Daniell Thomas Swale Robert Doughtie Richard Dockwray Henry Fenton	

The picture gained from the household furniture and contents, agricultural produce, equipment and livestock shown in the inventories over period of 168 years is one of an agricultural village with fluctuating wealth. Towards the end of the period, between 1623 and 1678, the highest valuation was that of Thomas Fenton, but from about 1560 to the end of the 16th century, valuations were higher and more evenly spread. The wealthiest occupant was Thomas Swale whose estate was valued at over £218 in 1619. (He may have been a kinsman of Dr Richard Swale who had purchased the manor from Thomas Vavasour in 1599.) It is tempting to conclude that the second half of the 16th century brought rising prosperity to some farmers in the village. Once the manor was sold in 1599 it became a revenue-producing investment and new leases and perhaps changes in traditional copyhold tenure meant that small farmers prospered less. The Civil War must have had a huge impact but unfortunately the records for that period are non-existent.

Arms and armour in the 16th century

Several of the inventories record the arms and armour held by the individual. These items must be considered against the politics of the time. Government anxieties about invasion by the French and war with Scotland during the 16th century led to requests for the numbers of men 'ready and able for the war' to be reported regularly to the crown by the lord mayor of York. To do this, musters were held in various locations in and around the City and the Ainsty; the constable of each township was ordered to bring his men, fully equipped with horses and arms, to drill and be counted.

Records of the Musters for York and the Ainsty found in York City Archives allow us to stand on the sidelines and visualise a day in the lives of 33 Copmanthorpe men in 1584.[5] Colton Moor, adjacent to the township boundary, was a location often used for the South Ainsty and on the appointed day, all would set off with an assortment of arms. Every man aged between 16 and 60 was liable to attend; for those without equipment, the common armour, held in some central place like the manor house or the church, would be lent.

Men were divided into bill men and bow men: a bill was a vicious curved blade on a pole (adapted from a billhook) and the bow men carried bows and sheaves of arrows. Some had protective equipment – the more wealthy had armour – and Anthony Wood turned up with his coat of plate and steel cap. Others had to manage with a 'jak', a thick padded leather jacket, but several also had steel caps and sallets – an old-fashioned kind of steel helmet. The common armour consisted of two jaks, two steel caps, a bow, a sheaf of arrows and a bill, so there was no excuse for those without. The Copmanthorpe men joined those from Colton, Appleton, Bolton Percy and other villages in the area; this could amount to over 200 men who were inspected by local gentry such as Sir William Fairfax of Steeton, along with aldermen or the lord mayor of York. Numbers were counted and drill performed, and for the men, a day away from their labours in the fields, meeting men from neighbouring villages and catching up on news and gossip, would provide a welcome change from every-day life.

4.2 Agricultural tools of the type that men would have taken to the muster
(© Catrina Appleby)

The inventories of the houses in Copmanthorpe made for probate purposes show that there was more armour around than is seen in the 1584 Muster Roll. Henry Vavasour, lord of the manor, who died in 1583, had some black armour as well as a coat of plate; he also had two bills (**fig 4.2**) and a halbert in the house. Widow Anne Thursby, who died the following year, also had a coat of plate in her house and in 1619 a battle bill is listed amongst Thomas Swale's possessions. Apart from the armour belonging to Henry Vavasour (who was on the up-and-up at this time), the rest could be left-overs from the Wars of the Roses, gathering dust on the walls of farmhouses and in the far corners of barns. Firearms figure in the inventories too and as early as 1557, Jenet Hodgeson had a weapon known as a caliver, an earlier and lighter form of musket. Thomas Swale had another in 1619 and later, William Swale mentioned a fowling piece and two shot moulds in his will dated 1626. Not until the Civil War did firearms became the

Double-edged

Single-edged

Blades:
45cm
120 cm with shaft
(approx)

norm in battle situations but fowling guns were popular in the countryside as hunting with guns became much more of a leisure pursuit for the
wealthy.

Notes

1 The documents can be identified in the Dean and Chapter Probate Indexes
2 The Catholic form of religion was replaced by Protestant doctrine in the
  1540s, after the Reformation; it then reverted to Catholicism in the time of
  Queen Mary and back again in 1558 when Queen Elizabeth reinstated the
  Protestant faith
3 Cartwright, J J (ed) Subsidy Roll for York and the Ainsty 1524/5 in *YAJ* vol
  4 1887 p 195
4 See chapter on Agriculture
5 YCA Muster rolls E41A

CHAPTER FIVE

Church and Chapel

MARJORIE HARRISON AND RUBY FOSTER

St Giles church

COPMANTHORPE WAS AN OUTLYING PORTION of the York parish of St Mary Bishophill Junior just off Micklegate, along with Holgate and Nether Poppleton. The fabric of St Mary's contains Anglo-Saxon stonework; parts can be dated to the early 11th century and it may have been built on the site of an earlier church (**fig 5.1**). These extra-parish arrangements probably also went back long before the Conquest when landowners gave rights to the cure of souls in their manors, along with the tithes, to churches elsewhere. So, the people of Copmanthorpe had a long walk to attend church until a chapel of ease, dedicated to St Giles, was built some time in the 12th century on the green in the centre of the village. It was still necessary however for villagers to marry and have their children baptised at St Mary's, and their dead were buried there until the burial ground next to St Giles was established in 1750, saving that last sad journey into York.

It has been suggested that 1180 was the date of foundation but there is no supporting evidence for this. In 1546 it was recorded that:

> There is no incumbent in the said chapel, but being ordained, made and built by the inhabitants there, of their own devotion, for their own ease, upon the ground that is now one Thomas Vavasour's, gentleman, and was built to the intent they might have mass there, because that sick, impotent and aged people could not come to the same parish church.[1]

The fabric of the small simple church of St Giles, cobbles and rough stone, indicates that there was no great benefactor to erect an elaborate building, reinforcing the idea that the people of Copmanthorpe themselves built it.

5.1　The church of St
Mary Bishophill
Junior
(© Marjorie
Harrison)

5.2　St Giles Church,
Copmanthorpe
– the picture
must date from
the early 20th
century as the
iron railings are
still in situ. Such
railings were
removed during
World War I to
make weapons
and ammunition
(Sanderson
Collection,
Copmanthorpe
Library; York
Library Service)

A long, low building with the nave and chancel all in one, it is similar is
shape and size to the churches at Askham Richard and Askham Bryan,
both late Norman in date (**fig 5.2**).

St Giles was a dedication often found in forest areas as St Giles
himself was a forest hermit. He became the patron saint of lepers, crip-
ples and blacksmiths, among others, who asked for his intercession. The

Ainsty was very well forested in the Middle Ages, so this may have been a factor, although the people of Copmanthorpe could have chosen St Giles because the blacksmith's shop was nearby. Travellers along the 'Streete' (now Top Lane) were not far away from the smithy at Copmanthorpe if they needed assistance. The dedication may have pre-dated the church as the well on Low Green was called St Giles' well in the past and could have been revered as a holy well.

The arrangements for the provision of priests by the mother church is not clear and there were times in the 14th and 15th centuries when problems arose because the vicar of St Mary's had not provided a chaplain for Copmanthorpe.[2] In 1411, complaints were made that a priest was illegally using a church called 'le Tempyll', just outside the village.[3] This is clearly a reference to the chapel that had belonged to the Knights Templar preceptory, closed down over 100 years previously, and the situation may have occurred because the people of Copmanthorpe were not well served in their own chapel.

The Reformation has left little mark on the parish. What was a small, poor chapel would have been stripped of statues and ornament and no record remains of local events in the 1530s and 40s.

Tithes and the glebe

Tithes were the traditional way of parishes supporting their own church and chaplain through the gift of one tenth of what each household produced. They were divided into great tithes (corn, hay and wood) which went to the rector, the person or body, frequently absent, who took the profits and appointed clergy (the Dean and Chapter of York in the case of Copmanthorpe); and small tithes, garden produce and such things as honey, eggs and fruit, which were collected by the vicar of St Mary Bishophill Junior. Glebe was land given to support the priest and church and in Copmanthorpe consisted of about 30 acres (c 12ha) scattered through the open fields, along with some property in the village. In the extended parish of St Mary, the inhabitants of Copmanthorpe saw their tithes carted off from the village with little benefit to themselves or their church. Initially the collection was a fairly simple affair but complications grew with time and by the 16th century the right to collect great tithes was frequently 'farmed' or leased out to laymen.

The Dean and Chapter of York farmed out the Copmanthorpe tithes and glebe land to men who could afford the fixed cost and take a chance on making a profit – in good years they would be well ahead despite having to pay a collector. The annual payment from the lessee did not go to the church or chaplain in Copmanthorpe but was absorbed into the coffers of the Minster. The rent in 1547 was £32 per annum and continued so for many years; at that time the Copmanthorpe tithes and glebe were leased to Thomas Vavasour, the Lord of the Manor. The lease gives details of the church property in the village: 'all that Rectory or parsonage of Copmanthorpe aforesaid with all the tithe corn and hay, glebe lands', and describes the properties:

> one old mansion house standing in and upon the site of the said rectory or parsonage, which is very ruinous and in great decay … and one tenement [the vicarage], two laithes [barns]. Thomas Vavasour to have free liberty and licence to take down and carry away, and to convert such timber and stone as is thereupon, to his own proper uses, saving one cross chamber standing in the east end of the said house, which the said Thomas Vavasour … to make up in one fair garner [granary] … and to maintain one tenement two laithes.[4]

This stone and timber mansion house, with a cross wing, would at one time have been a high-status village house but in 1547 it was about to be reduced to a granary.

Later evidence from the 1664 glebe terrier (an account of all the land and property belonging to the church) describes two houses: a parsonage house and a vicarage.[5] The parsonage house had a garth and croft; this property fronted onto Low Green and may have replaced the earlier house reduced to a granary in 1547. The vicarage was in the same garth of about one acre with the tithe barn. (A timber-framed tithe barn about seventeen yards (c 15m) long, with two threshing floors of clay, was still in existence in 1785.)[6] We must assume that when there was a curate serving Copmanthorpe he lived in the vicarage, but the function of the parsonage house is unclear. As the farmer of 'the Rectory', whoever was leasing the glebe and tithes may have had that house for his own use, or for anyone he sublet to. The vicarage house was described in the mid-19th century as 'a long brick building let in tenements, in a state of great dilapidation. In front, in plaster, is a date – 1719'.[7]

Most farmers of the tithes and glebe had little connection with the village: the Vavasours, who had lived there, were followed by John Milner of Barmby Moor. Later Richard Swale, Sir Francis Hildersby, Robert Sprignell of London and Sir Robert Harding were all lessees until John Wood obtained them in 1717. Wood had an ongoing dispute with the

Dean and Chapter about tithe for line (flax) and rape which had previously been judged to be small tithes and had been paid to the vicar of Bishophill.[8] Later, under the Tithe Act of 1836, the Copmanthorpe tithes were commuted into cash payments in 1837.

St Giles church in the 18th and 19th centuries

The church of St Giles had become much neglected, along with its parishioners. John Fuller, the vicar of St Mary Bishophill Junior, reported at Archbishop Herring's visitation in 1743 that there were about 40 families in the village, no dissenters and no meeting house. There was no public or charity school although some children were taught by a private master at the expense of their parents. There was no almshouse and no resident curate. Services were only held once a month at Copmanthorpe because he [Revd Fuller] had to attend to another chapelry (Upper Poppleton) as well as the mother church in York. Holy Communion was provided just once a year at Copmanthorpe and four times a year at St Mary's.[9]

A gallery was erected at the west end sometime in the 18th century and no doubt the Wood family made some attempts at improvements to enhance their status. The manor pew and oak pulpit (both no longer in place) may have been their gift, along with a silver chalice. As non-resident lords of the manor, they would rarely have attended at St Giles, although John Wood was buried there in 1740, as was his son, John Wood Boynton, in 1771.

Some 100 years later, Canon Dixon, writing in 1844, sums up the situation:

> This is the meanest religious edifice and the worst conditioned Chapelry in the district comprised within the limits of the Rural Deanery. It is a Peculiar of the Dean and Chapter of York [*a separate jurisdiction*] and is a Chapel of Ease to St Mary, Bishophill Junior. Divine service is performed only once a month, and the communion is administered only once in the year, at which there may be about twelve old people. The population in 1831 was 293, and the church accommodation was returned as sufficient; this must be understood as to the number actually attending, and not measured according to the population, even if the space within were arranged in the best manner possible.

> There are on the south side of the church four ranges of old oak stalls, and two large square pews on the north. The Manor pew is

on the south side near the pulpit, both of which are of fine old oak. The altar rails are modern, tho' of oak, and there is a very handsome old oak table, very massive, and oak benches near the Communion rails which are free sittings. There are some other benches under the Gallery also free, cold, damp and miserable which are occupied by a few old persons who partake of the Norfolk dole of bread.[10] Perhaps under the best arrangement of the sittings not many more than 50 could comfortably be accommodated. Taking the fabric itself and its present neglected and dilapidated state, the small amount of divine service performed in it and the great desecration of the church yard, it can be considered in no other light than as a disgrace to all those who ought to be interested in it. There is an entrance into the church yard from a public house adjoining, and it is used as a common drying ground. A Faculty was obtained in 1750 for inclosing the chapel yard for a burial ground; before which time, I suppose, funerals were taken in Bishophill. The present wall of the church yard, being of brick, bears the following inscription on the left hand post of the entrance: This wall was built anno Dom 1773 John Dawson Jonathan Hobson churchwardens.[11]

There were good reasons for the establishment of the burial ground; as early as 1732 it was recognized that the distance from York and the poor condition of the road created problems and there were other difficulties:

> Frequently they, or some of them of the poorer sort have been so intoxicated and overcome with much strong drink at the funerals or entertainment that they have not been able to get home the night after, but have been forced to lie in the lanes or fields till the next day – to their great scandal.[12]

Parish re-organisation took place in 1844 when the chapelries of Poppleton and Copmanthorpe were separated from St Mary Bishophill Junior. A Mr Atkinson was appointed as incumbent and came to live in the village at that time. Some renovations were undertaken and tables of the Commandments, the King's Arms and the font were brought to Copmanthorpe from the old St Andrew's church at Bishopthorpe which had undergone restoration in 1842 (this despite having been rebuilt by Archbishop Drummond in 1768).[13] Later, in 1866, Copmanthorpe became its own parish and the handsome vicarage, built by the Ecclesiastical Commissioners at a cost of £1400, was built on ground where poor houses had once stood (**fig 5.3**). The living was worth £250, and the vicar of St Mary Bishophill Junior had the right to appoint the vicar of

Copmanthorpe, thus preserving the connection. The Reverend Albert Willan MA then arrived at the beginning of a new phase in the life of the church of St Giles.

The growth of population in the 19th century forced an extension to the graveyard, created by gradual acquisition and the demolition of properties adjoining. Also, greater recognition by the Church of England of the, by now, very well-established nonconformist chapels in Copmanthorpe and elsewhere, led to other activity. St Giles was restored in 1889 and many alterations took place. The gallery was removed, the east end of the chancel rebuilt, and an organ chamber and vestry added. At this time a small Norman window was discovered in the south wall and opened up – it may have been a squint which allowed people on the outside to see what was going on within. Some of the old redundant stonework was removed to the Vicarage garden to add character to the rockery, and to puzzle its 21st-century occupants.

Nonconformism in Copmanthorpe

By the early 18th century nonconformism was making a significant impact on the English way of life. The increasing educational opportunities of the times, along with the effects of the 1689 Toleration Act allowing freedom of worship, had enabled religious dissension to take hold.

Here in York, nonconformism grew quickly despite the powerful presence in the city of the Minster and many established parish churches. The parish of St Mary Bishophill Junior (including Copmanthorpe) had just five dissenters in 1764.[14] However, between 1770 and 1790 Methodism was growing in York and the surrounding villages and hamlets. John Wesley, the founder of the movement, was known to have visited the York area at various times between the 1740s and 1780s, preaching in York, Tadcaster, Acomb, and even perhaps neighbouring Acaster Malbis.[15] It was not Wesley alone who spread the Methodist gospel in this area, but also a band of dedicated lay preachers. These lay preachers, either singly or in a group, held services in market places and on village greens. As winter approached they would arrange to hold services in the cottages of converts; these cottages became known as 'meeting houses' and continued in use until the first mission halls and chapels were established.[16]

At a time when Methodism was not a popular cause there was a strong network of mutual support. Each society was organised into classes with a leader and support was given to those who needed help in reading and understanding the bible. The early Copmanthorpe Methodists would have been active within the wider York area helping other classes to become established.

The Copmanthorpe Society

The 1787 and 1799 surveys of Wesleyan members[17] show that Methodism was introduced into Copmanthorpe in 1787. Six members formed the first Copmanthorpe Society class which became part of the York Wesleyan Circuit. By 1799 membership had increased to eleven: William and Margaret Batman, John and Ann Hobson, Elizabeth Scott, John Corner, Jane Dawson and four members of the Dixon family. Members of the newly formed Copmanthorpe Society appear to have been fairly prosperous as they began by sending 4s (20p) to the Quarter Board, quickly increasing it to 9s (45p) a quarter as membership increased. By 1811 there were 27 members.

Methodism in the village owes a great deal to two of Copmanthorpe's oldest farming families, the Batmans and the Hobsons, who were related by marriage. The Society was headed firstly by John Corner, who was quickly succeeded by William Batman, under whom it flourished. William Cammidge, writing in 1908,[18] explains how two villagers, Mrs Ann Hobson and Mrs Elizabeth Scott, worked tirelessly to spread the Methodist gospel among their friends and neighbours. Ann opened up her home at the York end of the village, establishing a meeting house, with services and prayer meetings held in the kitchen. Sunday was a very full day for Ann – what a character she must have been! Full of enthusiasm, out and about with the preachers, every Sunday her kitchen a hive of activity, full of Society members, new converts and preachers engaged in bible study, prayer and singing the new Wesleyan hymn tunes. Perhaps one or two reluctant farmhands were present. At this time when Ann was so active within the Society she was also a busy farmer's wife and mother of a large family of young children: baptismal records show that she had eight children between 1892 and 1912.

After Sunday morning worship, along with her friend Elizabeth Scott, she would accompany the visiting preachers to neighbouring hamlets and villages, often Colton, to help with services there. Ann eventually took over the Society leadership from William Batman, continuing in this post until ill-health and old age compelled her to retire. Although she went to live with relatives in York, she requested that her final resting place should be in Copmanthorpe. Ann played a huge part in the early Society and her grave-stone may be seen in St Giles' churchyard.

Ann's friend Elizabeth Scott, a well-to-do farmer's wife, provided accommodation for visiting ministers, both lay and ministerial. She set up an altar in her home, which was popular with the early Methodists; every morning she would gather together her family and any available farm-hands for morning prayers and bible reading.

Reverend John Scott (first principal of Westminster Training College)

Elizabeth Scott gave birth to a son, John, on 16 November 1792.[19] Brought up in a home where visiting preachers often stayed, his early years were influenced by both his devoutly Christian parents and those preachers. He developed into a very bright boy, intent on reading, bible study and learning. He attended meetings at Mrs Hobson's home and on Saturdays, along with his sister, would make his way to York to attend bible study and religious education classes. These were conducted by the Reverend Joseph Sutcliffe who was renowned for his work with young people and had a profound influence on John's religious life.

Meanwhile, John's widowed mother, Elizabeth, had remarried. His new stepfather expected John to take up the family business of farming. Although John was willing to do his share on the farm it was not what he wanted for his future career, so in his spare time he continued with his book learning. This caused some dissension between stepfather and son and, on more than one occasion, John was reprimanded.

John continued to enjoy the visits of the ministers to his home, listening to the discussions and gradually being able to take part in them.

Eventually he was able to debate eloquently and in 1810, when only eighteen, the Reverend James Macdonald arranged for John to preach at the Copmanthorpe meeting house. The sermon was such a success that it was discussed at the following Circuit meeting. John by this time had decided to dedicate his life to the ministry and the following year, at the young age of nineteen, he was accepted for training and he later travelled widely throughout Britain as a circuit minister, theologian and administrator.

His distinguished career included the following:[20]

1836–38   First principal of Westminster Training College

1836–68   Treasurer of the Foreign Mission Society

1843 & 1852 President of the Sheffield Conference.

John served the Methodist church for 56 years until his death at Blackheath in 1868. A plaque in the Methodist chapel on Main Street commemorates his work.

The Old Wesleyan Methodist chapel

In March 1821 John Hobson paid £10 for a property on Church Street; this was a school house known to be in use in 1815. Almost immediately he sold it on for the same price to the Methodist Society and it would appear that he was acting on their behalf.[21] The register of York meeting houses shows Mr Joseph Wade, farmer, of Copmanthorpe applying to the Archbishop of York for a certificate to licence the Church Street property as a place for the use of religious worship; this was granted on 6 September 1821 and the Copmanthorpe Society at last had their own place of worship.[22]

A short-lived Primitive Methodist chapel sprang up on an adjacent property in 1860. This occupied the site of the present Co-operative Store but by 1879 it had been purchased by the Wesleyans for £97 and converted into a Sunday School.[23]

A copy of the Trustees report for 1875–79 held in Copmanthorpe Library shows the wide-ranging nature of support for the Wesleyan chapel as illustrated by its four local trustees. They were: John Clark (railway inspector), Frederick Masterman (railway clerk), John Acomb (surgeon), and John Hobson (farmer), assisted by others from York and as far afield as Beverley.[24] In 1872 the Society paid £10 for the adjoining derelict

5.4 The old Wesleyan chapel built by the Society of Methodists in 1821 (now the site of the Co-operative store room) (Sanderson Collection, Copmanthorpe Library; York Library Service)

cottage, using it to extend the chapel. This extension is visible on the left-hand side of the chapel (**fig 5.4**). In 1945 the Trustees adopted Section 17 of the 1929 Methodist Act of Union, after which the Wesleyan Chapel became known simply as the Methodist Chapel.[25] In 1958 it was sold for £100 to a fish merchant, Mr J V Miller, subject to removal of all exterior evidence of it having been a place of worship and that the premises were not used for gambling, drinking or dancing.[26]

The chapel, situated in the village centre, has a fascinating history having done service in its time as school house, Methodist chapel, grocer's shop, joiner's shop, hardware and general store, and today, the store room for the Co-op.

Chapel reminiscences

The chapel, despite its small congregation, held a significant place in the life of the village. It is remembered with affection and humour by the small band of Methodists worshipping there up to its closure in 1958. Familiar names for this period were members of the Unwin, Pinder, Harper, Barnes, King and Ansell families along with Mr North. Mrs Simpson was the organist and Mary Thompson led the Sunday school. The outstanding class leader of this period was Mrs Grace Agar who was also chapel steward, communion steward, and treasurer, sometimes even all four at once, certainly until Mr Aubrey Ansell became treasurer in 1956.[27]

The chapel stood back to back with St Giles church, its plain exterior relieved by the front porch. It consisted of one high-windowed room. To the front, behind the communion rails, stood the pulpit, the font and the communion table, with the organ on the left. Heating was provided by a cast-iron stove with a long flue, often the subject of good-natured banter about which way the wind was blowing and whether it would belch out smoke into the chapel. The pews were tiered and provided a good view over St Giles' graveyard.[28]

The pattern of worship consisted of Sunday services at 10.30am and 6.30pm, bible study and prayer meetings. A monthly midweek preachers' meeting was held and special services of celebration took place throughout the year. Southlands chapel choir from York were frequently in attendance for these, the Revd Leslie Houldsworth being minister for both Southlands and Copmanthorpe chapels.[29]

Afternoon Sunday School classes for the younger children took place in the chapel, led by Mary Thompson. The older children went to the home of Aubrey and Mollie Ansell who had kindly offered their lounge, and pews were brought over from chapel for this purpose.[30]

Seasonal celebrations took place along with chapel and Sunday School anniversaries; harvest festival was always well attended by villagers and the chapel would be overflowing with home-grown fruit and vegetables and decorated with flowers and sheaves of corn. The old cast-iron stove took pride of place, bedecked with leaves and its long pipe entwined with foliage which had shrivelled up by the evening because of the heat. Favourite hymns were 'We plough the fields and scatter' and 'Come ye thankful people come'. The event culminated with a jolly harvest supper and an auction of the fruit and vegetables. The highlight of the year was the annual summer outing, a joint event with St Giles church. This was a train journey to Scarborough for a full day at the seaside.[31]

The closing years

In 1955 the decision was taken to erect a new chapel on Main Street costing £2750, half of this being funded by the Methodist Church and the other half by local fund-raising. Over the following three years the chapel members, under the inspiring leadership of Mrs Agar, pursued a vigorous campaign of fund-raising. Garden parties at the home of Mr and Mrs Ray Fox on Top Lane, cream teas, coffee mornings, jumble sales, concerts and sponsored bike rides were among the many events. The hard work and initiative of the chapel members along with village support ensured the required target was reached. Fittingly, the final service in the old chapel was the harvest festival: a service of thanksgiving.

Main Street chapel

The prospect facing the new chapel was a challenging one, its opening coinciding with the onset of the village housing boom and its attendant population explosion. The population of the village rose from 600 in 1958 to nearly 4000 in 1980.[32] How would the chapel cope with catering for the spiritual needs of a rapidly changing village?

The chapel opened in June 1958. For the Methodist stalwarts this marked the culmination of their hard work and dedication (**fig 5.5**). Photographs in their archives show Mrs Grace Agar turning the key in the chapel door watched by presiding clergy, officials and members. The service of dedication was conducted by Revd L Houldsworth, the Copmanthorpe minister, Revd N T Colley (superintendent minister of York Wesley circuit) and Revd Fowler, the vicar of St Giles.[33] Among the large number of trustees at that time were Mrs Agar, Mr Ansell, Mrs King, Mrs Goodwin, Mrs Pinder, Mrs Simpson, Mr Harper and Mr North.[34]

5.5   Laying the foundation stone of the new chapel, 1958 (Sanderson Collection, Copmanthorpe Library; York Library Service)

The building

The building itself demonstrates how it has adapted and changed over the past 50 years to meet the needs of the village. The chapel began as a single-storey structure, its double doors opening into the porch which led into the chapel.[35] At the opening, membership was 20, rising to 63 by 1966.[36] By 1976 two temporary wooden buildings had been added to accommodate increasing membership and the growing Sunday School. It quickly became obvious that these buildings demanded more and more maintenance and with pressure for yet more space, a permanent extension was needed.[37] A three-man team was appointed to oversee the project and plans were submitted by York architect David Greenwood.[38] The undertaking, costing £55,000, was funded partly by the Methodists themselves; 40% of this came from grant aid outside the village and a substantial amount was raised by local funding,[39] this latter once again demanding a huge effort by chapel members. The village newsletter, first appearing in 1970, proved to be a good vehicle of communication between chapel and village, carrying adverts for fund-raising events and articles about the new extension.

This extension replaced the wooden buildings with a worship centre capable of being adapted for large or small gatherings, and the original chapel was converted to a Sunday School and multi-purpose community centre. A dedication service at the opening on 13 June 1981 was conducted by the Copmanthorpe minister, Revd J Price, attended by the previous minister, Revd D Bowker, Revd P Morley (superintendent minister York Wesley circuit) and Revd P Kerridge.[40] By now there had been some reorganisation of the York Centenary circuit and the York Wesley circuit and the York South circuit had emerged, taking in Copmanthorpe.[41]

The chapel had 90 members and continuing expansion meant that just twelve years down the line yet more space was required. This second extension, costing in excess of £160,000, was funded by grants from various trusts and funds; the chapel itself raised £70,000 including £35,000 contributed at a gift day. A £40,000 loan provided by the Methodist Chapel Aid Association meant that fund-raising continued long after the opening of the new building. The extension opened on 5 September 1993 with a dedication service led by Revd R Moore, pastor of Copmanthorpe and Revd B Tibbets, superintendent minister of York South circuit. Mr Roy Piercy, chapel steward, welcomed the members and visitors. The extension enlarged the worship centre and replaced the single-storey Sunday School/community centre with a two-storey multi-purpose building able to accommodate local groups including village playgroups and the Brownies.[42]

Worship

The pattern of worship has continued in the tradition of the old chapel, with only slight alterations in the times of Sunday services. The village newsletters testify to this, also showing gradual increases in mid-week fellowship until today, when the chapel has a busy programme of worship. This includes united services with St Giles, united family services, early morning mid-week communion, mid-week vestry prayer meetings, ladies monthly fellowship, men's fellowship, healing services and house groups for prayer and bible study. Preaching has continued unchanged with the pulpit occupied by ministers, lay preachers and invited speakers.[43]

Sunday School

The first Sunday School records appear in the minute book of 1963 but a Sunday School had been in existence long before. At a meeting in September 1963, presided over by Mr Fox, Mary Thompson was elected as Sunday School superintendent, Miss J Thompson, secretary, Mrs King, treasurer and Mrs Holt took responsibility for the cradle roll. Four teachers, Mr Cooper, Mr Wilkinson, Miss Scott and Miss Thompson were named, along with Mrs Scanlon and Miss Scott, who played the piano and organ. Afternoon Sunday School continued with Mary Thompson leading until 1964, when after many years of devoted service she retired, to be replaced by Mr Coupe. Shortly afterwards classes began to take place in the morning.

The combining of the Methodist and St Giles' Sunday Schools from 1967 to 1978 brought changes, with the children being taught by both Methodist and Anglican teachers in a variety of venues including the WI hall. On reverting back to their own individual classes in 1978, the children began to be incorporated into adult worship. With the opening of the new extension in 1981 the children at last had their own permanent Sunday School which continued to meet before morning service until the opening of the second extension in 1993. Provision of a crèche enabled Sunday School and chapel to take place at the same time. Today the children join the adults for the first fifteen minutes of morning service before leaving for Sunday School.[44]

Fellowship

Fellowship has always been part of the Christian experience, the first Copmanthorpe Methodists demonstrating this as they travelled together around the villages helping other classes. In the old chapel it was visible in the joint annual outing and shared harvest suppers. The Revd Marion Bucktrout (Copmanthorpe 1991–99) writing in 'Ministers remember' for the chapel's fortieth anniversary celebrations in 1998 recalls chapel family walks, picnics, pantomimes, poetry reading, flower festivals and harvest celebrations (complete with borrowed milking machine).[45] It would appear that over the years chapel social events have become more secular. The minute book of 1958 shows the trustees 'discussing the business of dancing at Methodist functions', but in September 1985 the chapel advertised a barn dance! At appropriate times these social events have been combined with fund-raising. Today the chapel has a full programme of fellowship and social events, often shared with the wider Christian community.

Relations with St Giles

Relations between the two churches have been, and remain, cordial with significant mutual co-operation. The joint Sunday Schools and annual outings of earlier years were successful enterprises, while today, interdenominational services include frequent united Sunday services, a service of remembrance, a carol service and joint Lent courses. There is a strong non-denominational youth club with a monthly service alternating between the two churches and a joint holiday club. The traditional harvest festival is now celebrated jointly in the WI hall.

The Methodist Church today

Today the chapel serves the village well as a community centre and place of worship; it owes a great deal to the many Copmanthorpe members, past and present, who have been unstinting in their devotion to Methodism in the village. The present membership is 120 with 40 children at Sunday School. Three remaining members from the old Church Street chapel are still worshipping today: Mrs Dorothy Unwin, Mrs Dorothy Barnes and Mrs Barbara King.[46]

Little remains of the original building of 1958, it having been modified and enlarged until today when it is a substantial, partly two-storey Lshaped construction. It harmonises well with its surroundings and sits on an elevated site, facing on to Main Street. The interior is well laid out and its crowning glory is undoubtedly the main worship centre, an imposing room with a steeply sloping wooden ceiling creating a sense of height and space. The fittings and furniture of light wood further contribute to this.

The building incorporates two pieces of modern stained glass: a three-cornered 'Trinity' window over the entrance to the chapel and a half-moon-shaped window depicting eleven different species of wild flowers found within half-mile radius of Copmanthorpe. This was designed and made by chapel member Roy Jones. A link with the old Wesleyan chapel is the communion table, still in use today, while a carved stone, removed from the short-lived Primitive Methodist chapel, stands as a reminder of that venture in the grounds.

The Revd Bucktrout wrote in 1998: 'But wonderful also is this beautiful building in this fortieth anniversary year. A building with a touch of the monastics and a dash of the Scandinavians! God's joyful building.'[47]

Notes

1   Page, W (ed) *The certificates of the commissioners appointed to the survey of chantries, guilds, hospitals etc in the County of York* pt 1 SS vol 91 1892 p 81

2   Tillot, P M (ed) *Victoria County History* vol 1 History of Yorkshire: City of York 1961 p 389

3   Raine J (ed) *The fabric rolls of York Minster* SS vol 35 1858 p 54

4   YAS MS 214 Skaife, R F vol 5 *Materials for a history of the Ainsty* p 7

5   YCA M:60 Copmanthorpe Glebe Terrier 1664

6   NYCRO ZET/2598 Wood of Hollin Hall Papers 1779–91

7   YAS MS 214 Skaife, R F vol 5 *Materials for a history of the Ainsty* Canon Dixon's mss

8   Ibid

9   Ollard S L & Walker PC (eds) *Archbishop Herring's Visitation Returns 1743* pt 1 YASRS vol 71 1927 p 139

10 A charitable bequest by a member of the Norfolk family for bread given out to the poor

11 YAS MS 214 Skaife, R F vol 5 *Materials for a history of the Ainsty* op cit

12 BI D/C CP 1732/2 f

13 YAS MS 214 Skaife, R F vol 5 *Materials for a history of the Ainsty* op cit

14 Annersley, C & Hoskins, P (eds) *Archbishop Drummonds Visitation Returns 1764* vol 3 York 2001 p 162

15 Beckerlegge, O *John Wesley comes to York* York 1988 pp 2, 5, 9, 15; Appleby, C & Smith, D *Of Malet, Malbis and Fairfax* 2000 p 48

16 Cammige, W *Copmanthorpe: introduction of Methodism into the village* York 1908 p 4

17 B I MRC/1/11 Census 1787 MRC/1/1/3 Census 1799 MRC1/1/5 York Society book 1807–20

18 Cammidge, W op cit p 5

19 Ibid pp 6, 7

20 John Rylands University Library, Manchester: Methodist Archives

21 Johnson, J *The Copmanthorpe Story* op cit p 20

22 CL Copmanthorpe Wesleyan Methodists Trustees Report 1875–79

23 YCRL Bulmer, T History & Directory of North Yorkshire 1890

24 B I Register of Meeting Houses 1821 Register 1

25 Johnson, J op cit p 20

26 Mr A Ansell to RF

27 Ibid

28 Mrs D Unwin to RF

29 Mrs M Ansell to RF

30 Mrs D Unwin to RF

31 Mr A Ansell to RF

32 CL Village Newsletter April 1980 p 3

33 YCRL Y287 *Ministers remember: Forty years on Main Street: Copmanthorpe Methodist Chapel 1958–1998*

34 BI MRC 3

35 Mr A Ansell to RF

36 YCRL *Minsters remember* op cit & BI MRC **1/1/4**

37 CL Village Newsletter April 1980

38 YCRL *York Evening Press* 18 June 1979

39 Mr A Ansell to RF, also *York Evening Press* 8 April 1980

40 YCRL *York Evening Press* 13 June 1981

41 BI MRC 2 Launching of York South circuit commemorative booklet

42 YCRL *York Evening Press* 6 September 1993

43 Revd P Worth & Mr R Piercy to RF

44 BI MRC COP 10 & Mr R Piercy to RF

45 YCRL *Ministers remember* op cit

46 Mrs F Unwin, Revd P Worth and Mr R Piercy to RF

47 YCRL *Ministers remember* op cit

CHAPTER SIX

A history of the agriculture of Copmanthorpe

DAVID BREWER

The lie of the land

I T IS IMPORTANT TO UNDERSTAND the geography and under-lying geology of the area to appreciate why the cultivation of the land developed as it did. Copmanthorpe is situated on the southerly slope of a terminal moraine created by the last Ice Age, with the highest land lying to the north-west of the parish and the lowest to the south-east where it meets the Foss. (It should be explained that this is not the same Foss that runs through the centre of York; the name, derived from the Latin *fossa*, a ditch or trench, is very common in the area.) The lowest point, which is less than 9m (29.5 feet) above sea level, is at the most southerly end of the parish below Copmanthorpe Grange where the Foss leaves the parish. The Foss then continues through Appleton Roebuck, where it changes its name to the Fleet, and ultimately joins the Wharfe at Nun Appleton, at which point the Wharfe is still tidal. The mean high water mark at Nun Appleton is 7m (23 feet) above sea level which suggests that with so little fall between Copmanthorpe and this point the natural drainage would have been quite poor, and backing up of the water would have been significant when the Wharfe was in flood. This poor natural drainage of the lower-lying land around Copmanthorpe is not helped by the fact that the soil type for the whole of this area is classed as 'clays to loams with impeded or slow drainage'[1] although there are local variations to this. Below the top soil is 'clay till'[2] deposited by the glaciers, which is the cause of the impeded drainage. The low-lying area is to the east and south of the village, extending from York Field, through Temple Field and the Moor, right up to the south end of Low West Field.

The natural drainage for the area is provided by the Foss to the south-east and by a watercourse, also known as the Foss on some maps, to the

• 73 •

west. It is also possible that the courses of Town Ings drain, High and Low West Fields drain, and Low West Field drain are also principally natural. In fact the natural features suggest that the water course now followed by Town Ings drain may well have extended as far as the area of Low Green and the site of St Giles' Well. The site of the well, at the foot of a slope where the underlying soil is predominantly clay, is a common location for springs. The type of land and the original vegetation is clearly chronicled in the field names given in old documents, and such is the quantity of information available, it has been possible to compile a detailed list of the field names giving their possible origins (see **Appendix**). Briefly, it can be seen that many of the outlying areas were decidedly wet, with names such as moor from Old English 'mor', for waste/barren ground tending to be wet, and carr from Old Norse 'kjarr' for marsh/low-lying ground, or wooded/scrubby ground as indicated by 'rudding' – Old English meaning clearing. Some of the names even include the indigenous plants such as broom, sedge and gale (also known as bog myrtle).

Early farming

Any traces of the earliest farmers have been eroded by time. The written record begins with Domesday which indicates that farming was already well established, although the amount of land being cultivated is very difficult to estimate. Copmanthorpe is listed as containing six carucates of taxable land. A carucate was supposed to be the amount of land a team of eight oxen could plough in one year. The actual area therefore would vary according to the local soil conditions, with heavier soil taking longer to plough. In this area it has been estimated that one carucate was approximately 120 acres (*c* 48ha), so on this estimate six carucates gives an area of around 720 acres (*c* 291ha). By the time of Domesday, however, the carucate was more of a tax measure than a real area of land. It must also be remembered that the Domesday survey was carried out in a very short space of time, approximately two years, so the quoted area of land would have been at best an estimate and at worst nothing more than a guess. Bearing this in mind, it is possible to see an approximate equivalent to this area on the 1722/79 map where the original outlines of High West Field, Low West Field, York Field and Temple Field can clearly be seen, covering in the region of 750 acres. So by 1086 nearly half the parish (total 1658 acres; *c* 671ha) had already been cleared and was being farmed to some degree.

Farming was obviously an important part of the local economy in 1086, and by 1284/5[3] the cultivated/taxable land had increased to 11 carucates (c 1300 acres; c 526ha) showing that additional fields may have been created from the more difficult to work land. It could also indicate that the king was desperately trying to squeeze more taxes out of everyone! By the time of the dissolution of the Knights Templars in 1307/8, wheat, maslin (mixed corn), barley, peas, oats, rye and beans were all being grown, and the domestic animals included cows, bullocks, pigs, sheep, hens and geese, with both oxen and horses used for ploughing and transport. Later that century the Poll Tax return of 1379 shows only five people doing a particular job or trade and the assumption must be that everyone else was involved in agriculture.

Copmanthorpe's open field system

Copmanthorpe had four open arable fields which are still clearly iden-tifiable today (see **fig 8.5**). Each field consisted of a large number of strips which contained anywhere between a quarter of an acre and about two acres. These strips were organised into blocks known mainly as flatts, but they were also referred to as furlongs. Between the flatts were balks, narrow strips used for access but occasionally cultivated. Some balks also existed within the flatts, again presum-ably to aid access. Originally each villager would have had one or more strips in each of the open fields, distributed so that good and bad land was shared more or less equally. However, this resulted in no-one having all their land together. As late as 1722, when the open fields were owned by just thirteen people, none of the land holdings had been amalgamated. As an example of how this ancient system still persisted in 1722, Hasacre flatt in York Field had a total area of six acres one rood, divided into thirteen strips, owned by eleven different people, with none of them having any adjacent strips.

Initially individual strips may have been worked separately, but event-ually it would have become clear that working blocks of strips together had distinct advantages, especially when crop rotation became better under-stood. In the days before artificial fertilizers, the health of the soil was maintained by occasionally allowing it to rest, or lie fallow, and crops were grown in a rotation to ensure maximum output and minimum disease. In Copmanthorpe, crop rotation and the use of a fallow year is clearly shown in Mr Wood's field book of 1811[4] which indicates that rotation was done by field since Low West Field was given over entirely to fallow in that year. Leaving a whole field fallow gave the opportunity to turn grazing animals onto it as soon as the last crop had been cleared in autumn. They would eat anything remaining, plus any re-growth, and in the process added their own nitrates back into the soil. In spring and early summer of the fallow year the ground would be ploughed regularly to help kill any perennial weeds that had become established. Over the summer the land would usually have been too dry and hard to plough, so the field would have been left and it would have eventually turned green with a mixture of annual weeds and remaining corn. This would again be grazed before being ploughed ready to take the next year's crop. In this way the fertility of the land was restored.

In 1811 High West Field had only wheat listed. Having all the wheat in one field would have made both sowing and harvesting much easier and eliminated a lot of travelling. The next part of the four field rotation would most likely have been in Temple Field where beans and clover were grown. Both of these are legumes which have the ability to fix nitrogen from the air back into the ground in the form of nitrates, thus boosting the fertility of the soil. Beans are high in protein and clover was very important as animal fodder; this would have been cut then carried to the animals in other fields or made into a very rich hay. A small quantity of oats was also grown in this field. In 1811, York Field seems to have been in the fourth year of the rotation cycle which would generally have featured mainly root crops; it is the only field where turnips and potatoes were grown that year. However, these were not grown in great quantities, probably reflecting the fact that they were only for local consumption, so oats, wheat, barley, beans and clover were also being grown in York Field. The broad mixture of crops in this field, where every flatt contains more than one crop, seems to reflect the fact that, for that year, each strip holder seems to have been responsible for their own plots and may just have grown what they felt the land would take. This could also explain why some of the strips are left fallow, as they could already have been weed infested and needed cleaning, or it could just be that weather conditions had not been favourable at seedtime.

The land outside these open fields may originally have been common grazing for the whole village and would have been a mixture of moor, forest, marsh and scrub which is confirmed by some of the names that survive. Over the years, after the open fields were cleared, these more marginal lands would have gradually been enclosed for use as pasture and hay meadows. Enclosing these fields as they were cleared made sense as the grazing cattle and sheep would have been much easier to manage than if they were left to roam. Conversely, when hay was being made, they could be excluded. These fields would not have been divided into strips like the open fields; instead, individuals may have carried out the reclamation on the understanding that they were then entitled to at least some, if not all, that they reclaimed. By 1722 only the Moor (45 acres 3 roods 22 perches) and the Common (1–2–26) had not been reclaimed from the original marginal land, and the size of each of the open fields had been considerably reduced by enclosures (intacks) taken from them. This meant that by 1722 the majority of the land in the parish, 1056 of the 1658 acres, had already been taken into private ownership and enclosed. Of these 1056 acres, Mr Boynton (247 acres), Mr Wood (413 acres), and Mr Adams (153 acres), owned 813 acres (77% of the total). All these gentlemen had a direct connection with the Lordship of the Manor. This left the rest of the land in the hands of seventeen other individuals with an average holding of just over 14 acres (c 5.5ha) each. Obviously Messrs Boynton, Wood and Adams were not going to get their own hands dirty, which would have been difficult from their residences in Ripon and the East Riding, so their lands were rented out. This concentration of land in the hands of absentee landlords, with the other land holders having their holdings spread over the whole parish, resulted in the total absence of outlying farms in the parish, as no one working farmer possessed sufficient lands adjacent to each other to create a viable separate farmstead away from the village.

Enclosure Award 1840

Formal enclosure of open fields and common land had been in progress across England for more than 150 years when the Copmanthorpe Enclosure Award was made in 1840, and in 1820 'less [sic] than 50 townships in Yorkshire'[5] retained the open field system. So, why had Copmanthorpe not been enclosed earlier, and why did the landowners decide to go to the considerable expense of an Act of Parliament specifically for the enclosure of Copmanthorpe at that very late stage. The simple answer to the first question seems to be that the major land holder, the Wood family, had become so deep in debt that they simply could not afford the cost. Despite owning nearly half the land in 1810, Mr Wood was even in debt to his own tenants, owing Thomas Norfolk £150, Henry Wade £50 and John Batman £1000.[6] The imminent arrival of the railway seems to be the answer to the second question (see chapter 7).

Enclosure had a number of objectives, providing benefits both locally and nationally. One was to increase the productivity of the land already in cultivation: the open field strip system operating in 1811 was far from efficient and needed modernising. On a national scale the aim was to bring all the remaining marginal land into useful production in an effort to make the country more self-sufficient. By 1840 the only remaining areas of common land in Copmanthorpe were the Moor, to the south of the village, and the common, which may have been to the north of Temple Field. Both these areas were overseen by the local Manor Court, and a system of beast pastures and gates was used to ensure that the common areas were not overgrazed. However, at least one dispute had to be resolved at the York Quarter Sessions where in 1659 Edward Love was prosecuted 'for erecting a cottage on the corner of Common of Copmanthorpe and stopping a sure [sewer ie drain in this case] which was a watering place for the whole towne'.[7] In an effort to improve the productivity of all the land, enclosed or unenclosed, a system for improving the drainage for the whole parish was included in the Act of Enclosure. Nineteen field drains were specified in detail in the act for Copmanthorpe, as well as improvements to the few that already existed. Even today with the addition of sub-surface drainage tiles (or perforated plastic pipes) assisting these field drains, the land can still become waterlogged, so imagine what it was like before all these improvements.

Finally, enclosures were encouraged in order to lay out formally all the public rights of way from footpath, to bridle path, to highway and thus improve the infrastructure of the whole country providing benefit to everyone. In fact the rights of way thus specified in the acts form the legal basis of all our public rights of way to this day. The main effect of the Act of Enclosure for Copmanthorpe, apart from the obvious benefits detailed above, was for the land in the open fields to be rearranged so that landowners had blocks of land together rather than scattered strips. Ironically, despite the name of Enclosure, the act did not create many new enclosed fields in Copmanthorpe. Leighton's Trustees' land holdings were consolidated predominantly to Low West Field where they became the sole owner and no new divisions were made apart from those created by an access road. Mr Wood acquired part of the Moor which was adjacent to his existing land so it became subsumed into existing fields and similarly some of his allocation from York Field.

FROM COPPENTHORPE TO COPMANTHORPE

Produce from agriculture

The presence of the Knights Templar preceptory in the parish provides us with a valuable insight into the economy of the area in the late 13th/early 14th century. At the time of the suppression of the order, three inventories were made between 1308 and 1311 detailing their holdings in Copmanthorpe which show a considerable variety of crops and livestock. Bread would have been a staple part of the diet, being made from the wheat, maslin and rye mentioned. Also listed were oats (used mainly as animal food but also to make porridge), peas and beans (valuable sources of protein for both humans and animals), and barley (the main ingredient for ale which, having been boiled in its production, was much healthier to drink than the water). The livestock consisted of 10 cows, 10 heifers (a young female cow that has not yet produced calves), 3 bullocks, 8 pigs, 246 sheep, 5 geese and 1 cock and 1 hen. The nominal cock and hen may reflect the fact that the peasants paid their 'customary rent' for their cottages in kind such as eggs, which explains why 360 eggs are mentioned later, so the brothers did not need to produce these themselves. The large number of sheep emphasises their value for wool and hides as well as meat. The cows would have been producing milk so, although not listed, cheese and butter would have been made. Draught animals included eleven oxen for ploughing, four cart horses, and six plough horses. This is a relatively early use of horses for these purposes and may indicate that some of the knights' horses were then being used for domestic purposes.

One of the inventories also mentions a dovecote. Doves (probably pigeon) were a useful additional source of protein which were generally reserved for the lord, or probably in this case the brothers. The doves helped themselves to the corn in the fields, *everyone's fields*, so they were frequently a cause of friction between the few who had the privilege of eating them and the many whose crops they decimated. A windmill is also listed which would have brought in an income from its use by other farmers in the area. It is probable that the windmill was sited in the field called Mill Hill on the 1722/79 plan as it lies close to the site where the preceptory is believed to have been, but there is no evidence of it either in the field or on later maps.

It is some time before such detailed lists occur again, but it is fortunate that a large number of wills and inventories have been preserved for Copmanthorpe. One of the earliest of these is the inventory taken after the death of William Featherstone in November 1528 (see chapter 4).[8] Winter corn is mentioned indicating that even at this early date varieties of wheat or barley (or both) had been developed for autumn sowing. This would have been of real benefit to farmers because although there is usually some loss of plants over winter this would be outweighed by the fact that the resulting harvest could begin a few weeks ahead of the spring-sown crop. Corn for the market then became available at a time when the previous year's corn would be deteriorating in store (storage itself being an expensive operation) so the first of the new season's corn would have been sold at a premium. Also included in Mr Featherstone's inventory is an item which may be 'two loads of woad'. Woad is always associated with the ancient Britons from the first millennium AD, but it was an important source of blue dye and was grown in parts of England until indigo was imported from the tropics. Indigo itself was eventually superseded when aniline dyes were created from coal tar in the 19th century. Woad (*Isatis tinctoria*) is of the same family as brassicas (cabbage etc) and would have been a useful occasional rotation crop, especially in some of the poorly drained fields as it does not mind wet conditions. Part of the complex process of extracting the dye involves fermentation with ammonia, which was extracted from urine, and gave off such a stench that 'Queen Elizabeth issued a proclamation that woad production had to cease in any town through which she was passing'.[9]

The inclusion in John Thresher's inventory (1580) of salt beef, and of a salting tub in Henry Vavasour's (1583) is a reminder that preservation of perishable goods was quite a problem. Most of the cattle were slaughtered before winter and the beef salted to preserve it. However, if the climate was temperate enough to over-winter corn, and hay was a major crop, then it could be argued that over-wintering cattle, which would naturally grow a winter coat, may not have been such a problem. The cost of providing suitable shelter may have been the deciding factor, and there was of course the period of the Little Ice Age in the 17th century. Perhaps the introduction of the turnip in the 18th century was the turning point when it became profitable to over-winter cattle. Thomas Fenton's inventory (1588), which includes two hives of bees, gives a reminder that sugar from cane was not freely available until well into the 17th century. Honey was valued as a sweetener and preservative and the wax had many uses such as in the making of polish, for waterproofing cloth, and to make candles. The scale of honey production is best illustrated by the will of Robert Foster (1622) who had one and a half gallons (seven litres). Some products and crops seem to escape the early records: no specific mention is made of grass or clover until 1811, being no doubt included previously in pasture, and potatoes are also mentioned for the first time in 1811, despite having been grown in this country by then for over 200 years. This latter omission is even more surprising since the land in this area is particularly suited to root vegetables such as potatoes and sugarbeet.

The record of tithes paid shows that rape was grown occasionally.[10] It is another of the brassica family and is grown for its oil, which is extracted by crushing the seed. Rape was originally introduced in the 15th century as a way of reducing olive oil imports and was used in the cloth trade and industry. Today farmers are once again growing rape, but now the rape-seed oil is for use in the food industry, where, amongst other things, it is still a substitute for olive oil. The 'Tyth for Lin' also confirms the cultivation of flax (*Linum usitatissimum*) which grows to about one metre in height and produces long fibres which are then made into linen, canvas, twine and even writing paper. The fibres are extracted by pulling the plants up by the roots and soaking the whole plant, including roots, for a few days in water to dissolve the vegetable matter, a process known as retting. This method is confirmed at Copmanthorpe in a letter of 1810 to Mr Wood from Wm Kilvington who says 'I am very sorry to inform you that W Batman I think has taken a very unwarrantable liberty in digging a line pond at the bottom of Temple Field'. Copmanthorpe even had the facility to take the production of linen to the next stage as a note in Copmanthorpe library from Mrs Catherine Burton, confirmed by a tape interview with Mrs Beedham in 1975,[11] mentions the Flax Mill on York Field Lane. This mill can be identified on the 1910 OS map, and in 1861 Richard Cussons is listed as a flax dresser (ie a person who prepares flax) in the census returns. There is also reference to hemp (*Cannabis sativa* not *Cannabis indica*) in the tithe record, and in 1622 Robert Foster's inventory includes a 'hemp brake', a tool for breaking up hemp fibres during the retting process. The hemp fibres were used primarily to make twine and rope.

Another crop of real importance to both lord and peasant alike was wood. For centuries this would have been the only fuel available and would have been almost a by-product of land reclamation. York City Muster Roll of 1584, the document created when every man had to assemble at the Knavesmire complete with his arms, shows that by far the most common weapon was a bill. Although a design of bill was developed specifically for use in battle, William Fenton's inventory of

1555[12] shows clearly that his bill was the everyday tool used for cutting and chopping wood (see **fig 4.2**); its use as an offensive weapon was only co-incidental! Wood, in the form of standing trees, was a one-off but major source of income for the Lord of the Manor. In 1798 Richard Wood sold 521 trees in the hedgerows at Copmanthorpe and 2505 trees in Copmanthorpe Wood, along with 164 trees in the hedgerows at Dringhouses for the then small fortune of £1710.[13] This almost certainly would not have gone down well with the locals as not only did this remove a source of firewood for them but the trees in the hedgerows would have provided the only shelter, summer or winter, for their animals. In addition to all the obvious uses of wood, the bark of the oak was also a valuable source of tannin for the leather industry. Stripping the bark from the wood before it was cut up for other uses provided 32 man-days of work for the locals according to Mr Wood's accounts for May 1796.

In addition to the crops grown in the fields, fruit and vegetables would have been grown in the garths attached to most dwellings. These were rarely listed in inventories, although Robert Foster's of 1622 confirms the existence of apples. Later, in 1722, some of the garths are referred to as orchards, although the term had been used in an indenture of 1678. Fruit such as pears, plums, quinces and even medlars could have been grown in these orchards, but it is the apple that seems to have had a particular importance for Copmanthorpe. At least one variety was named after the village, the Copmanthorpe Russet, which was exhibited under that name as late as 1934 and there may have been another variety called Copmanthorpe Crab, although it must be remembered that in some areas the words crab and apple were interchangeable so the varieties may have been one and the same. It is possible that Copmanthorpe Russet was just a local name for the Dutch Mignonne variety but John Lindley, secretary of the organisation that became the Royal Horticultural Society, writing in 1852 asked quite reasonably how an apple named after a small village outside York could have become confused with a well-known continental variety and he suggests that further investigation may have confirmed them as distinct varieties. The very fact that the village had its own named variety, regardless of its origins, and the fact that the record indicates apples being grown over so many centuries, shows just how important this humble fruit was to the economy of the village.

Associated trades

From the earliest times the people who worked the land around the village of Copmanthorpe would have generated work for others although the subsistence nature of the very first farmers probably meant that they had to be virtually self-sufficient, either individually or as a group, so most of the skills required would have come from within their own community. Initially the people who acquired these extra skills would have continued to work their own plots and would still have considered themselves farmers, but eventually there would have been enough demand locally to support specialised tradesmen. As early as 1308 there was a windmill associated with the Knights Templar establishment in the village which would have provided someone with almost a full-time occupation. There was a working windmill in the tenure of John Vary in 1678[14] who is the only miller named in the documents. It had been assumed that the only mill site was at Mill Hill as mentioned previously, but the survey of 1722 refers to a Mill Hill Flatt located in York Field. By 1811 this name has been replaced by Street Gate Flatt, which is clearly located to the south of Street Gate on the 1840 Enclosure map. Street Gate is the point where Top Lane meets the York to Tadcaster road. This area to the south of Top Lane is raised above the rest of York Field at one of the highest points in the parish and would have been a much more suitable location for a windmill than along Acaster Road (Temple Lane).

The 1379 Poll Tax return suggests that the majority of males over the age of sixteen were employed in some way on the land (31 out of 36) as only five had their trade specified: weaver, tailor, carpenter, bailiff, and smith. William Bishop is listed as weaver, practising his trade in his own home. Weaving remained very much a cottage industry even after the introduction of power looms in the manufactories of the late 18th century. The spinning and weaving of wool and linen may have been carried out in most households both for personal use and, in the 18th and 19th centuries, as a serious contribution to the family income. William Fenton, husbandman, had clearly produced all the raw materials as in 1555 he left wool, hemp and lyne, and Jane Hodgson (1557) left one spinning wheel. In fact this lady seems to have had a significant business as also listed were 4 stone (25kg) of wool, 5 yards Lyneclothe (linen), 12 yards of harden cloth (a coarse fabric also made from flax or hemp), 9 yards of carssea (kersey, a coarse wool cloth), 13 yards of lynn clothe, and 10 yards of cloth yarn. This trade even provided work for the blacksmith: in 1622 Robert Foster, blacksmith, left wool and tow (flax or hemp) cards, the tools used to comb out the fibres made of wire teeth set in leather or wood. Associated with the weaving of cloth is the task of making it into clothes and in the same Poll Tax return of 1379 John Hobell is shown as cissor (tailor). The carpenter was one John Wright, who had clearly continued in the profession that originally gave his family their name. The Old English word 'wyrtha' meaning to work or build was generally associated with working wood, hence wheel-wright, and at that time the carpenter would have been an important person in the village, building houses and making all manner of carts, implements, furniture and kitchen utensils for the villagers, with a little input no doubt from William Marshall who is shown as a faber (smith). For the smith, in addition to helping make carts and implements there would have been the obvious requirement to shoe horses and, as the name suggests, he would also fabricate anything required from metal such as the tools used in house and field. He would also have been the knife sharpener as he was one of the few with a grindstone. In 1807, John Morley is not only the blacksmith but also the tenant of the Royal Oak, and even as late as 1893 the smithy is shown adjacent to this inn, although by 1910 it had moved down Moor Lane where it remained in living memory. For a while at least, it seems there was sufficient work to keep blacksmiths employed at both locations.

One skill that does not appear as a specific trade in the records is that of thatcher. We know that in 1808 'the houses at Copmanthorpe are all very ancient and chiefly thatched'[15] so someone must have done the thatching. The raw materials for thatching were readily available being the straw from either rye or wheat, or reeds from the sedgepitts.[16] One possible explanation is that the farmers and farm workers were all quite capable of doing it for themselves. It was not possible to store all of the corn and hay under shelter on a farm once it had been gathered in, so most of it would have been stacked in the stack-yards (hence the name). When they had finished building these stacks the farmers would give them a peaked or rounded top to help throw off the rain. More often than not this was done by thatching, using the materials to hand, although later the thatch was replaced with a tarpaulin (a canvas sheet, similar to sail cloth, treated with tar to make it water-proof). Thus basic thatching was a skill learnt 'on the job' by farmers and labourers, although there were undoubtedly specialist thatchers in some villages.

Records become much more abundant as the 19th century progresses, with both private directories and the national census information giving details of everyone's occupation. Baines' directory of 1823 shows Thomas Batman and Richard Harrison as butchers, a long-established trade, while John Taylor is listed as a gamekeeper, a profession more often associated with the 'big house' occupied by the main landowner. At that time the Wood family did not live at Copmanthorpe so there was no grand house. The same directory lists a John Kirkman as a gardener, which is believed to mean market gardener. This is the first indication that vegetables are being grown rather than the traditional agricultural crops; the trade of market gardener then features in all the census information through to the last available in 1901, a reflection of the demand for such produce from the expanding cities and towns.

Another notable entry in the 1823 directory was David Dykes – portable threshing machine maker and worker. This really was the early days for the mechanisation of the threshing process, with the first threshing machines only being patented in the late 18th century. These would have been fixed permanently inside a building; portable machines only became available early in the 19th century so David Dykes was decidedly on the cutting edge of technology for his day. No doubt he used the services of Thomas Kilner, the wheelwright in 1823, to make some of the wooden gearing necessary to drive the mechanism in his machine. The actual driving power for the threshing machine would have been a horse wheel of some description which could also be portable, so having pulled the machine to the next farm the poor old horses then had to power it as well! Before mechanisation the grain was separated from the straw and husks by means of threshing flails; the next part of the process, separating the grain from the chaff, is shown in Thomas Fenton's inventory of 1658 by his winnowing cloth, which would have been spread on the ground to ensure that none of the grain was lost during this process. We also know that in September 1785, 'the tithe barn was occupied by B Hobson who had his corn in it and was about 17 yards long with 2 threshing floors of clay'.[17] We do not know how successful Mr Dykes was with his threshing machines, but by the census of 1841 he preferred to be listed as a farmer. This probably reflected the sharp decline in the use of threshing machines in the 1820s and 1830s caused by discontent among farm labourers who saw them as a serious threat to the little winter work they had. This, combined with their already extremely low wages, led to civil unrest and protests which became known as the Captain Swing riots with associated executions, deportations and imprisonments. Such was the seriousness of this unrest that even some of the major manufacturers abandoned the production of threshing machines during this period. By the time Joseph Hobson was a 'threshing machine proprietor' in 1909 it would be most likely that his machine was factory-made by the likes of John Fowler & Co of Leeds and powered by steam in some form or other. Any problems with labour unrest were long gone by then due to the migration from the countryside to the new industrial towns and cities.

Reducing dependence on agriculture

Although the first census of the country was carried out in 1801, a detailed census did not occur until 1841 when it showed just how dependent Copmanthorpe still was on agriculture. Sixty-six out of 95 males aged over thirteen were employed either directly in agriculture or in one of the associated trades (blacksmith, joiner, butcher and gardener). The directories and census returns confirm just how adaptable, even entrepreneurial, some of the farmers were, with Joseph Dickinson (1851) branching out as a carter; Thomas Moyns progressing from market gardener, to carrier, to potato dealer; and John Wright also expanding from market gardener to include carrier in his occupations. By the start of the 20th century, agriculture and its related occupations were becoming less important to the economy of Copmanthorpe: the 1901 census shows that although nearly the same number of male adults was either directly or indirectly employed in this industry (67), the adult male population had increased to 112. Over the course of the 20th century the numbers employed in agriculture declined rapidly, although in 1936 the number of farmsteads was still similar to that of 1871 at fourteen, compared with approximately 20 in 1722; today only three working farms remain.

This reduced number of farms and the associated reduction in workforce in the second half of the 20th century can be explained in one word – power. Mechanisation had been a continuous process, begun centuries earlier with the introduction of innovative implements such as the mouldboard plough, Jethro Tull's seed drill, the threshing machine, and Cyrus Hall McCormick's grain reaper. All these allowed more and more land to be taken into production, but the motive force had been the horse or the ox, which were both still in use in Yorkshire well into the 20th century. Mr King, interviewed in

1975, had clearly only ever worked with horses on the farm, and Jim Barker's recollections of working at Copmanthorpe Lodge show that horses and tractors worked alongside each other until the late 1950s. As tractors became more and more powerful the amount of land that could be worked by one man rapidly increased. In the 1940s Mr Barker was doing well to plough an acre (0.4ha) a day with a team of shire horses and a Ransomes single furrow plough at Copmanthorpe Lodge.[18] Today, Rob Schofield would hope to do nearer 30 acres (12ha) in a day using his Massey Ferguson 2720, still with a Ransomes plough attached but this time a five-furrow reversible – but then it is rated at 150 horse power! To maximise this increased power, and to improve efficiency, small fields were amalgamated to form larger fields, although this process was not as marked in Copmanthorpe as it was in many other parishes, since many of the original fields were already substantial, a consequence perhaps of the late enclosure. The greatest increase in efficiency was achieved when the small farms were taken into larger farms. As a result of all these changes, today there are now very few people in the parish who actually make their living, either directly or indirectly, from agriculture.

Notes

1 Askham Bryan College – Soil map of the Vale of York
2 Askham Bryan College – Map reference 631,424274
3 Skaife, R H (ed) *Kirkby's Inquest, Knights Fees & the Nomina Villarum for Yorkshire* SS vol 49 1866 p 24
4 NYCRO Wood of Hollin Hall Papers 1811–13
5 Barker A R H & Butlin R A (eds) *Studies of Field Systems in the British Isles* Cambridge 1980
6 NYCRO Wood of Hollin Hall Papers 1807–11
7 YCA F 7/418 22/7/1659
8 All the wills and inventories quoted in the text can be found in the Dean and Chapter Probate records at the Borthwick Institute
9 Hurry J B *The Woad Plant and its Dye* Oxford 1930
10 NYCRO, Wood of Hollin Hall Papers, Notes on payments for tithe leases, fee farm rents copyhold rents etc 1745–78
11 Taped interviews 1972–75: Mrs Beedham
12 '4 forks, a spade, an axe, a bill and 2 iron forks'
13 NYCRO Wood of Hollin Hall Papers 1798–1803
14 NYCRO Wood of Hollin Hall Indenture dated 30 December 1678

15 NYCRO Wood of Hollin Hall letter dated 8 September 1808 from
    Kilvington
16 Appendix 1
17 NYCRO Wood of Hollin Hall Papers 1779–91
18 Taped interviews 1972–75: Mr King & Mr Barker

CHAPTER SEVEN

A history of Copmanthorpe based on maps

DAVID BREWER

T HE MAPS OF COPMANTHORPE ARE fascinating, absorbing and very informative. The content ranges from a dot with 'Coppenthorpe' next to it positioned vaguely to the south-west of York, to complete surveys specifically of Copmanthorpe showing every field, stream, ditch, road and building in great detail. Each map gives a snapshot of life in the village at one specific period in time and thus the logical approach is to begin with the early maps and work through to the present day highlighting how Copmanthorpe has changed and developed. The earliest maps, such as Saxton's *Map of Yorkshire* (1577) and John Speed's *Map of the West Riding* (1610) just confirm Coppenthorp's exist-ence at these times. It is not until larger-scale maps appear that the basic shape of the village can be seen, along with the routes taken between the villages and the main centres of York and Tadcaster. The first large-scale map dedicated to Copmanthorpe is surprisingly early and contains a valu-able amount of detail about the whole village (**fig 7.1**).[1]

(Extracts from key maps are reproduced here; copies of all the maps mentioned are available for inspection at Copmanthorpe library or the City of York Reference Library.)

'A Reduced Plan of Copmanthorp (Taken from a Survey made in the Year 1722)' by Edward Watterson Jnr 1779

The survey referred to was 'The Survey of Copmanthorp, The Estate of John Wood Esquire, Taken November 1722 by Robert Kershaw of York'. Sadly there is no trace of the original 1722 plan but the field names and numbers from the 1722 survey and the 1779 plan do correlate, so it may be reasonable to assume that the 1779 plan reflects the situation in 1722. This assumption is further supported by the fact that in 1780 an entirely

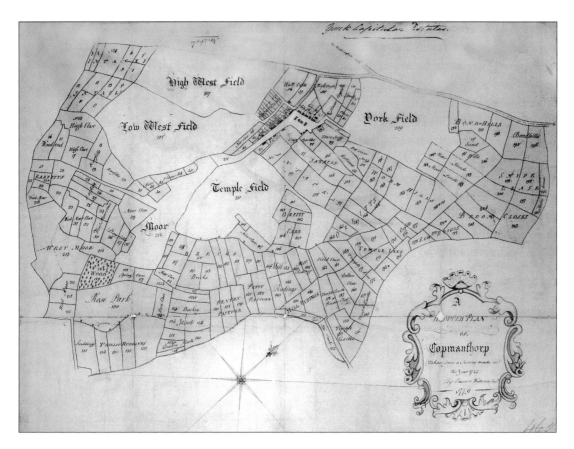

7.1 *A Reduced Plan of Copmanthorp (Taken from a Survey made in the year 1722) by Edward Watterson Jnr, 1779 (Reproduced by permission of the Borthwick Institute, University of York; CC D/C 11/21)*

new plan was produced which is very different from the 1722 plan (see below) and that Edward Watterson Junior is recorded only as a copyist rather than an actual surveyor.[2] Robert Kershaw on the other hand is a known surveyor[3] who is recorded as having worked in the North and East Ridings as well as in Cumbria on estate and parkland projects. It is also recorded that he was married in York Minster[4] on 8 January 1723 to Alice Day, so he was a man of some standing. His work on the 1722 plan is recorded through a payment made on 27 September 1724[5] to Mrs Kershaw by Mr Wood's agent described as 'more towards maps of Copmanthorpe'. It is an indication of the quality of this plan that it was still in use by the Wood estate in 1811.[6]

Two examples of the 1779 copy of the 1722 plan are known to exist today. One came from the Wood estate and is lodged in the archives at York Reference Library; the other was made for York Capitular Estates (responsible for the possessions of York Minster) and is now held by the Borthwick Institute at York University. Both were made by Edward Watterson Junior as he worked for York Capitular Estates between 1775 and 1788,[7] and they were produced as part of the negotiations 'for a new lease of the glebe and tyths of Copmanthorpe'[8] by Richard Wood. In 1722 John Wood held half of the Lordship of the Manor and owned more than a third of all the land, so a full inventory of all the lands under his control would have been very useful, especially as he no longer lived in Copmanthorpe. More importantly, he needed to know the detail of what everyone else owned as he was responsible for collecting the tithes on behalf of York Capitular Estates. Consequently, the plan concentrates on the land rather than the buildings, which appear to be no more than representations although the number may be correct.

The 1722/79 plan shows the basic shape of the village as we see it today but there is much more space around the church, which itself does not seem to be drawn accurately or in quite the exact position. There has clearly been considerable encroachment onto the village green over the years as can be seen when the map of 1722 (**fig 7.2**) is compared with the New Plan of 1780 and the Tithe map of 1840 (**fig 7.3**).

The encroachment taking place during this period perhaps reflects the fact that not only was the Wood family not resident in the village,

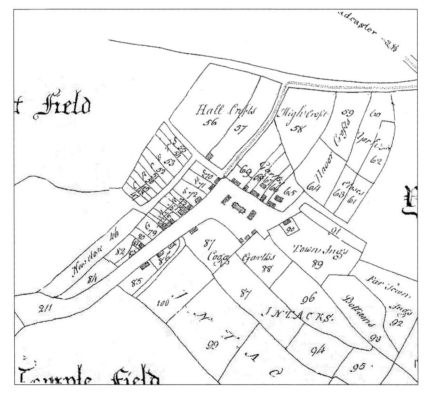

7.2 The layout of the centre of the village in 1722 (as shown on 1779 copy map) (Reproduced by permission of the Borthwick Institute, University of York; CC D/C 11/21)

but neither was their agent. This encroachment has resulted in Low Green, which was part of the original large green around the church, now seeming somewhat detached. Unfortunately, because the buildings were not drawn in detail or to scale, it is not possible to distinguish any high-status properties. Research suggests however that a property known as Copmanthorpe Hall existed in the area numbered 87 on the map and indeed it is on the largest plot. Relatively few houses are shown to the east of the church and this may always have been the case as the field names (Ings and Bottams)[9] suggest this area was quite wet.

Most houses have a small plot of land attached indicated by the word garth, from which the word garden is derived, and there are small additional plots called crofts associated with some of the houses, especially to the north and west of the church. This is the true context for the word croft as historically it meant an enclosed field associated with a house, rather than the dwelling itself. Garths are also shown well away from the main settlement, to the side of the road to Acaster in an area called Temple Garths. These garths are situated in the area that is believed to be the site of the Templar Preceptory (see chapter 2) and may indicate land associated with the preceptory complex. There is no other specific indication for the preceptory on this map but the use of the word garth in this area so far away from houses is most intriguing.

The layout of the roads is easily recognised with the routes of today's Horseman Lane, School Lane, Hall Croft Lane, Top Lane, Tadcaster Road, York Road, York Field Lane, Back Lane and Main Street all clearly shown. However, the road which looks uncannily like St Giles Way is just coincidence as the road shown was obliterated with the Enclosure Award of 1840. Roads connecting with adjacent villages are indicated in parts but none completely, a reflection probably of whether the fields were enclosed or not. All these routes would have been little more than rough tracks with minimal if any surfacing or drainage. With a little imagination it is possible to discern a route north-east to Bishopthorpe on a very similar line to today's footpath; a route south-east to Acaster Malbis following the route of the present Temple Lane; a route due south to Appleton Roebuck following Moor Lane and the present footpath round Copmanthorpe Wood; and a route due west to Colton along Moor Lane then cutting across along the line of today's footpath.

All these roads could well be much more ancient than one might imagine. For instance the route south is known to have continued through Appleton Roebuck down to Nun Appleton where a ferry existed across the Wharfe to Ryther, allowing access to the major market at Selby. It is even possible that during dry periods the Wharfe could have been forded at low tide, making it possible to drive cattle in this direction thus reducing the reliance on York as the only market. The original line of the Roman road running west from Hall Croft Lane had been reduced to a minor lane by the Middle Ages, when a small detour took it on to the line of the present-day A64. It is known that the Roman road had been encroached upon and obstructed by the middle of the 13th century in Colton[10] where 'Lord Wm de Scotenay made an encroachment from a King's Highway' and 'Philip de Faukenberg and Gazo de Calido Monte have obstructed the rest'.

A number of other features are also shown on the 1722/79 plan. The most obvious is the open field system, which was still operational at that time (see chapter 6). Much of the remaining land has been acquired and at least partially enclosed by landowners and tenants, with very little common land left. The resultant patchwork of fields is clearly shown. One area of woodland still remained, as it does today. This wood, or a larger wood, is referred to in an inventory of the Preceptories of the Knights Hospitallers at the time of their suppression by Henry VIII (1539) when Thomas Vavasour is described as keeper of the King's woods of Copmanthorpe. This suggests that the wood had been owned by the Knights Templar which would date it back to before 1300. The name 'Mill Hill' appears beside the Foss to the south of the road to Acaster, but there is no symbol for a mill and it is not mentioned in other documents; nor does it appear on later maps suggesting it was perhaps short-lived and certainly by 1722 was no longer in operation. Its location at some distance from the main settlement would have made it inconvenient for the villagers to use, so it may well have been abandoned at the same time that the preceptory site was. Finally there are no buildings shown away from the township; the reasons for this are discussed in chapter 6.

The New Plan 1780

The Wood family accounts for 1779–80[11] record a payment made on 10 March 1780 to William Dawes, their bailiff at that time, for 'A Survey and Plans …' which is obviously for a new survey and associated plans.[12] This survey was carried out by William Dawes, who is known to have been a competent surveyor,[13] and in a letter that went with these accounts, Mr Dawes says 'that there appears to be upward of 100 acres more in the present than in the old survey', confirming differences between the new survey and that of 1722. Other comments in his letter make it clear that the Dean and Chapter's information (presumably from their 1779 copy of the 1722 plan) could be taken advantage of as it was not up to date! So from 1780 the Wood family had two estate plans, one from 1722 and the other from 1780. Changes to some of the fields between these dates necessitated a new set of numbers be used in the 1780 survey. This is confirmed in 1811 when a field book[14] produced for the estate refers to 'Numbers on the Old Canvass Plan' which coincide with the 1722 information, and 'Numbers on the New Plan'.

Between 1722 and 1780 encroachment onto the village green had occurred from existing properties to the north and west of the church, and entirely new houses and garths had been created to the east of the church, taking substantial chunks from the village green. The 1780 plan shows the enclosure of the churchyard around St Giles, confirming the faculty granted by the Dean and Chapter on 1 February 1750 to allow for 'the interment of the bodies of the dead in all future times'. Numbers from the New Plan are used in sale particulars from 1813, which have a plan attached showing just the fields, garths and crofts associated with the farms being sold.[15] It is clear from this plan and the associated particulars that in 1813 neither Bond Hills nor Copmanthorpe Lodge existed; it may have been this sale that allowed the formation of these farms as it included separate lots which covered the blocks of land that went to make up these farmsteads.

Other early maps

It is not until the Enclosure/Tithe map of 1840 that such comparable detail is shown, but in the intervening years many maps of York, the Ainsty, and the West Riding were published which show the development of the village. Francis White's map of 1783 shows the Copmanthorpe woods extended and the roads to Acaster Malbis, Colton and Appleton Roebuck are more clearly defined. Manor Heath and the road to Askham Bryan are now shown, and while no track is shown to Bishopthorpe, Snape Stile is indicated, the crossing point of the Foss for the present footpath from Copmanthorpe to Bishopthorpe. There is confirmation that encroachment has begun onto the village green as detailed in the 1780 plan, and four open fields are named. No mill is shown within the parish, the closest being that at Askham Bryan; this had a near perfect site, being located on high ground to take advantage of the 'Askham blows'.

John Cary's map of 1808 includes the word 'Chap' under Copmanthorpe (note the 'e' at the end for the first time), an abbreviation for Chapelry, indicating a 'chapel of ease' rather than an independent church (see chapter 5). The next, apparently unrelated, map is the Enclosure Award map for Askham Bryan of 1812, but in fact the land to the north of Top Lane and Hall Croft Lane up to the 'York to Tadcaster Turnpike Road' lay in Askham Bryan parish as late as 1967. Field number 250 (3a 3r 36p) is the triangular plot where the Fox and Hounds stands today but there is no indication of a building there at that time. It is shown as being owned by John Hobson who was a resident of Copmanthorpe. Another Copmanthorpe name shown is that of Joseph Munby, who purchased land in Askham Bryan from S Croft Esq at the time of the Enclosure in 1812. The link from the A64 to the junction of Manor Heath/Hall Croft Lane was formally laid out as 'Copmanthorp Road 30 feet' (wide).

The first map to show the outlying farms known today as Copmanthorpe Grange, Copmanthorpe Lodge, and Bond Hill Ash, the latter (confusingly) being named 'Grange', is that published by Greenwood in 1818. Indeed, this is the first map to indicate any buildings situated outside the main village. A most unexpected map to have significance for Copmanthorpe is the 1821 Askham Richard Enclosure Award. Field number 175 (approx 3 acres/1.2ha) has 'Copmanthorpe Poor' written across it. This field was purchased using money from Thomas Norfolk's Charity, created by his will dated 15 August 1775.[16] This left £100 to be invested, with the interest originally providing bread for the poor attending divine service in the church, but part of the money was later used to purchase this field. Since it appears as 'Allotments' on the early OS maps, one must assume the Poor were allocated land on which to grow food for themselves. Another point of interest is that Ann Buckle is shown as owner of the inn then named Half-way House; today it is The Buckles. In 1832 Robert Cooper depicts many more buildings in the village but later information suggests that some or all the farm buildings have been included, as well as domestic residences. The school may also be shown, the 'Roman Road' is named as such for the first time, and Copmanthorpe House is the first building shown where the Fox and Hounds now stands. Today's Copmanthorpe Grange is named as Greenland House, Garden of Eden is shown for the first time, and a pond is shown to the north of Temple Lane which is later given the name of Brick Kiln Pond, suggesting it may have been dug as a clay pit to supply a small brick works.

1840 Tithe map and 1840 Enclosure Award map

These two maps are almost identical and seem to have been based on the same survey (**fig 7.3**). This is not surprising as the associated Acts of Parliament were passed in 1836 and 1837 respectively. By the mid-19th century, the medieval tradition of paying tithes in kind had almost disappeared, and had been replaced by a system whereby the tithes were leased out to an individual or family who paid a fixed sum to the church, but could charge what they liked to the villagers. Tithe maps were drawn up in order to enable the Tithe Commissioners to commute all the tithes from goods to money. Once the tithes had been given a monetary value, theoretically the payments had to be transparent. So after 6 November 1840 – the date stamp on the Tithe map – it is assumed that payment was made direct to the church although the document attached to the map still refers to 'the appropriate Rectors or their Lessee'.[17]

The process of enclosure had been going on for centuries, but the redistribution of the land was notoriously biased in favour of a few people. Consequently from 1709 Parliamentary Acts of 'Inclosure' were required for each parish wanting to re-organise their open field system and fence off their common land. The precise reason why it was felt necessary to go to the expense of promoting an Enclosure Act for the parish is not at all clear, since by this time all of the land in the open fields already had recognised owners, and by 1840 the so-called common land was down to less than 50 acres (20ha). There were however other benefits besides the formal allocation of land. For Copmanthorpe, one objective, critical to the success of agriculture in the parish, may have been to improve the drainage of the whole area. The Copmanthorpe Award specifies nineteen new drains, which when complete must have made a tremendous difference to the state of the fields, especially during winter.

A second benefit was the formal specification of roads in the parish with their course and width all clearly defined:

> The Acaster Road of the width twenty feet clear of the ditches on each side thereof commencing at the south end of the town street of the village of Copmanthorpe near a gate called Gales Gate and extending from there in an Easterly direction over and between ancient Inclosures belonging to Thomas Batman numbered 147 and 148 upon the said plan and on the north side of that part of the said open and common arable meadow and pasture lands and

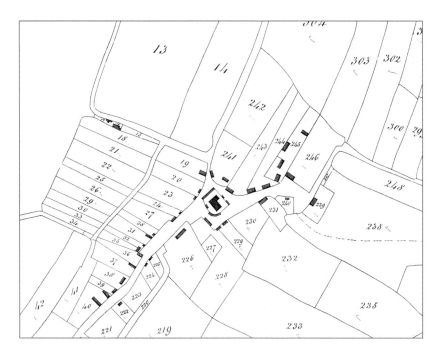

7.3 Extract from the
Tithe map of 1840
(Reproduced by
permission of the
Borthwick Institute,
University of York;
TA651L)

fields agreed divided allotted and inclosed called Temple field and
crossing the York and North Midland Railway in the same field
to and ending at an Ancient Highway in the said Township of
Copmanthorpe leading from there to the village of Acaster Malbis.

Footpaths were also formally laid out at this time, with the footpath to
Bishopthorpe closely following the line of today's path. York Field footpath linked York Field to the York to Tadcaster road following the line
of the railway. The Colton footpath is today's path from Moor Lane to
Colton, and the Temple Field footpath gave pedestrian access into the
fields off Acaster Road/Temple Lane.[18]

Having gone to the expense and trouble of creating all these roads
and drains, their repair and maintenance were also carefully specified to
ensure maximum and lasting benefit. Initially 'two proper persons being
inhabitants of the said Township of Copmanthorpe and interested in [ie
with an interest in] the lands agreed to be divided allotted and inclosed
as surveyors of the private carriage roads and public drains to take the
management and superintend the repairs ...'. The maintenance of the
roads has long since passed to what is now North Yorkshire Highways
but the field drains are still maintained by the Appleton Roebuck and
Copmanthorpe Internal Drainage Board. Obviously at some time the two
local drainage boards merged because of their common interests, and the
AR&C Internal Drainage Board has recently joined the York Consortium

of Drainage Boards. At the time of writing the whole system is 'under review' and it is probable that the organisation, created by the Enclosure Award of 1840, will become part of a much larger public body and will cease to exist as a separate entity.

The scale of the Enclosure map makes it possible to compare it directly with the 1722/79 plan. The encroachment on to the green shown in 1780 is confirmed, and the number of buildings has increased from 28 to 43, with four of the additional buildings shown attached to the churchyard. It must be remembered that some or all of these buildings could have been blocks of cottages, so there would have been more than 43 families. One curious omission from both the 1840 maps is any mention of the four outlying farms. They are known to have existed at that date and the lack of reference to them either on the maps or in the associated documents is difficult to understand.

Finally, perhaps the most obvious feature of these maps is the arrival of the railway which virtually cuts the parish in two. It is possible that the railway prompted the Enclosure Award, as it is believed to have done in a number of other parishes. It would have been extremely laborious for the railway company to have negotiated for the separate purchase of parts of individual strips of land that were crossed by the railway in Temple Field and York Field. It could also have been very problematic to acquire legally parts of the still common land known as the Moor. However, if the land was rearranged into larger holdings, and the ownership legally formalised by the process of enclosure, the purchase by the railway company would have been far easier. Even without the complication of the Moor, Temple Field and York Field, the railway crossed 20 other fields. No doubt all this provided work for many solicitors and surveyors! Having discussed the 1840 maps in such detail, it must still be remembered that much of the information included was an agenda for what was going to happen once the Enclosure Award had been implemented: the new field divisions, the roads, footpaths and field drains mentioned did not actually exist in 1840. To see what was actually implemented, maps after 1840 need to be consulted.

Ordnance Survey

The first maps for this area produced by the Ordnance Survey are dated 1849 for sheet 190 and 1851 for sheet 191. Inevitably Copmanthorpe lies across two maps (making the historian's life more difficult), being to the north-west corner of sheet 191 and to the north-east corner of sheet 190, with the join just to the west of the village. These maps are of the scale 6 inches to one mile or 1:10,560 which gives nothing like the detail or clarity of the 1840 maps which are to a scale of approx 1:1250 but it is still possible to see quite clearly that most of the 1840 Enclosure Award had been implemented. The new fields created by the Award from the open fields and the Moor are also shown but with additions. This is not surprising as some of the fields specified were too large to work as one unit with the machinery available at that time. So for instance Low West Field, which was awarded as two fields of just over 64 and 53 acres (26 and 21ha respectively) to Leighton's Trustees, had been divided into eight fields averaging more than 14 acres (5.5ha) per field – still a large area to be worked by horses. Most of the older field boundaries are shown dotted with trees giving a much more enclosed feel to the area, with none of the distance views seen today.

The first OS maps also confirm the existence of the village school on the corner of what are now School Lane and Horseman Lane. The Queen's Arms Inn has replaced Copmanthorpe House as the name for the Fox and Hounds and it was by then clearly an inn. Brick Kiln Pond is indicated also, confirming its existence as originally shown on the 1831 map. The layout of the centre of the village remains very similar to the 1840 map, with the name Copmanthorpe Hall added to what is now Manor Farm. The 'Site of a Preceptory of the Knights Templars' is indicated near the fields called Temple Garth, the first ever mention of this site (see **fig 2.5**). This is the only map to refer to the village as 'Copmanthorpe, formerly Temple Copmanthorpe'. The Ordnance Survey did not produce larger-scale maps for this area until much later in the 19th century; the first ones are dated 1892 and 1893 and are to a scale of 25 inches to one mile (1:2,534) (**fig 7.4**). By then the centre of the village has developed into what is recognisable today, and the map of 1958 (**fig 7.5**) shows the wider layout.

The 1892/3 maps are the first to name several features, although in some cases, such as the smithy attached to the south end of the inn (Royal Oak), its existence at this point had been documented since 1823.[19] The Sunday School is shown to the north of the church, the Methodist Chapel is in the vicinity of the Co-op, and the Vicarage is in its current location. A Post Office is also shown to the east of the church, and Copmanthorpe Station is still to the west of the railway line. The Fox and Hounds is named as such for the first time and the Allotment Gardens exist. The Brick Kiln Pond is no longer shown, but a building just out of the village

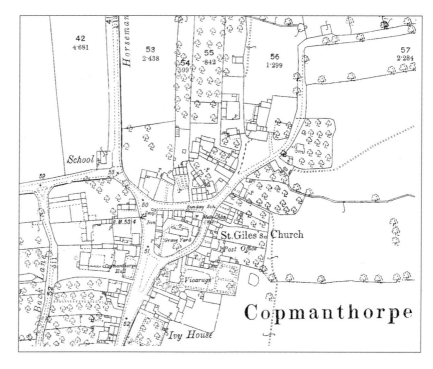

on York Field Lane which is shown for the first time is believed to be a flax mill. More than 20 water pumps show that domestic water still had to be hand pumped at that time.

By the time of the 1910 OS map, the ancient route south to Appleton Roebuck had become nothing more than a footpath beyond the boundary where the parishes meet. Since the advent of the railway markets were now much more accessible, and the ferry at Nun Appleton was long gone. Copmanthorpe Station is now to the east of the railway line (see chapter 11), along with a coal depot. The smithy has now moved out of the village down Moor Lane. At this point in time, apart from the encroachment onto the village green, the extent of the village had changed little since 1722, and the number of buildings is similar to the number shown in 1840 (approximately 43) but with a slightly higher population (330 in 1909 compared to 284 in 1841). In fact the number of households in 1910 was little more than the number at the time of the Poll Tax returns of 1379 when, it is estimated, there were approximately 36 households. By the time the OS map of 1930 is produced major expansion has taken place: there are then approximately 130 buildings spreading down Moor Lane, along Station Road, and along School Lane and Manor Heath. In addition there are 50 new houses to either side of Top Lane and ten new houses near Foss Bridge on Acaster Road. Drome

Road and Temple Garth have also been developed with 38 new houses. All this means that the village had grown from just over 40 houses in 1910 to approx 228 houses in 1930. This rapid expansion is reflected in the population growth to 591 by 1931, although this suggests a very low average occupancy rate for each property. Perhaps there had been speculative house building in the early 1920s, but the depression of the late 1920s may have resulted in many properties standing empty. After this major expansion of the village there is then little development shown on the maps until the OS revised edition in 1971 when the area to the north of Hall Croft Lane is completely developed, as is the area to the west of Horseman Lane. By 1981 there is continuous development both sides of York Field Lane, and the new school, the Recreation Centre, and St Giles way have all been built. The developments off Station Road/Moor Lane, Back Lane/Low West Field Road, and Wilstrop Farm have all taken place within the last 20 years.

7.5 The extent of the village as shown on the OS 6" map of 1958

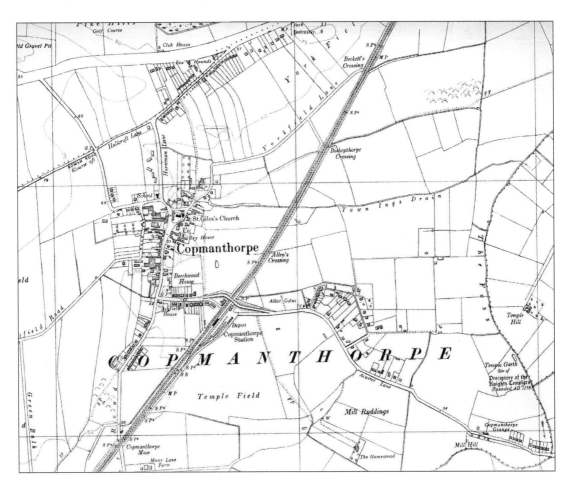

Ironically the latest OS map, which was revised in 2006, shows the boundary between Copmanthorpe and Colton, an ancient boundary recorded unchanged on all the maps from 1722, depart from the line of the ancient boundary and wander off into Hagg Wood for no known reason. So much for progress![20]

Notes

1   Borthwick Institute CC D/C 11/21
2   Bendall, S (ed) *Dictionary of Land Surveyors And Local Map Makers of Great Britain And Ireland 1530–1850* London 1997
3   Ibid
4   York Minster Archive
5   NYCRO ZET/2271 Wood of Hollin Hall, Papers 1724–47
6   NYCRO ZET/3279 Wood of Hollin Hall, Papers 1807–11
7   York Minster Archive index p 99
8   NYCRO ZET/2465 Wood of Hollin Hall, Papers 1758–88
9   See Appendix on field names
10 English, B ed *Yorkshire Hundred Rolls 1274–75*, YASRS vol 151 (1993/4) p 89
11 NYCRO ZET/2598 Wood of Hollin Hall, Papers 1779–91
12 WYL 466/17 'A Survey and Plans …' by William Dawes, 1780
13 NYCRO ZET/2598 Wood of Hollin Hall, Papers 1779–91, letter dated 27 Nov 1787
14 NYCRO ZET3403 Wood of Hollin Hall, Papers 1811–13, a collected Account of Lands held by different Tenants under Mr Layton and Mr Fawcitt at Copmanthorpe taken in 1811
15 WYL 466/17 'A Particular of property at Copmanthorpe intended to be sold …16th November 1813'; particulars are based on the New Plan of 1780
16 Lawton, G *Collections Relative to Churches and Chapels Within the Diocese of York* London 1842 p 99
17 BI TA 651L, Copmanthorpe Tithe map, 1840
18 The road from Copmanthorpe to Acaster crossroads is today known as Temple Lane, but is defined as Acaster Road on the Enclosure Award
19 Baines, E *History, directory and gazetteer of the County of York* Leeds 1823 vol 2 p 142
20 This is almost certainly the result of the digitisation of the OS data – there were numerous examples of this in the early days of computerisation

CHAPTER EIGHT

Ancient families

PHIL BATMAN

The Vavasour family: royal connections

THE VAVASOUR FAMILY, A FAMILY with royal connections and Catholic persuasions, make their first appearance in the documentary annals of Copmanthorpe in 1484, when a York cleric bequeathed Richard Vavasour all his goods at the village.[1] It is not known if Richard lived in Copmanthorpe, but his wife was Margaret Hodgson;[2] she may have been connected with that substantial yeoman family living in the village in the 16th century.[3] Subsequently the Fairfax family, who owned much of the land in Copmanthorpe and the surrounding area, sold the manor to Richard's sons, Thomas and Richard Vavasour, in 1545.[4]

These members of the Vavasour family stem from the Vavasours of Weston, who in turn were a lesser branch of the Hazlewood family. Locally they were connected with Appleton Roebuck, Acaster Malbis, Bilbrough and Askham Richard, where different members lived at varying times.

Thomas leased the Rectory of Copmanthorpe from the Dean and Chapter of York in 1547, together with its glebe land and crops. He held the lease for a term of 30 years at £16 a year, under curious conditions. Upon the site of the Rectory at that time stood an old mansion house in a state of ruin and decay: the church 'condescended' to permit Thomas the liberty of dismantling the house and using its timber and stone, save for one chamber. Come the expiry of the lease, Thomas undertook to return to the Dean and Chapter one house, a garden, and two barns in better repair than he received them.

Thomas Vavasour was active in local affairs: he was one of the gentlemen of the Ainsty who promised to assist the Lord Mayor at the king's visit to York; he collected taxes in the Ainsty; and advised on

8.1 Portrait of Anne Vavasour by Jan de Critz (Reproduced by permission of the Armourers' Hall)

possible sites for a beacon in preparing resistance to potential invasions from France. Politics were not his only local interest: notes from the Visitation books tell us that Margaret Lazenby, a single woman of Huntington, had a child by Thomas Vavasour of Copmanthorpe, a married man, by both their confessions. His will made provision for his son Henry to give ten shillings a year, via the hands of the gaoler, to the prisoners of the Castle of York, and he left £20 to charity. A generous man, he arranged for himself a yearly obit mass or dirge for 20 years after his death; let us hope it was effective.

Such shafts of historical light as fall on Thomas Vavasour fall also on many of his siblings, ancestors and descendants. The Vavasours of York were prominent Elizabethan Catholic recusants, prosecuted for their religious faith and beliefs. Thomas' grandson, Sir Thomas Vavasour of Copmanthorpe, Knight Marshall, distinguished himself in a naval fight against Spain, whilst his great-grandson, William Vavasour, Baronet, commanded for King Charles I in the Civil War. Following the Royalist defeat at the Battle of Marston Moor in 1644, barely a stone's throw from his ancestral village, William left England for Sweden. Perhaps the most glamorous Vavasour of all, Anne (**fig 8.1**), Thomas' granddaughter, served at the feet of Queen Elizabeth in her court, in a culture which could not have been further from her parochial ancestral home.

The Wood family: absentee Lords of the Manor

Richard Wood, son of Giles Wood of Pickering, gave land in Copmanthorpe to his son Anthony on his death in 1568, our first documented connection of the Wood family to the history of our village (**fig 8.2**). Anthony Wood was buried in 1626 in the Church of St Mary

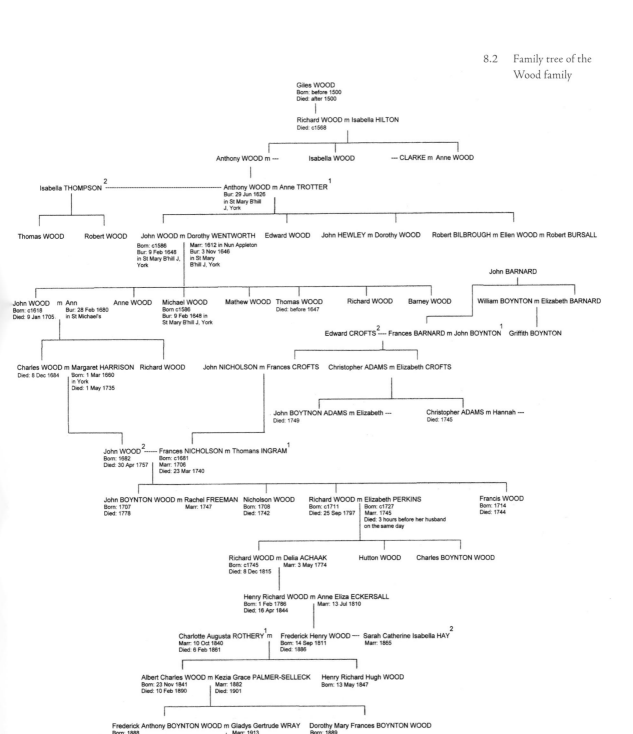

Bishophill Junior in York, the mother church of the chapel in Copmanthorpe. His descendants, successive squires of the village, extracted rents from the tenants and distributed charity to the poor there for generations to come.[5]

The Wood family display all the trappings of the landed gentry, including a love of horses, affliction with the gout and haemorrhoids, and sumptuous wealth acquired by guile and careful marriage then squandered by feckless youth! By the 18th century, the seat of the family was not in the village of Copmanthorpe itself but at Hollin Hall, a mansion near Ripon 25 miles or so distant as the crow flew. Hollin Hall, a magnificent country house complete with landscaped park and lake, was bought by John Wood at a cost of £1600 in the year 1718 and remained in the Wood family until the end of the 20th century. The Woods were largely absentee landlords, conducting their financial affairs with their tenants, and hearing their grievances (sympathetically or otherwise), by way of advisers who visited from time to time.

Two members of the family do, however, lie at rest in the vault of St Giles church in the village: John Wood (1682–1757) (**figs 8.3 and 8.4**) and his son John Boynton Wood (1707–78). This family held land not only in Copmanthorpe, but in many other far-flung places: Staveley, Leake in the county of Lincoln, Bishop Monkton in the Liberty of Ripon, Dringhouses near York, West Herrington in the county of Durham, not to mention three houses in London. John Wood practised as a barrister at Lincoln's Inn and married exceedingly well. His wife had inherited from her father both land in County Durham and property in Newcastle upon Tyne, and her mother had inherited property from her grandmother, Lady Frances Boynton, and her grandmother's sister, Elizabeth Boynton, which included shares of the manor of Copmanthorpe (see p. 30). By such complicated family connections was the name Boynton coupled to that of Wood in the Lords of the Manor of Copmanthorpe. John also bought a half share in the manor house in the village from his wife's cousin, and rebuilt the old house. Putting aside his power, influence and wealth, John nevertheless seems to have had great affection for his villagers in Coppenthorpe (by which name he referred to it), and, judging from the family papers, the feeling was reciprocated.

8.3   Portrait of John Wood (Reproduced by permission of *Country Life*)

Sacred to the memory of
John Wood, Esquire,
formerly of Hollinclose
in this county,
who rests in the tomb
at the foot of this memorial,
and of Frances his most beloved wife,
who is buried in the church of St Andrew,
Holborn, London
She died on the 23rd day of March, 1740 aged 59,
he on the 30th day of April, 1757, aged 74
They have attained eternal renown.

Transcription of inscription on Wood family tomb in St Giles church

8.4   The Wood family memorial in St Giles church
(© Mike Rogers)

John Wood had his freeholding in the village fields surveyed in 1722. The Boynton Wood family held then about a half of the acreage in the old common fields of the village, and a substantial part of the remaining enclosed fields in the parish (**fig 8.5**).[6] John's was a kindly disposition: he bequeathed his farm in Coppenthorpe to his younger son Richard, and the furniture in his Coppenthorpe house to his other son, John Boynton.[7] The farm was held in trust, 'the better to enable Richard to educate and provide for his children', and he beseeched his son not to sell it. His will made provision for ten shillings for the five poorest people in the village and the same sum for poor widows in St Catherine's Hospital. He wished to be interred in a vault in Coppenthorpe Chapel 'without any kind of pomp'. All this spelt out in his own hand, his script accidentally and delightfully imprinted with the whorls of his thumb whilst the ink was still wet on 15 November 1756 (**fig 8.6**).

John Wood worried: as a squire about his villagers, and as a father about his children. He implored his two surviving sons not to argue if they had any regard for their father or his memory, or to listen to reason if they did, but trouble lay head. John Boynton, his wayward son, had been blessed (or cursed) by inheritance. He had received property bequeathed by his distant aunt Elizabeth Boynton (on condition he adopt her surname), a share of the manor of Copmanthorpe, and, on his father's death, Hollin Hall as life tenant. He found, or was found, an eligible wife.

But all this privilege exceeded his capacities. By the early 1740s he had accumulated debts amounting to £7000 (£650,000 in today's terms) and he fled. He hid in several places, and made his will, signed with the pseudonym William Bateman (for 'economy and privacy's sake'), whilst an inhabitant of Carmarthen, in South Wales. John Boynton was unkind, attested his father, and his marriage was unhappy and barren. He penned a letter rueing his mistakes and seeking reconciliation with his wife, but died miserable and alone, having been bedridden for three years.

John Wood and his ancestors had accumulated a healthy income and status through hard work and careful consideration, but his descendants to a large extent reversed that trend. John's younger son, Richard, pursued a legal career in his father's footsteps, and inherited Hollin Hall upon the death of his irresponsible elder brother. Richard inherited also, it seems, his father's kindly disposition to his tenants in Copmanthorpe. He yearly had his agent tot up his rents and assessed his income from the village. Needless to say, he also attempted to increase his rents in times of adversity, although the correspondence with some of his tenants suggests he may have heeded their objections; their pleas seem to have been successful. Lists of debts

8.5 Copmanthorpe Freeholders Survey, based on map of 1722/79 (© Phil Batman/ Mike Rogers)

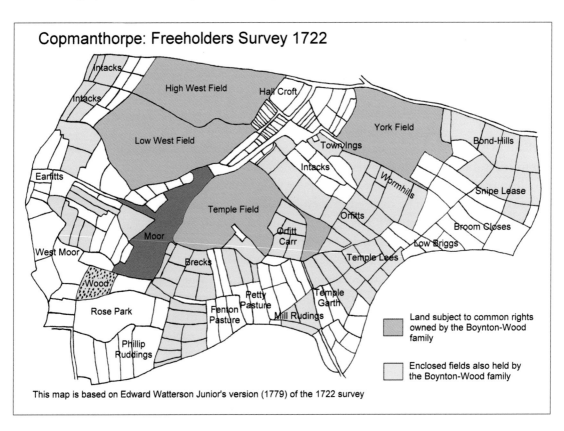

Copmanthorpe: Freeholders Survey 1722

Intacks
Intacks
High West Field
Hall Croft
Low West Field
York Field
Bond Hills
Town Ings
Intacks
Earfitts
Wormhills
Snipe Lease
Temple Field
Orfitts
Moor
Orfitt Carr
Broom Closes
Low Briggs
West Moor
Temple Lees
Brecks
Wood
Petty Pasture
Temple Garth
Rose Park
Fenton Pasture
Mill Ruddings
Phillip Ruddings

Land subject to common rights owned by the Boynton-Wood family

Enclosed fields also held by the Boynton-Wood family

This map is based on Edward Watterson Junior's version (1779) of the 1722 survey

and unpaid policies abound in the family archives, and some forty years after John Wood's death and his wish to keep in the family the farm in Copmanthorpe, John Batman loaned Richard Wood £1000 with the farm as security. The last dated entry for Copmanthorpe in the Wood archives is in the year 1840, and the last male descendant of Giles Wood of Pickering died in 1998, when Hollin Hall lapsed from the annals of Copmanthorpe.

John Batman (1783–1873): tenant farmer

The Batman family, wealthy yeoman farmers, lived in the village for a longer span of years probably than any other family. Records show they earned their living off the land from the 1600s or before until the late Victorian period when they migrated into York.[8] The Batman family tree (**fig 8.7**) shows the generations tumbling down from the 1500s to the present day. At the centre of the tree is the figure of John Batman. He sits comfortably there: at a crossroads in the life of the Batman family. He was born in the year William Pitt the Younger became Prime Minister of Great Britain (1783), and was aged ten years at the outbreak of the Napoleonic Wars. He first comes to our notice, however, on 11 October 1805, when the British people held their breath in anticipation of Nelson's imminent battle with the Franco-Spanish fleet at Cape Trafalgar, but John Batman's mind was focused sharply on matters much closer to home. He stood alongside his brother Thomas in the courtroom of Quarter Sessions in York, on pain of a fine of £50 each. His crime was a shameful one: he was guilty of fornication.[9]

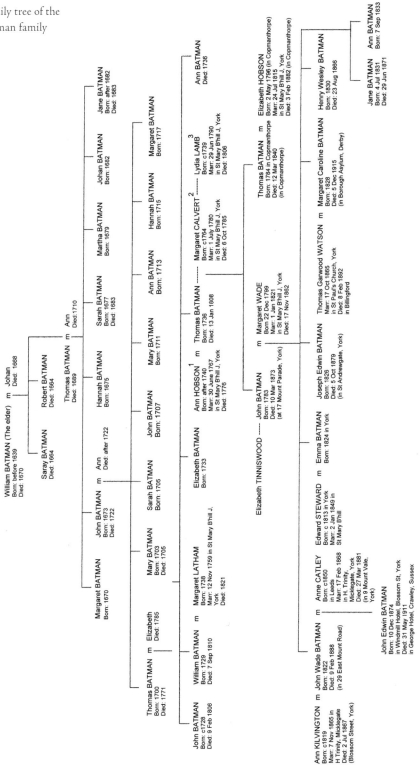

John brushed this episode aside and subsequently prospered. His standing in the village community was considerable, as a wise, imposing and enlightened figure. In reality, his manner may not have been so alluring: farmers of his generation were reputedly ignorant rustic dullards, highly resistant to new ideas in their working practices and politics.[10] Whether he was agreeable or otherwise, however, he prospered for the two reasons why men have always prospered since time immemorial: good fortune, and good sense! Whether luck or sense is what counts in the choice of a wife is debatable, but John chose well, marrying Margaret Wade on New Year's Day 1821.[11] John was 37 years of age, and his bride 21. Why John should have married so late in life is a mystery. His father was long dead, he was financially self sufficient, and besides, the days when parents chose their children's spouses for them were past. Margaret, on the other hand, could not have married at a younger age without her parents' consent. It is unlikely however that John and Margaret's match would have met with disapproval, for they were similar in social standing. Perhaps John was simply particular in his choice of bride, had unattractive habits, or was just plain ugly! At any rate, their union was blessed.

Margaret had been born in Hambleton, near Selby, after being conceived romantically on her parents' wedding night. Both John and Margaret lived in Copmanthorpe at the time of their marriage, and journeyed to St Mary Bishophill Junior in York for the ceremony. Indeed, Margaret was of Copmanthorpe stock. Her father had been born in the village,[12] and her grandfather lived and died there. Margaret brought to the marriage her own share of status. Her brother Thomas, a wealthy farmer and staunch Methodist, retired to the Nunthorpe area of York and was generous towards Margaret and her family in his will, leaving Margaret £200 and her four daughters similar amounts of money and a share in his estate.[13] His considerable estate comprised properties in Nunthorpe, Barlby, Selby and Sherburn, which passed down to his numerous nieces upon his widow's death. Margaret's grandfather was just as affluent for his time, but perhaps not quite so generously minded.[14] Margaret benefited from his will to the tune of £100, but his benevolence was marred by his carrying over a grudge beyond the grave. His eldest son Thomas stood to inherit farms at Fewston near Ilkley and at Copmanthorpe, but the latter only if he did not marry Ann Bewlay, daughter of William Bewlay of the village. Even if father could not forbid his son's choice of partner, he could exert his influence in hard economic ways. The Bewlays had lived in Copmanthorpe for generations, but the day a Wade married one, he lay disinherited. Some parents can't resist exerting control over their children even from beyond the grave, and marriage was far too important a matter to be left entirely to the individuals concerned. We shall never know what caused this feud but suffice it to say that no marriage of one Thomas Wade with one Ann Bewlay is to be found in the registers. Isn't that a pity? Perhaps we would have had more admiration for his spirit (if not his business acumen) if it was?

John Batman's enormous good fortune was that he was born of sound farming stock and prospered from the golden age of Victorian high farming in the middle decades of the 19th century. He inherited wealth and was able to build on it. His father left him a farm in Nun Monkton with 30 acres (12ha) and the lease of a farm in Copmanthorpe with 40 acres (16ha) of land.[15] John inherited this property at the age of 25 years. Some 30 years later, the enclosure of the open common arable acres as well as the meadows and pastures of the village was ordered by of Act of Parliament, and John Batman's scattered lands, which had been farmed for centuries by communal agreement between neighbours, were consoli-

8.8   Principal land-
holdings on the
Tithe map of 1840
(© Phil Batman/
Mike Rogers)

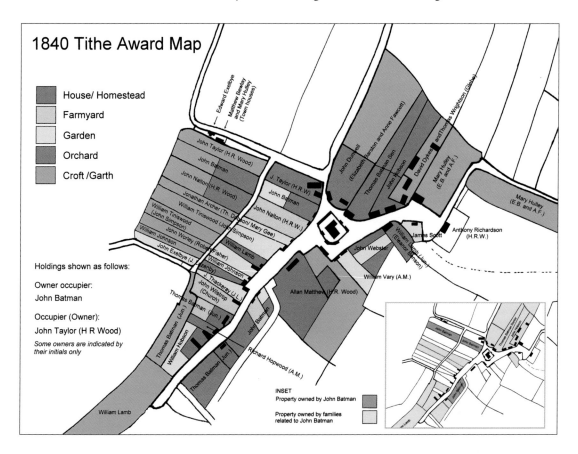

dated into 29 acres (c 12ha) in High West Field.[16] He was obliged to dig ditches and plant hedges around his allocation of land. At the time of the Tithe Survey of 1840, his total land holding in the village stood at 126 acres (51ha).[17] He had concentrated his farm in Copmanthorpe and sold 13 acres (5ha) in Nun Monkton. He also rented a further 17 acres (c 7ha) in Wood End and York Field in his home parish. The total area of farming land in the village fields in the Tithe Award was 1600 acres (648ha); only two landowners possessed greater acreage than John, namely the Lord of the Manor, Henry Richard Wood Esquire and his distant relative, the Reverend Francis Leighton.

The Tithe Map of 1840 draws 29 plots of land clustered around the streets at the nucleus of the village (**fig 8.8**), with some 24 farming households (including John's) managing these plots. John was related in some way to no fewer than seven of these families. Towards the southern end of the main street lived Thomas Batman junior, who was the son of John's recently deceased brother. Thomas Batman senior, a cousin, lived over the opposite side of the church. John Hobson and his distant cousin William also lived in the village; John was married to Ann Batman, another of John's cousins. In short, John Batman cannot have wished for a stronger family network.

At the age of 58 years, John Batman was in the prime of life when he answered his door to the knock of the village schoolmaster, the Census enumerator, on 12 June 1841. The owner of Trowel House Farm (**fig 8.9**) was a wealthy man: the enumerator was able to write down the word 'Independent' for John's occupation, not farmer. On the day of this conversation, John stood in possession of three houses (two in Copmanthorpe and one in Nun Monkton) and 143 acres (58ha) of farmland. His men worked 109 acres (44ha) of his own land in Copmanthorpe and a further 17 acres (c 7ha) rented from Martin Burnell. He collected rent from his house in Nun Monkton and 17 acres of land there.

In 1841, Trowel House Farm at the heart of the village was only a few years old, but John had built it with elegance and style. The door onto the street was (and still is) adorned with columns, a cornice hood and a spider's-web fanlight. The farmstead behind was designed to accommodate the processing of crops from arrival at harvest time to delivery to the mill. A barn complete with huge archway for receiving wagons laden with wheat, the threshing barn with holes high in the walls for engine beams, and the cart sheds survive in the yard to this day as nostalgic reminders of a horse-drawn moon- and candle-lit age.

John had not only wealth, but also enterprise. Over the next three decades, he acquired the freehold of a further four farmhouses in Hessay, a village somewhat smaller in size than Copmanthorpe and five miles to the north-west. John evidently was not the rustic dullard like many of his contemporaries. The end of the Napoleonic Wars had heralded a sudden and steep fall in prices which caught many small and some wealthy large farmers, who retrenched or failed.[18] Rents were low, and tenants felt no desire to purchase land. Farming could produce a good ten per cent or more profit on capital expenditure. It made more economic sense to the tenant farmer to produce a good return by buying new equipment and broadening the scale of his farming than to purchase the farm from a good landlord and save the small rental. In acquiring more farms and land in the early decades of the 19th century, John swam against the tide.

The map of the streets and houses of Copmanthorpe in 1840 portrays a static snapshot, which is of course illusory. Nothing ever stays the same. Within a few years John had left the village of his birth for an easier life in a suburb of York, and acquired his farms in Hessay possibly without ever setting foot on the land there. He came by some of this land through the generosity of his distant relative and former close neighbour William Hobson. Although William didn't live in Hessay either, he had consolidated a holding of land there in the enclosure of the communal fields in 1831.[19] Shortly after John left the village, old William Hobson died, and bequeathed John his 98 acres (40ha) of Hessay fields with a house, Cromwell House Farm.[20] From the comfort of his armchair in retirement, John acquired a further house (Croft Farm) and 36 acres (14ha) or so of land in Hessay from William Calvert. He sold Croft Farm with 75 acres (30ha) of old Hobson and old Calvert land in 1865,[21] but continued to collect rent from the farmers of Hessay until his death. The name of John Batman must have been as well known in Hessay in the second half of the nineteenth century as it was in Copmanthorpe in the first half. At one time or another, three houses in the parish, and more than 134 acres belonged to John Batman's family.

John left the rustic common sense of his 18th-century farmhouse in his native village for a splendid new town house in Mount Parade, a fashionable suburb just to the south-west of the walled city of York.[22] He moved to the Mount area of York at more or less the same time as other members of his family, their radical uprooting from country to city living setting a precedent which generations of other landed families were destined to follow.

No doubt he took pride in the growth of his little empire: from the lease of the farm and 40 acres of land he inherited in Copmanthorpe, to an estate of seven houses and nearly 400 acres (162ha) in his village and neighbouring Hessay, not to mention his small but sustained interest in Nun Monkton.

The portrait of John Batman drawn here so far is one of a successful businessman and farmer. Of course, his life was much more complete than just that, and his marriage was equally fruitful. Margaret bore him three sons and four daughters, all of whom took their first breath in Trowel House Farm and were christened across the village street in St Giles church. Their first child arrived ten months after John and Margaret's wedding on New Year's Day 1821, and their last twelve years later. What is more, not one of their babies died in infancy.[23] Margaret died in Mount Parade in 1862, leaving John a widower for the remaining ten years of his life.

This severing of ties with farming and cutting adrift from Copmanthorpe in the nineteenth century was, without doubt, the most momentous event that had ever happened to the Batman family, and many others like them, for many centuries. At the back of John's mind during his acquisition of land in Copmanthorpe and Hessay must have been the thought that he was establishing farms for his three sons to inherit. However, he lived through a time of change; ever since the foundation of the village, the people of Copmanthorpe had belonged to the land and to the cohesive village community but the economic pull of the city of York and of industry elsewhere became irresistible to John's children. John's precious land became purely a commodity to be bought and sold in the wake of the parcelling up by hedges and lanes of the sweeping open communal fields.

The three sons turned their backs to working the land. What of them? An innkeeper, a solicitor, and even (did old farmer John approve?) an artist. John died at home on 10 March 1873 at the old age of 90, and his will made provision for all of his land and property to be sold privately or by auction for the benefit of his eldest son, the innkeeper John Wade Batman.[24] From this fortune (as it must have been), his eldest daughter Emma inherited £800, his second daughter Margaret Caroline £1000, and his third surviving daughter Ann £100. John's only other living child was the artist, Joseph Edwin, and he received the security of an annuity of £20 for the rest of his life (whether he was financially insecure or just thought to have slippery fingers with a lump sum, we shall never know!). Sure enough, a year after his death, John's son John Wade repossessed the farms and land in Hessay and sold them to one Richard Wilson Skilbeck of the nearby village of Bilton.[25] This sale was the deathblow to the Batman family's dependence on the land.

John Wade's retreat from farming was timely indeed. The final quarter of the 19th century after the land was sold in 1874 was a period of seemingly unending disaster for the arable farmer.[26] John senior's will reads like it predicts just such a catastrophic dependence on the soil. The combination of foreign competition and low prices hit hard on those farmers who relied heavily on crops. Then came natural adversity: the remaining years of the 1870s were noted for cold wet summers with poor harvests. In 1879, the rain arrived in spring and lasted until the autumn, and the following winter was bitterly cold. The eighties produced little respite. A blizzard lasted for over two days in January 1881, and little wheat could be sown in the wet summers of 1881 and 1882. The summers of 1885 and 1887, by contrast, were droughts. The early nineties brought greater misery with harvests blighted by unremitting rain, prolonged drought, persistent frost, and deep drifts of snow over Copmanthorpe for weeks on end. Many a farmer was forced into bankruptcy. John's children (with the one exception of his daughter Margaret Caroline) fortunately avoided the slump in agriculture in the late Victorian era, having moved to the relative security of the trades and professions of the city; and they had their inheritance. What became of the small fortune from John Batman's endeavours remains a mystery to this day

The Swale family: debtors

The Swale family were prominent yeomen freeholding farmers whose generations spanned the centuries from the earliest registers in the 1600s to Victorian times. The Swales had stature: in the early 1700s for example, the elders, John and Henry, attracted the honorary title of 'Master' in the parish records, and a Henry Swale who died in 1728 had the distinction of 'schoolmaster'. The family with the largest number of mouths to feed was that of another Henry Swale. Nine children born between 1724 and 1740 (five of whom seem to have survived into adult life) ran through his house; a help with the harvest but no doubt a worry to feed. Henry Swale held a sizeable acreage of land in the four great common fields of the village when he appears as a freeholder in the survey of 1722. Indeed, only three other landed gentry owned more land than the Swales at that time.

Four wills of the Swale family survive, although we cannot see precisely how these three men and one woman fit into the extended family tree. The earliest record to survive is the inventory of Thomas Swale whose goods and chattels are listed in a beautifully scripted document of 1557.[27] His neighbours toured his house and land, and recorded (evidently having retired to consider the matter), amongst other possessions to the tune of £95, '3 score holde sheype 15 lames, 10 swyne, 3 downgforkes, 1 spayd, 1 showall with other houselmentes not remembryed'. He left debts (as did most people) to Thomas John Wilson of Dringhouses and 'to my chyldren of the gift of my mother Woode'. He had spent his children's 'gift'!

In 1619, another Thomas Swale left his affairs in chaos.[28] 'Beinge sicke in bodie yet of good and perfect memorie' upon his deathbed, he wished his servants to fetch some of his neighbours. John Wilkinson, Joanne Swale and William Batman attended the sick bed,

> who when they were come to him they asked him how he did and he answered he was very sick whereupon [they] willed him to set all things straight and Thomas Swale replied that he was in much debt, then [they] told him that he had good and enough to pay it all. And thereupon Thomas Swale … said that when his debts were paid there would not remain so much as his son William was worthy of and that he would give all his goods his debts being paid to his said son William, except some legacies which he would give, but he did not then express what the said legacies should be nor on whom he would bestow them …

We do not know how this dispute, which evidently was aired in court, was resolved. His inventory included his bees worth 45 shillings, magical insects which Thomas would have chased rattling basins and kettles when they swarmed.[29] His estate was assessed at £218, a goodly sum in the early 17th century.

William Swale, who died in 1626, bequeathed his 'bowe and arrows and my fowlinge peece' (a shotgun), his 'worke daye apparel', and to 'everie poore householder six pence'.[30] Evidently a man of generous spirit but perhaps not as wealthy as his relative Thomas. The only woman of her family to leave a record, Margaret Swale, bequeathed her worldly goods to her children and her soul to the 'Almightie ... whensoever it pleaseth God to taike me out of this Transitory world ...', which He did in 1643.[31]

The Tinniswood family: outcasts!

People break the rules, and they always will. The rules of sexual conduct in the Copmanthorpe of past centuries were enforced by the church. Bastards were a financial burden on the parishioners, and those villagers whose fornication out of wedlock impoverished the community were publicly humiliated, made to pay penance in church, and possibly fined.

The register shows that 21 illegitimate babies were born in Copmanthorpe between 1759 and 1837.[32] A complex web of social and economic factors caused these girls to break the rules. Possibly poverty and high mortality encouraged migrants into the parish. Poor landless lonely souls stood little chance of accumulating sufficient wealth to set up a permanent dwelling; their prospect was marriage to a poor man. Faced with a dismal future, and a short supply of marriageable men, a girl would flaunt her sexuality with as many young men as possible in the hope of catching a husband.[33]

Some families were sexually incontinent out of fecklessness or despair. One such family was that of Francis and Hannah Tinniswood and their daughters Elizabeth, Jane and Ann. This desperate household yielded no fewer than four bastard children in Copmanthorpe in the early years of the 19th century. Francis Tinniswood arrived in the village from Stillington, North Yorkshire, and married Hannah Norfolk, from a family with strong local connections. They produced five daughters and a son over the ensuing fifteen years. The son and one daughter obeyed the morals of the day, married locally, and raised seven legitimate children between them, unlike three of their sisters.

Mary, bastard daughter to Elizabeth Tinniswood, was born in the village in 1805. She died prematurely, as was often the case in such circum-stances, before she reached her fifth birthday and received a Christian burial in the churchyard. David, bastard son born to Jane Tinniswood in 1818, was fathered by David Dykes, who remained in the village as a tenant farmer. Eleanor Tinniswood, bastard, was born to Ann in 1821 and died soon afterwards, and in 1825 Ann bore an illegitimate son, David. Nothing more is known about the lives of these poor wretched folk, other than the fate of one mother, Ann Tinniswood. She married a local man, William Lamb, 25 years later, and subsequently emigrated to Canada.

The Tinniswood family was notorious and indeed they may have been outcasts from village life. While their lives remain largely hidden from view, the father of one of these illegitimate children is a much more visible character. On 11 October 1805, John Batman appeared in the Courtroom of Quarter Sessions in York accused of 'begetting Elizabeth Tinniswood with child'. He was not alone: curiously enough, there were more illegitimate babies born in England in 1805, in comparison with the number of children born within wedlock, than there had been in any year for more than 250 years. We might think that illegitimacy peaked in 1805 because couples delayed marriage then until the vigour of youth had passed, but we would be wrong.[34]

In fact the age at which men and women married in 1805 was at an unprecedented low. In centuries past, marriages postponed or marriages foregone had been associated with fewer bastardies, not more of them as might be expected. John fornicated with Elizabeth Tinniswood at the age of 22 years, some four years or so younger than the age at which most of his contemporaries would marry. Elizabeth then vanishes from the historical record; John Batman meanwhile remained a bachelor, whether celibate we know not, for fifteen more years, then flourished in our village of Copmanthorpe.

Notes

1   Kaner, J The Vavasours of Copmanthorpe and the Court of Elizabeth I in *YAJ* vol 72 2000, p 107

2   *Ibid* p 108

3   Cartwright, J J Subsidy roll for York & the Ainsty 1524/5 in *YAJ vol 4* 1887 p 19. Edward Hogeson had taxable goods to the value of £3 – a high amount & BI Dean & Chapter Probate Index: Inventory of Richard Hodgson 1563. This shows goods and chattels to the value of £206.

4   Collins, F *Yorkshire Fines vol 1* YASRS 1887 p 113

5   NYCRO ZET Wood of Hollin Hall papers

6   BI CC D/C 11/21 1779 copy of 1722 survey of Copmanthorpe

7   BI Will of John Wood of the City of York Prerogative Court July 1757 vol 101, f 139

8   YFS Parish registers op cit

9   YCA F28 York Quarter Sessions Minute Book 1801–08, p 258

10 Mingay, G E *Rural Life in Victorian England* Stroud 1998

11 YFS Parish registers op cit

12 *Ibid*

13 BI Will of Thomas Wade of York 11 September 1862

14 BI Will of Francis Wade of Copmanthorpe 4 June 1808

15 BI Will of Thomas Batman of Copmanthorpe 6 February 1808

16 West Yorkshire Deeds Registry (WYDR) B37 Copmanthorpe Enclosure award

17 BI TA651L Tithe award for Copmanthorpe

18 Mingay 1998

19 Newman, P R Absentee landlords and the enclosure of the open fields: Hessay in the Ainsty *York Historian* **3** 1980

20 BI Will of William Hobson of Copmanthorpe 19 April 1853

21 WYDR Indenture 1865 Batman to Kirk, registered 31 July 1865

22 1851 York Census; Parish of Bishophill Junior

23 YFHS Parish records op cit

24 BI Will of John Batman 9 June 1873

25 WYDR John Wade's sale to Richard Skilbeck; Indenture registered 12 May 1874

26 Mingay 1998

27 BI Will of Thomas Swales of Copmanthorpe 1557 Dean and Chapter wills

28 BI Will of Thomas Swales of Copmanthorpe Dean and Chapter wills 1619/20 and DC CP 1620/3

29 Thomas, K *Man and the Natural World: changing attitudes in England 1500–1800* Harmondsworth 1984

30 BI Will of William Swale of Copmanthorpe Dean and Chapter wills March 1626

31 BI Will of Margritt Swaile of Copmanthorpe Dean and Chapter wills Sept 1643

32 YFHS Parish records op cit

33 Scott, S and Duncan, C J, Interacting factors affecting illegitimacy in preindustrial Northern England. *J Biosoe Sci* vol 29 1997, pp 151–69

34 Laslett, P *The world we have lost: further explored* London 1994 pp 159–61

CHAPTER NINE

Changing Society 1600–1900

PATRICK SOLICH, DOREEN FELTON
AND MARJORIE HARRISON

WHEN CONSIDERING THE HISTORY OF a particular community, people frequently ask what the population was at different points in time. Even today, such figures are not always very accurate – the modern census is carried out at ten-year intervals and much can change in a community in a decade (see **fig 9.2**).

It was the past, counting people was primarily a means of establishing how much tax could be raised. During the medieval period, occasional snapshots are provided by events such as the Poll Tax in the late 14th century, and some church documents may shed light on the size of a community. It must be remembered, however, that such documents tell only part of the story: they record only those who are liable or have the means to pay tax, not the women, the children and the very poor. Thus any figure based on a medieval document has to be scaled up to achieve an approximate overall population figure. In the case of the Poll Tax of 1379, some 51 individuals are listed for Copmanthorpe, but when other family members and servants are added in, the likely total is nearer 170 (see chapter 2).

It is not until the 17th century that records become sufficiently numerous to attempt an accurate survey of population changes over time, and even then the records can be uneven, as is the case for Copmanthorpe. Using the sources available, this chapter examines how the population of Copmanthorpe has grown over the years and how families have come and gone.

The seventeenth century

During the 17th century, certain taxes begin to be collected on a regular basis, allowing the size of the population to be tracked. The village of

9.1 Graph showing Baptisms and Burials in Copmanthorpe, 1675–99

(© Mike Rogers)

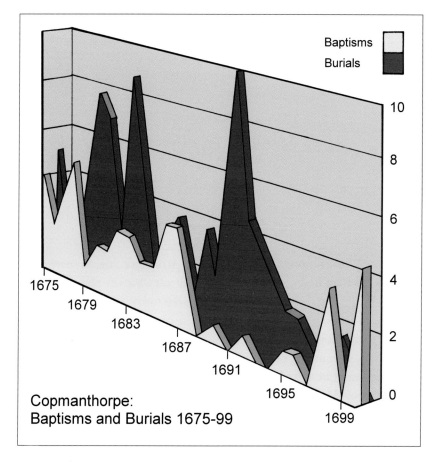

Copmanthorpe seems to have grown somewhat throughout this century. The Hearth Tax returns show 21 households in a survey dated 1665, rising to 24 in the survey of 1671, and no fewer than 26 families appear in the returns for 1674.[1] Such figures suggest a rise in the population from probably about 90 souls in 1665 to about 112 nine years later. The burial register shows no dramatic increase in the size of the population, although there were more annual deaths on average in the second half of the century than in the first.[2]

On average, the inhabitants of Copmanthorpe could expect three of their community to die each year. The changing fortunes of this little community from year to year were affected by the harvest more than by any other single influence. In good years, and there were eleven such years in this century, nobody in the village succumbed to old age, childhood infections, death in childbirth, or any other earthly disaster. In bad years, however, the mortality rate could rise to three times the average and more. The city of York suffered severely from an outbreak of plague in

FROM COPPENTHORPE TO COPMANTHORPE

1604 when more than a quarter of the population died, and it seems likely that this epidemic spread to outlying villages. A glimpse at the average mortality rate over the ensuing century then shows waves of excess deaths, one occurring in the first quarter of the century and four at roughly equal intervals in the second half (**fig 9.1**).

If we can pinpoint a mortality crisis in a village which buried an inhabitant only once every four months or so throughout this century, then that crisis occurred in the year 1690: no fewer than ten villagers died that year. And with the exception of just one child, all were old, established members of this close community. They included five old men (Thomas Batman, Leonard Nicolson, Richard Powell, Henry Swale and Thomas Marshall) and a widow (Ellin Hunter) whose names appeared as heads of households in the Hearth Tax returns of 20 years or so before. Three members of the Hunter family perished. This crisis claimed considerably more deaths than usual, and wise old heads at that.

The eighteenth century

In Copmanthorpe, time seems to stand still in the 18th century as very few records exist to tell us of the daily lives of the people and changes within their village. The evidence from Copmanthorpe wills and inventories fades away as the rural population became poorer; even the lord of the manor fell into debt and was bailed out by his tenant farmers. National census returns, which provide an accurate account of population and occupations, were not in place until 1841 and parish registers give little information about Copmanthorpe – an area removed from the church of St Mary Bishophill Junior sited just off Micklegate in York.

Life went on of course in the usual way and changes were gradual. At the beginning of the century the church was the only religious meeting place and Archbishop Herring's Visitation of 1743 tells us that there were about 40 families in the village and no dissenters had yet appeared. Services were held only once a month at St Giles church and communion, only once a year, so there was little spiritual provision for the inhabitants unless they walked or rode in to York. This was to change dramatically by the end of the century as recorded in chapter 5. The evangelical preaching of John Wesley had woken up the poor in towns and villages up and down the country and there was a realisation that individuals could receive education and improve themselves.

Herring's investigation revealed that there was educational provision only for people who could afford to pay the schoolmaster – and who could spare their child from agricultural or domestic tasks. Child labour could make a difference to a family with a small income and they were set to work as soon as they were able. It was not until the 19th century that children in Copmanthorpe had better educational opportunities.

Housing was poor in a village where most families were tenants of the lord of the manor; at the beginning of the century houses would probably have been timber-framed and thatched with brick gradually being introduced as the old houses became no longer fit for habitation. However, chapter 6 on Agriculture talks of houses described as 'all very ancient and frequently thatched' as late as 1808 so we can imagine that living conditions were poor.

We have learned from the chapter on Ancient Families that John Wood and his descendants were distant landlords, and land ownership was complex. The administration of the estate was in the hands of bailiffs and the Manor Court was still going through the motions in the 1780s. There was little change on the land until the 19th century when first the railway, and then enclosure, hit the village like a bombshell and propelled the men and women of Copmanthorpe forward into a better future.

The 19th century: census evidence

The first census of population was taken in 1801, and thereafter every ten years until the present date, with the exception of 1941 during the Second World War. From this Census data (**fig 9.2**) we can trace the rise (and fall) of the population in Copmanthorpe during the 19th century and then the substantial rise in numbers during the 20th century. The population rose by just 115 people in the 1800s, a modest amount considering the rise in the overall population of the country during that century. However, it is interesting that the figures rose steadily from 184 in 1801 to a peak of 350 in 1861, after which the population of agricultural villages gradually began to decline. This drift away from the land to expanding cities such as Leeds, where people could find work in the new industrial factories, and also emigration to America and Australia which offered hope of better prospects, was accelerated in the 1870s as an agricultural depression took hold. Poor weather and cheap imported wheat combined to affect the profitability of farming at this time and many tenant farmers and their labourers lost their livelihoods. Associated trades were also affected. In near-by villages, the fall in population is marked by the number of empty

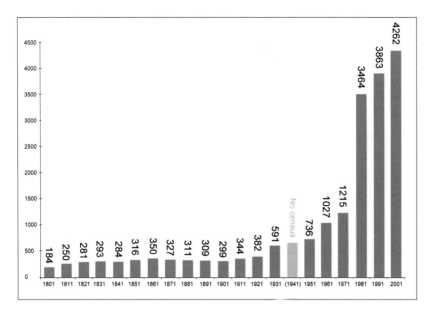

9.2 Population of Copmanthorpe from Census data, 1801–2001 (© Doreen Felton/ Mike Rogers)

houses in the 1871 and 1881 censuses, but in Copmanthorpe it would appear that any increase in vacant houses had taken place between those years and by 1881 there were fewer than ever before (three). Lower household numbers were accounting for the reduced population.

By 1901 the population had fallen to 299 but then began to rise; the arrival of the railway had earlier provided some employment opportunities and later, allowed men and women to travel easily into the growing city of York to take up jobs there. During the 20th century the population of Copmanthorpe rose rapidly, with large rises during the 1960s and 70s, chiefly due to the housing boom of those years and the fact that the road network was improved and commuter travel was becoming increasingly fashionable; Copmanthorpe is ideally located for travel to both York and Leeds.

During the 19th century, the largest percentage of the population of Copmanthorpe was employed in agriculture, from farm owners to agricultural labourers, and associated trades such as blacksmiths, carters, grooms, cartwrights, flax dressers, shepherds and market gardeners. The 1861 census lists other trades in Copmanthorpe including carpenters, tailors, dressmakers, shoemakers, a clock dresser, schoolmaster, shopkeepers and house servants including sick nurses, a pupil teacher and a governess. The Railway Company employees included a station master, clerks, labourers, porters, grooms and a gate man and boy. Craftsmen such as blacksmiths, tailors and shoemakers often employed apprentices who usually lived with them.

Although census returns have been taken every 10 years since 1801, from which it is possible to track population movement over the past two centuries, it was not until 1841 that the statistics collated included a house-to-house breakdown of occupants showing their occupations and ages. From 1851 far more information was given including the relationship of each occupant to the head of household, their employment, gender, marital status and accurate age at census date, and of importance to historians and researchers, where each person was born. Looking at the movement of individuals, we find that railway workers tended to move around during the Victorian era, often moving from one station to another in order to gain promotion, much as is the case today. Using an example of railway employee Thomas Fawbert, born in Londonderry, North Yorkshire in 1818, it is possible to track him from 1861 when he was working in Copmanthorpe as a railway porter. He resided there with his wife, who had been born in Holtby, his eight-year-old son born in Carlton Miniott, near Thirsk, and his five-year-old daughter born in York. By 1881 he was living in Moss, Doncaster and was employed as station master. In 1891 he had returned to Carlton Miniott, where he was still working aged 68 as a railway lavatory attendant; Thomas died in Thirsk in 1895, aged 73. The railway provided wider employment opportunities even for labourers; in 1861, James Harrison, born in Copmanthorpe in 1818 to Thomas and Mary Harrison, was living in Copmanthorpe with his wife and family, and was employed as a railway labourer, but by 1871 he was in Skirpenbeck working as a farm hand. In 1881 he was in Norton, Malton, back with the railway as a porter, before returning to Copmanthorpe where in 1891 he was again employed as a farm labourer. He died in 1895, aged 76. Both these examples show how the working classes, with no pensions to support them, had to work until they were incapable, although in both of these cases the men attained a reasonable age for those harsh Victorian years.

Village life 1850–1900

As we have seen, the small agricultural village of Copmanthorpe was growing in the first half of the 19th century. This upward trend reflected the national growth in population which in itself provided an increasing demand from the towns and cities for the produce of the land. The rapid expansion of the railway network facilitated this, helping farmers and industrialists alike to reach their markets quickly and the population to travel with greater ease.

Enclosure of the open fields had transformed the village landscape. Along with the associated increased efficiency, the introduction of new farming methods and machinery, such as the threshing machine belonging to David Dykes, was changing the agricultural scene. By 1851 the railway had become well established and the station at Copmanthorpe was providing farmers with an easier way of getting stock to market, saving many man-hours driving cattle into York. This was alongside many other benefits to the local community.

By the 1860s central government policy was beginning to have a greater effect on local communities. Poor Law Unions had been created to replace the old Elizabethan Poor Law and deal better with poverty and ill health. Attempts to create a better-educated society were made; the 1870 Education Act aimed to fill the gaps left by the hit and miss voluntary system. This Act provided a framework for state education, although it did not become compulsory until 1880, and then only until the age of ten. By 1891, elementary education had become free to all.

We have seen in a previous chapter (5) the strength of nonconformism in Copmanthorpe. By 1850 the Methodist church boasted a strong congregation to take its place alongside its Anglican counterpart. The Methodists brought ideas of self-improvement to ordinary people and were a strong force educationally through Sunday schools, which not only taught the Bible, but helped with reading and writing too.

'Stayers' or 'core families' occupied villages up to the beginning of the 19th century. These were families with ties to the land, be it through ownership or labouring and although village populations had never been static, their identity changed only slowly over the years. The 19th century however saw new patterns developing; some families began to push out their roots beyond the boundaries of a single parish. They moved on, some taking their trades with them, and so villages became more open to new families and the changes they brought.

Census information shows that Copmanthorpe was no different to many other villages and parishes of the time. It was never a self-contained village. It retained its history of the core family, but inward migration was always evident throughout this period. Although some men and women came from near-by townships, the 1851 census shows that the origins of the majority were much further afield, albeit mainly in Yorkshire.

The arrival of the railway offered some opportunities for work beyond that of agriculture. New faces appeared in the village and the evidence for this can be seen in employment patterns; who worked where, and what new business was brought in over a period of time. In this respect, the popular local 'Directories' are an invaluable source of information to historians, as they must have been to the communities of the time. It can also be seen in family names that appear, and how new families became part of the village alongside the core families.

In 1851 we find Copmanthorpe dominated by farming. Agricultural work took many forms: those at the top of the socio-economic scale were the landowners. They had large households and large acreages and were important people in the parish, undertaking positions such as Overseers of the Highway or Overseers of the Poor. John Nalton, with 155 acres, and the Allan family are two examples of this in Copmanthorpe. The job opportunities offered by these families were various, although in the 1851 census most were noted as 'agricultural labourers'. One position which occurs frequently is that of servant, and in many instances these were teenage girls and boys from the village. They could be house maids, laundry maids, stable boys, or simply 'servants of husbandry', indicating outdoor work on the farm. As the details recorded in the census improved in later years, the agricultural job descriptions become more revealing (horsebreakers, dealers, shepherds, to name but three).

The other sector of employment, the railways, was different in make-up to that of agriculture. As previously seen, workers often came from elsewhere and it offered a variety of jobs, from platelayers, porters, and gatekeepers to 'head of railway', as well as good promotional prospects.

These two themes of employment and migration are continuous throughout the period, but small-scale changes are apparent, reflecting the pace of social change that was filtering through to the rural areas. A butcher's shop, owned by a Charles Forth, born in Askham Bryan, opened in 1871. Charles remained in his shop for many years and employed apprentices (in 1891 he had two, one from York and the other from Dringhouses) but not until 1901 is a Copmanthorpe lad, Thomas Lindsell, seen in this role.

Kelly's West Riding Directory for 1877 lists thirteen farmers in Copmanthorpe; associated trades were the blacksmith, joiner and wheel-wright. There was a market garden, the pub and one shop. John Wright was the carrier, William Gresham the tailor and Richard Chandler the shoemaker. The village was weathering the agricultural recession and would begin to see more diverse occupations in the future.

Clerical jobs began to appear in the later census years as well as a wider variety of occupations. Arthur Batman and Harry Piercy were solicitor's clerks, possibly travelling daily into York along with George Batman, a pawnbroker's apprentice (1881). A merchant's clerk is listed in 1891 and Bertha Johnson was a typist (1901).

Other occupations in 1881 include a druggist, Arthur Fox, born in Pontefract; a toll collector (Richard Cussans); a clock cleaner (John Exelby); and a commercial traveller, John Markham, born in Doncaster. Charles Wheatley was a telegraph wire-worker and two retired men, one an engine driver and the other a coach smith, lived in the village – a wonderful illustration of the changing world in the late 19th century. The old male-dominated village trades of shoemaking and tailoring were still continuing but Elizabeth Gresham, continuing her father's business, is recorded as a tailoress, with a female apprentice, rather than the more usual dressmaker. A nurse and a midwife are represented in 1881.

The returns of 1891 see more new occupations: the postmistress (Ellen Hudson), and a retired veterinary surgeon (Charles B Spencer, born in Otley). Edmund Woodlock was a timber merchant's clerk, there was a cattle dealer, and an agricultural machine driver. By contrast, Ann Gisburn, a 62 year-old widow, was eking out a living as a gatekeeper on the railway.

By 1901 a newsagent – Joseph Milner – had arrived in Copmanthorpe and Robert Gray, a builder, along with the manageress of a laundry and a French polisher. A basic village-based occupation was performed by George Eastwood and William Brown, each described as a 'Parish labourer on the roads'. They would be known as a 'lengthsman' responsible for keeping the village street swept of dung, and mending potholes.

This material indicates some development of the village economy and opportunities for future employment as the village moved on into the 20th century. Some of these new tradespeople were born outside the village, showing that there was no barrier to in-migration.

The Allan family name offers a fine example of a three-generational presence within the village, a 'core family' within Copmanthorpe. The name is steeped in an agricultural working past. The family lived at Ivy House Farm and in 1861 the youngest son, George (now 28), became head of the household, with his own family in its infancy. Between 1861 and 1891 the nucleus of the family remained, with some new arrivals and others who may have migrated. In the 1901 census, one of George's sons, also called George, had now become head of the family, resident at Ashfield House with his wife and two daughters, Edith and Florence.

The other strong family name that is worthy of note is that of Beedham. The family was headed by William in 1851, with his wife Anne and six children, only one of whom was born in Copmanthorpe (William). In 1861 he was still at home with an older sister but the other four were no longer there, either working away from home, or overtaken by illness and death. Their places were taken by new siblings: Robert, Thomas and Elizabeth. In 1881 we see the original family unit still present; however one of the older boys, Henry, now has a family of his own (his daughter Mary Agnes was born in Naburn, which may suggest evidence of return migration). By 1891 Robert had set up his own family home, married with two children. Thomas had also started his own family, with a wife, a son and two daughters. The Beedhams married into another important Copmanthorpe family, the Thompsons. In 1901 these many offshoots from the original Beedham family were all present and increasing in numbers. Following in the family tradition, two of these third-generation Beedhams are noted as working as servants.

These families show us different ways in which a name remained within the village. The Beedhams show how a name could spread around the village without ever having a landholding presence; this was a common occurrence in rural villages for those lower down the social scale. They also give an example of families in the village marrying within it. Core families in the village, as can be seen, had vastly different experiences.

For those who moved in, the experience would offer even more challenges. The names Leng, Jacques, Cussans and Lindsell appear throughout the latter part of our period and enable us to see how a migrant family developed its own place within a community. For instance, by 1901 Robert Leng, whose father (born in Norton) moved into the village as a joiner in 1861, had become the parish clerk. The majority of these newcomers were all from relatively nearby places, although in 1881 the Lindsell family were introduced. Head of the family Charles was born in Ireland, and his wife in West Hartlepool; Charles was employed on the railway. By 1901 his son Robert was a servant with the Allanby family, and another son, Thomas, was the assistant to the butcher, Charles Forth.

The families that settled successfully were able to establish their own presence and enjoy a stable lifestyle. The majority of these were from towns and villages not too far away, although the Lindsell story shows how the patterns may have started to change as the 20th century beckoned.

Notes

1   YCA M30:22/47, M30:25 M30:26 Hearth Tax returns
2   York Family History Society (YFS) The Parish Registers of St Giles, Copmanthorpe, York 1759–1837 YFHS Publications no 3

CHAPTER TEN

Copmanthorpe at war

MARTIN MURPHY

The Copmanthorpe War Memorials

The Copmanthorpe War Memorials were erected in 1920. As well as the stone memorial on the Green (**fig 10.1**), which gives the names of eighteen men from the village who gave their lives in the two world wars, there is a brass plaque within St Giles church which names all the men from the village who served, who were wounded, and who died in the Great War. The investigation of the names recorded on the memorials provides some interesting insights into the families living in the village at the time.[1]

The Great War (1914–18)

There are ten names on the memorials of men who died between 1914 and 1919 (**fig 10.2**).

Unusually, the names on the stone memorial are not arranged alphabetically, and do not seem to be in the order of date of death, nor according to the date of enlistment.

The names as given are:

ALFRED ANDERSON	ALFRED BEEDHAM
GEo Hy BRIGGS	RICHARD BROWN
JOs E GERMAIN	FRANK HARDWICK
IVAN VICTOR REED	THOMAS SPENCE
ARTHUR WALTER LT	CHARLES WILDING

IN PROUD AND GRATEFUL
MEMORY OF
OUR MEN WHO GAVE THEIR LIVES
FOR US IN THE GREAT WAR.
1914 – 1919.

ALFRED ANDERSON. ALFRED BEEDHAM.
GEO HY BRIGGS. RICHARD BROWN.
JAS E. GERMAIN. FRANK HARDWICK.
JOHN VICTOR REED. THOMAS SPENCE.
ARTHUR WALTER. LT. CHARLES WILDING.

10.1   Copmanthorpe
        war memorial
        (© Catherine
        Pemberton)

10.2   Detail of WWI
        names on
        memorial
        (© Catherine
        Pemberton)

Similar memorials elsewhere give soldiers' regiment or corps, and the date on which each died. Their absence on the Copmanthorpe memorial makes identifying some of the men and their families difficult, and while it has been possible to find information about most of them,[2] two cannot be linked to the village with any certainty.

The following men have definite association with Copmanthorpe:

Alfred Ernest Beedham

Alfred was one of the five children of Thomas and Annie Beedham. Thomas was a shepherd at Manor Farm and earned fifteen shillings a week. The 1901 Census records that the family (all of whom were born in Copmanthorpe) lived in a three-roomed cottage and at that time included Alfred's older sister Blanche, and John, his younger brother. John, who would have been eighteen in 1914, also fought in the Great War, and was wounded. At the age of 86, Blanche spoke to an interviewer about her memories, but sadly did not mention her brothers.[3]

Alfred Beedham enlisted in Wakefield, giving the town as his place of residence. When he enlisted is not known, but the date of his death suggests that he was one of the hundreds of thousands of young men who volunteered before the introduction of conscription. He served as a gunner with 'W' 8th Trench Mortar Battery of the Royal Field Artillery in France. This unit fought at the Battle of the Somme, when nearly 20,000 British soldiers were killed on its first day, 1 July 1916, but Alfred died some months later. He was killed in action near Bethune, aged 25, on 29 September 1916. As the date of his death does not fall within any specific military offensive, and as mortar units tended to attract enemy shelling when fired (making them unpopular with other front-line troops), it is possible that Alfred was killed by retaliatory artillery fire in everyday operations. He is buried at Vermelles British Cemetery in France.

Ivan Victor Reed

Ivan Reed was born in Skelton, the son of William and Louisa Reed and moved with them to Hurton Villa, Copmanthorpe, along with at least two brothers and a sister. It seems that his was a 'respectable' and responsible family. His father was a parish councillor and a church warden, and his sister was a teacher.[4] Ivan's brother John Frederick (Fred) followed their father onto Copmanthorpe Parish Council and served for 36 years (29 as chairman), until 1970. A bachelor who continued to live in Hurton Villa, Fred came to the village in 1910, at the age of eighteen. He worked at the railway headquarters in York, but served in France in the Great War with the Machine Gun Corps and was taken prisoner in the last German offensive before the Armistice.[5] Fred died at the age of 80. Another brother, Alan, died in 1988, aged 90 (see **fig 10.5**). He had been a lieutenant in the Royal Flying Corps during the War.[6]

Ivan Reed was killed in action on 1 April 1918, aged 23. He was a Corporal of D Company, in the 20th Battalion of the Machine Gun Corps, after having enlisted at Hull with the East Riding Yeomanry. Enemy machine-gunners were generally regarded with hostility by the infantry soldiers of both sides because of the slaughter they inflicted on advancing troops, and were often given no quarter when captured. Ivan was one of 14,000 British soldiers killed in March and April 1918, during the last German offensive, who were never found and have no known graves. He is commemorated on the Pozières Memorial, near the Somme battlefields in France.

Joseph E Germain

Joseph was the son of William Germain, who was from Slingsby, and his wife Ester Ann, born in Robin Hood's Well (a hamlet near Doncaster). At the time of the census in 1901, William and Ester were living at 3 Railway Cottages, Copmanthorpe, with their baby daughter Olive, and seven sons who ranged in age from four to sixteen. Joseph, then six, was the second youngest boy. Harry, the eldest, was working as a railway porter, while Frank (aged fifteen) was a railway lamp-lad. William Germain was a signalman and his work on the railways would have taken him around Yorkshire, for Harry was born in East Cowton and Frank and Fred in Moss; both are villages which lie alongside railway lines. The family must have moved to Copmanthorpe by 1890 because all the younger children (including Joseph) were born in the village.

The plaque in St Giles church shows that Harry and Robert (who was three years older than Joseph) also served in the Great War, although Harry as a railway worker could have been exempt from conscription. Records show that Joseph enlisted in the Army at York (though not when) and was a private in the 23rd (Tyneside Scottish) Battalion of the Northumberland Fusiliers, when he was killed in action in France, aged 22, on 6 December 1917. Like Alfred Beedham, the date does not occur within any specific offensive on the Western Front, so he may have fallen victim to routine shelling or sniping. He is buried in the Guémappe British Cemetery, Wancourt, near Arras, in France. He had given as his next of kin only his mother, living at 56 Doncaster Road, South Elmsall, Pontefract; she would have been 53 then, and his father (if still living) would have been 56.

Arthur Walter

Arthur Walter is the only officer listed on the stone memorial for the Great War, and was a second lieutenant in the 1st Battalion of the East Yorkshire Regiment. Arthur was a professional soldier and his Battalion was in York in August 1914; it landed in France on 10 September 1914. Arthur was killed in action nearly four years later, on 21 March 1918, during the desperate last German assault of the war, which forced the Allied armies back across the former Somme battlefields. He was 37, which is old for a second lieutenant (the most junior commissioned rank) and since he held a Military

Medal, which was not awarded to officers, he had clearly served in the ranks before being commissioned. Commissioning from the ranks was not uncommon as the war progressed; it has been suggested that by its end two-thirds of officers had been commissioned in the field.[7] He is also commemorated on the Pozières Memorial, and not by a grave, which means that his body was never found.

Officers at the Front had a higher casualty rate than other ranks, as they were specifically targeted by snipers in the trenches and when they led their men 'over the top' and across No Man's Land to attack enemy lines, but as well as greater responsibilities, they had greater freedoms and privileges. Arthur would have received an individual commission from the King, reading 'George by the grace of God ... to our trusty and well-beloved Arthur ...', and referring to the King's special trust and confidence in Arthur's 'loyalty, courage, and good conduct'. His pay would have been much greater than a soldier's, whose basic pay was one shilling (5p) a day, usually paid irregularly and in arrears.[8] A new second lieutenant's total income from pay and allowances was £200 (on which he paid income tax of £6). His outfit allowance easily paid for two service dress uniforms and a greatcoat and accessories, as well as a sword and revolver[9], for unlike soldiers, officers bought their own uniforms and weapons. He could afford to supplement army rations with delicacies from Harrods, and his food in the trenches would have been prepared by his batman, the soldier-servant allocated to each officer. Hampers from home might have contained whisky (then costing £3 10s, or £3.50, a bottle) or brandy, whereas other ranks, unlike officers, were not permitted to drink spirits, even at cafes in towns behind the lines during rest periods. At base camp Arthur would have shared a tent with another officer, but ten of his men would have occupied one tent, and if wounded, he would have received better and more sympathetic treatment.[10] Arthur is likely to have worn a moustache, because until 1917 King's Regulations made them compulsory for officers, though not for men.

As a second lieutenant, Arthur Walter would have commanded a platoon of 48 soldiers and four non-commissioned officers, who were divided into sections of twelve men under a sergeant or corporal. The 1st Battalion of the East Yorkshire Regiment, at full strength, would have consisted of 1,007 men, including 30 officers. Arthur's platoon would have been one of four making up a company, commanded by a major with a captain as second-in-command. There were four companies and a headquarters unit to each battalion, which was commanded by a lieutenant-colonel, with a major as second-in-command.

Arthur was the son of William, a labourer, and Alice Walter, who lived in Watford, and gave his residence as Tidworth (a military base in Wiltshire) when he married Hannah Milburn Tomlinson, spinster of Copmanthorpe, in St Giles church on Christmas Eve, 1912. Hannah was the daughter of William Henry Tomlinson (deceased), and was aged 35; Arthur was 32.[11] When Arthur was killed, Hannah was living at 118 Albemarle Road, The Mount, York, and his mother Alice was a widow.

Richard Brown

Richard Brown was born in Church Fenton. Richard enlisted in York and was a lance corporal in the 11th Battalion of the West Yorkshire Regiment (Prince of Wales' Own). He was aged 28 when he was killed on 7 June 1917, near Ypres in Belgium. It was the first day of the Third Battle of Ypres, when the British army launched a major assault at Passchendaele. He is commemorated on the Menin Gate memorial to the missing in Ypres, which means that his remains still lie somewhere in the earth of Flanders' Fields.

Richard was the son of William Brown, a railway porter, and his wife Mary, and at the time of the 1901 Census was aged twelve and was living with them and his sister Sarah at 2 Railway Cottages, in Kirk Fenton (as it was then called). However, on enlisting he gave as his next of kin his brother Edward Brown, of 11 Mayfield Terrace, Tadcaster. This proximity suggests that Richard himself may have lived in or near the village, though no Copmanthorpe address is given to explain why his name is on the Memorial. It is possible that his parents were dead or infirm (in 1917 they would have been aged 59 and 64), or that he was estranged from them, and so named his brother as next of kin. As his brother was not recorded as living with his parents by the census, it seems that he would have been at least two or three years older than Richard, possibly leaving home for work in his early teens.

There is less certainty about a connection with the village of the following names:

George Henry Briggs

It is probable that George Henry was Private G H Briggs of the 14th Battalion of the London Regiment (London Scottish), who was the son of Mr F F Briggs of 20 Trinity Lane, Micklegate, York.[12] When he enlisted in Glasgow, he gave his place of residence as York. He died on 7 November 1916, age unknown, and is buried in the Laventie Military Cemetery, near Lys, in France. He is commemorated on the St Mary Bishophill Junior Church War Memorial in York, and in the York King's Book[13] and it is not clear why his name also appears on the Copmanthorpe memorial.

Charles Wilding

Private 17330 C Wilding, age unknown, who was killed in France on 6 January 1916, may be the Charles Wilding whose name appears on the Copmanthorpe Memorial, but this is cannot be confirmed.

Frank Hardwick

It is possible but not certain that the Frank Hardwick of the Memorial may be Private 1812 Frank Hardwick who belonged to the 5th Battalion of the West Yorkshire Regiment (Prince of Wales' Own) and died in France on 27 September 1915, aged nineteen.

Thomas Spence

It is not possible to identify with certainty the soldier commemorated on the Memorial, although he is likely to be one of two Spences who died whilst serving in the Yorkshire Regiment, either Private 11446 Thomas Spence of the 6th Battalion, or Private 2302 Thomas Watson Spence of the 4th Battalion.

Alfred Anderson

It is not certain which of the eleven entries for 'Alfred Anderson' in the national records, or of the further 64 for 'A Anderson', is the Alfred Anderson of the Copmanthorpe Memorial.

It is not clear now by what criteria names were placed on the memorials, and whilst there are ten names for those who fell in the Great War, Fred Reed was recorded as saying: 'We lost five villagers, including my own brother', in the War.[14] As neither Fred nor his brother were born in Copmanthorpe, he must have counted as 'villagers' men who lived in the village, wherever they originated from, but may not have included those who lived in the surrounding countryside, or who lived further afield but worked in Copmanthorpe.

Others who served

The plaque in St Giles church lists another fourteen men who were wounded, and a further 51 who served, during the Great War, giving a total of 75 Copmanthorpe men who went to war. In 1911, the census recorded 178 males living in the village, of whom about 117 would have been of adult working age (16 to 65, which is wider than the eventual liability-to-conscription age range of 18 to 51). This suggests that during the course of the war, more than 60% of the eligible men in Copmanthorpe served in the military.

Of those who served, 13.3% died; this is more than the national average for Britain of 11.8%.[15] The deaths represent 8.5% of the population of adult males of working age in the village, compared to the national 6.3% of males aged between 15 and 49 who died.[16] Not all who served in the Great War fought on the front-line, where the great majority of the deaths occurred. There were more soldiers behind the lines in support roles, though there is disagreement about how many more; the Army Council maintained that there were only three support troops to each fighting man, but an officer at the Front estimated the true ratio at fourteen to one.[17] The death ratio for Copmanthorpe's soldiers suggests that a higher than average proportion served in units fighting at the Front.

Memorials to the fallen often contain the names of two or more members of the same family. This is not the case in Copmanthorpe, but the church plaque records that John Beedham, brother of Alfred, was wounded, as was George H Eastwood. George H was the son of George Eastwood (parish labourer and road-mender) and his wife Jane, and older brother of Thomas, who also served. Similarly, G W Ackroyd was wounded, when S H Ackroyd (who may have been his brother) was not. A Wilding is recorded as having served, and he may be related to the Charles Wilding who appears on the memorial to the fallen. It is not now possible to identify relationships unless the family appears in the 1901 Census returns, and only ten of those listed do. The release of the 1911 Census returns may help to clarify some of the uncertainty.

The plaque lists around sixteen family names who may have been brothers or fathers and sons serving in the War. It was not uncommon for brothers (and sometimes fathers and sons) to serve together in the same unit. It is known that there are at least 184 instances of brothers (or fathers and sons) being killed on the same day, usually (but not always) in the same location. There is a headstone near Cambrai commemorating a corporal in his 30s which has an inscription by his family saying that he was one of five brothers who fell, 'each a hero', and also a cemetery by the Somme battlefields in which are buried three pairs of brothers.[18]

Some of the fourteen men who were wounded may have been maimed or permanently disabled, while most others would have made a full physical recovery (the War Office concluded that 55% of wounded soldiers who were not mortally wounded returned to active service). All who went away to war would have come back changed, and many of those who endured the horror and the terror of the trenches and the battlefields will have carried mental and emotional scars for the rest of their lives.

World War II (1939–45)

There are eight names on the Copmanthorpe War Memorial of men who died between 1939 and 1945, 'for Justice and Freedom'. They are arranged (almost alphabetically), as follows:

ERIC SWIFT BARKER

REGINALD CARTER

WILLIS COLLIER

ROBIN KING

HAROLD STANLEY JARRATT

ALFRED MAY

JOHN HERBERT RODGERS

REGINALD BASIL WRIGHT

The names are sufficiently distinctive to allow positive identification through national records for most of them, though as with the Great War, the connection to Copmanthorpe is not clear in every case. The fate of some of these men illustrates well the wider theatre of action of World War II.

The following had a definite connection to the village:

Reginald Carter

Reginald Carter was a Major, aged 47, when he died on 14 September 1944. He was the son of John and Mary Ann Carter (address unknown), and husband of Violet Victoria Carter 'of Copmanthorpe, Yorkshire'. Major Carter is recorded as being on the General List (rather than serving with a specific unit), and is buried in the Stanley Military Cemetery in Hong Kong.

By 1941 it was recognised that Japanese annexation of Hong Kong could not be prevented, but nonetheless there was stubborn resistance. The colony was taken by the Japanese on Christmas Day 1941, after seventeen days of intense fighting, and it is probable that Reginald was captured then and held in the officers' camp in Stanley. Some of the prisoners-of-war and civilian internees were executed, but Reginald almost certainly died (after more than two years in captivity) of disease, exacerbated by malnutrition and harsh treatment; it is alleged that the Japanese withheld available drug treatment from the prisoners.[19]

Alfred Allan May

Alfred May was a gunner with 61 Anti-Tank Regiment, Royal Artillery, and died in North Africa on 27 October 1942, at the age of 33. He was killed in action during the Battle of Alamein, which began four days earlier. He is buried in the El Alamein War Cemetery, some 80 miles west of Alexandria in Egypt. Alfred was the son of James William and Ada May of Copmanthorpe, and husband of Dorothy Hannah May, who lived at 14 Drome Gates, Copmanthorpe. He had been employed at the LNER carriage works. His death was reported in the *Yorkshire Evening Press* on 1 December 1941, which showed his photograph; this is the only known local newspaper report of a village soldier's death.[20]

Reginald Basil Wright

Reginald Wright died aged 23 on 9 December 1940, and is buried in the churchyard at Shawbury, in Shropshire. He was in the RAF Volunteer Reserve, and was a Leading Aircraftman who was training to be a pilot. Shawbury is a village near Shrewsbury, and it is possible that Reginald was killed in an accident whilst learning to fly at a nearby airfield (during World War II, casualties from accidents in flying training and exercises in Britain were high).

Reginald was the son of Joseph Henry and Florence Anne Wright of Copmanthorpe.

Harold Stanley Jarratt

Trooper Harold Stanley Jarratt of the 8th Royal Tank Regiment died, aged 28, on 23 November 1941, and is buried in the Knightsbridge War Cemetery, Acroma, Libya. Acroma is not far from Tobruk, where the Eighth Army had an advance fuelling station and airfield. The cemetery contains the remains of servicemen retrieved from scattered desert battlefield sites in the surrounding area, and Harold is likely to have died during the resistance to the German advance towards Suez. No address is given for his parents, but his name is distinctive (and unique in the national register); he is remembered locally as being from the Fox and Hounds.[21] On 18 October 1944, 25-year-old Muriel Jarratt, also of the Fox and Hounds and daughter of Harold Wilks Jarratt, grocer, married a Canadian airman.[22]

Robin King

There is only one Robin King in the national register. He was a Lance Corporal in the 2nd Battalion of the East Yorkshire Regiment, and died, aged 23, on 16 October 1944. He is buried in the Mierlo War Cemetery in the Netherlands, suggesting that he was involved in the fighting to liberate Holland which took place from September to November 1944. Robin was the son of Frederick John and Mary Alice King. His parents' address is not given, but they appear in the Copmanthorpe Register of Baptisms when Robin was baptised on 14 August 1921. Frederick's occupation was recorded then as being that of farm labourer. The baptisms and marriages of their children Alice and Hubert are also recorded.[23] Hubert was born on 17 April 1926, and was married in 1946; when he joined the Home Guard, he gave his occupation as an acting fireman for the LNER, and his address as 15 Moor Lane, Copmanthorpe.[24] As this was before he married, when he was aged seventeen or eighteen, it is likely that this was the parental address. Robin's wife is named in the national register as being Peggy Louisa Mary King of Grantham, Lincolnshire.

The transcript of a taped interview recorded in the mid-1970s with Mr and Mrs King seems to indicate that they were Robin's parents, Frederick and Mary. Mrs King (who was then 90) says that she had 'nine lads and four girls: we lost two, one son was killed in this last war and then I lost a girl in the first war, she was two years and ten months'. They make no other reference to Robin.[25] Frederick was born in Shipton, but Mary was the daughter of Charles Lindsell of Copmanthorpe, a railway platelayer. The couple married on 10 June 1905[26] and returned to Copmanthorpe from Shipton.

John Herbert Rodgers

John Rodgers was serving with the 7th Battalion of the Green Howards (Yorkshire Regiment) when he died, aged 26, on the 26 October 1942. He died three days after the start of the Battle of Alamein, and is buried in the El Alamein War Cemetery. He was the son of John William and Nellie Christabel Rodgers, and the husband of Winifred Mary Rodgers, of Acaster Malbis. While his parents' address is not given, it seems likely, because of the proximity of Acaster, that they lived in Copmanthorpe.

These names have less certain connections with Copmanthorpe:

Eric Swift Barker

The Debt of Honour Register records that Eric Barker was a Gunner with 77 (The Duke of Lancaster's Own Yeomanry) Medium Regiment of the Royal Artillery. He was 28 when he died on 12 April 1945. He is buried at the Rheinberg War Cemetery in Germany, indicating that he was killed during the final advance into Germany, just weeks before VE [Victory in Europe] Day. Eric was the son of Walter Ernest and Alice Barker, and the husband of Jane Barker, of Newry, Co. Down, Northern Ireland. No address is given for his parents, but there is only one Eric Swift Barker in the Commonwealth War Graves Commission records, so it seems that he is the soldier commemorated on the memorial. Either Eric and Jane, or Walter and Alice, may have lived in Copmanthorpe at this time.

Willis Collier

There is a Corporal *William* Willis Collier of the Royal Dragoons in the national register. Aged 33, he died on 28 December 1941, whilst serving with the Royal Armoured Corps in North Africa, and is commemorated on the Alamein Memorial at the El Alamein War Cemetery. There was fighting in the area from 1940 to 1942, culminating in the Battle of Alamein in late October 1942. Corporal Collier's death was long before that Battle, and as he has no grave, it seems that he was killed in action somewhere in the desert and that his body was never found. William Willis was the son of John and Kathleen Collier, and was the husband of Eveline G Collier of Elvington, Kent. No address is given for his parents, but as his name is distinctive, and unique in the register, it seems likely that his link to Copmanthorpe is through them. Willis is an unusual forename but it appears in the village in the 1901 Census, and later in local Home Guard records, when Willis Exelby Dykes, butcher, of Rose Cottage, enrolled in the Bishopthorpe detachment on 30 June 1940, a month after Dunkirk, and two weeks after the Fall of France, when he was nearly 37.[27]

Copmanthorpe aerodrome

While men from Copmanthorpe went off to the battlefields of France and Flanders in 1914, the War came closer to those they left at home with the establishment of an aerodrome on the outskirts of the village. Aeroplanes were new and unfamiliar then, and the activities in Drome Road airfield must have been fascinating for local residents, particularly young boys.

The Royal Flying Corps (RFC) aerodrome just outside the village (**fig 10.3**) was in operation from the middle of the Great War until after it ended, and early fighters – slow, fragile biplanes made of wood and wire and fabric – flew from Copmanthorpe to intercept marauding Zeppelin-type airships.

The airfield was one of a number intended to form a home defence chain from Dover to Newcastle.[28] There had been recognition before the Great War that the long range of the German airships meant that Britain was no longer safe as an island securely protected by its navy but was

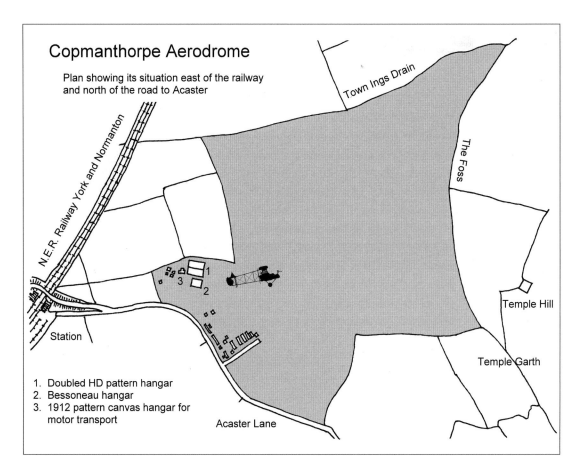

Copmanthorpe Aerodrome

Plan showing its situation east of the railway
and north of the road to Acaster

Town Ings Drain

N.E.R. Railway York and Normanton

The Foss

Temple Hill

Temple Garth

Acaster Lane

Station

1. Doubled HD pattern hangar
2. Bessoneau hangar
3. 1912 pattern canvas hangar for
motor transport

10.3 Copmanthorpe
Aerodrome
(Based on original
map in archives
of the Yorkshire
Air Museum,
Elvington)

open to 'aerial invasion', and this caused much public concern and demand for new defences. The North East was especially vulnerable to bombing raids because it was nearest to the airship bases across the North Sea, and was the target of the first Zeppelin attack on Britain, on the night of 1 January 1915. Aiming for Hull, the Zeppelins in fact bombed towns in Norfolk, killing several people and injuring more, causing fear and alarm and a national and international outcry. The press referred to 'helpless victims of a wanton outrage', the Archbishop of York condemned the raid as 'cruel', and French and American papers used words such as 'barbaric' and 'savage'; there were suggestions that in attacking Norfolk, the Germans were trying to kill the King at Sandringham.[29] In its aftermath, citizens of York were requested by the Chief Constable to reduce lighting and to screen windows in the event of an air-raid, and shop-keepers were asked to subdue the illumination of window displays.[30] London and other cities were bombed in 1915, but Zeppelins did not come to York until the following year.

York was attacked first on the moonless night of 2 May 1916 by a single Zeppelin, which at 10.45pm dropped bombs on Dringhouses, killing two people, and then moved south-eastwards and released further bombs which killed nine more people.[31] The raid lasted ten minutes and the slow-moving Zeppelin, because of its elevation and great size, would have been clearly visible from Copmanthorpe, and may have passed over the village. Blanche Beedham, then aged 27, many years later recalled seeing a Zeppelin, and described standing in the street with other frightened villagers in their night-clothes, watching the dark shape of the huge vessel as it droned over Copmanthorpe;[32] it is likely that it was this first raider that she saw. Another attacked York from 11pm on 25 September 1916, dropping nine bombs without causing casualties, before being chased away by a new anti-aircraft gun at Acomb and moving off towards Leeds. The raid of 27 November 1916 by three Zeppelins was more serious, when bombs were dropped on the eastern side of the city, causing deaths and injuries and destroying property. One of the airships may have been damaged by the Acomb gun.[33]

The aerodrome was completed just after the Zeppelin raids took place, and covered an area of 550 by 650 metres, east of the railway line and north of the road to Acaster. It was a grass field, without runways, and aeroplanes would take off and land along the grass in a direction dictated by the wind. The site was cleared and levelled by 'Cat C' troops unfit for service overseas, with the assistance later of Canadian timber-men.[34] Miss Beedham remembered that there was a pond, with a willow tree, which had to be drained and filled. Another villager, Fred Reed, interviewed in the 1970s, revealed that the air-field was found to be too low-lying, and that the military had planned to build a replacement aerodrome on higher ground alongside the road to Colton if the War had continued beyond 1918.[35] Initially the aircraft were housed under canvas; later there was a large hangar (40 by 37m) built of wood, and a smaller one, for the planes (**fig 10.4**), and a canvas hangar for motor vehicles. Temporary huts provided accommodation for airmen, but permanent buildings were erected in the vicinity of what became Drome Road. These would have included a kitchen and bath-house for the officers and a cook-house and ablutions-block for the men, and separate mess buildings for the different ranks, as well as other necessary structures like munition stores and guard-houses. It has been said that a subsequent civilian dwelling incorporated part of the non-commissioned officers' mess,[36] and that this was the house next to 16a Drome Road,[37] while another had been the officers' mess, but nothing is apparent in the front view of the present houses in this part of the village.

A search-light unit, one of six planned to ring York, was established on the aerodrome before the aeroplanes arrived. In World War II, search-lights were usually operated in pairs at a distance apart, so that the height of an enemy aircraft could be estimated accurately by triangulation, but this consisted of a single light. It was operated by volunteers from the village, led by Thomas Russell of The Bungalow, Horseman Lane, and included Fred Weatherill and Herbert Knowles, both of Main Street, and Stanley Dykes of Yedmondale, Low Green. The volunteers were responsible to Captain F Egerton, OC 'A' Flight, No. 76 Aeroplane Squadron of the RFC, and undertook their duties until September 1917, when the Royal Engineers took over the search-light operations. Papers relating to this voluntary duty were lodged with the village library, apparently by Mr Dykes, and include his permit to enter the aerodrome and a letter of thanks from the Brigadier General commanding 6 Brigade, RFC, expressing appreciation of the men's 'patriotism at a very critical time'. (Also deposited was a newspaper report of the funeral in 1935 of Captain Francis Egerton of Melbourne Hall, at which the Archbishop of York officiated.)

Captain Egerton's squadron was the second unit to fly from Copmanthorpe. The aerodrome was occupied first by 'B' Flight from No. 33 Squadron, RFC, which had been flying from the Knavesmire race-course, and which was detached to become No. 57 Squadron, under the command of Major A L Pattinson MC, at Copmanthorpe on 8 June 1916. Three months later, No. 76 Squadron, formed at Ripon race-course on 6 September, sent its 'A' Flight to operate from Copmanthorpe. The pilots of both squadrons underwent training at the aerodrome, and Miss Beedham recalled 'a lot of flying', by night as well as day. Owing to the prevailing wind being from the south-west, mostly planes when taking off would have flown away from Copmanthorpe, but in landing would have come over the village. Inevitably there were crash-landings near to the village: two were recorded in the fields south of Temple Lane[38] and one beyond the railway line by the gatehouse at Moor Lane Crossing.[39]

It is not known how many personnel were stationed at Copmanthorpe aerodrome. Miss Beedham thought that there were under 200, and Mrs Mary Alice King, interviewed in the 1970s when she was aged 90, said that there were not as many as 100, but it is likely that there were more than that. Each flight (of which there were usually three per squadron) would normally have consisted of eight aircraft,[40] and as each squadron

10.4 Interior of hangar
      at aerodrome in
      1920 showing
      blocks manu-
      factured there for
      the new YMCA
      building
      (Sanderson
      Collection,
      Copmanthorpe
      Library; York
      Library Service)

was equipped with two-seater aeroplanes there would have been as
many observers as pilots. Other officers would have included the station
commander, a 'recording officer' with an administrative staff of two or
three non-commissioned officers ('NCOs') and ten airmen of other ranks
('ORs'), an armaments officer (with five ORs), an equipment officer (with
five), and a transport officer with over twenty men (and eight motor-cycles
and five lorries). There would have been craftsmen and artificers to care
for the aircraft: half-a-dozen carpenters, four each of sail-makers and elec-
tricians and copper-smiths, a couple of black-smiths, fifteen riggers, two
dozen engine-fitters, a welder, three instrument repairers, and a vulcan-
izer.[41] These would have been highly skilled, conscientious, reliable men,
whose pay recognised their importance: 45 shillings (£2.25) per week
when the basic pay of a private soldier was 7 shillings (35p). In addition,
there would have been others to do the varied less-skilled work required
at a military base. Blanche Beedham recalled that some villagers were
employed at the aerodrome as cooks, waitresses and mechanics.

   Miss Beedham told of how the airmen would come into Copmanthorpe
for social events, including concerts, held in the old school. She described
how other entertainment, such as music-hall shows and singers and
comedy turns, was also put on there, and it is known that there were
dances held in the large room above the Royal Oak.[42] Some of the contact
between the young RFC men and the village girls would have resulted
in romances, and in more than one instance led to marriage.[43] Although
she herself never married, Blanche Beedham commented that 'through

10.5 The airmen would have been issued with flying gear like that worn by Lt Alan Reed, RFC. Alan, from Copmanthorpe, survived the war and died aged 90 in 1988 (Sanderson Collection, Copmanthorpe Library; York Library Service)

all the War, we had good times. There were Australians, Canadians, and Americans …' In her late 20s at the time, she thought that the airmen were generally aged about eighteen (**fig 10.5**). Certainly, the pilots and observers would not have been much older, and more often than not from a public school background. Glamorous figures in dashing uniforms, they would have been high-spirited, and it is recorded[44] that sometimes they would land their aeroplanes at Grange Farm to enjoy a drink with the farmer, Arthur Hall, though almost certainly this use of their aircraft would have been frowned upon by the RFC authorities. Most of the pilots would have lived on the airfield, but some officers were billeted in the village, and a resident is recorded[45] as remembering the commanding officer striding from his billet in Ivy Farm House to the aerodrome with his swagger-stick under his arm, and his riding boots gleaming in the sun. Two pilots said to have been billeted at Manor Farm are described as South African and are named as a Lieutenant Dale of No. 76 Squadron,

who came from a farming background, and Wolf Joel, said to come from a family with diamond mining interests; each seems to have survived the war.[46]

No. 57 Squadron finished its training first and on 16 December 1916 was moved to France. While the rest of the squadron crossed the channel by steamer, the pilots would have flown their own aircraft over. It has been written that 'within a month, they were all dead',[47] but that is not correct. It is true that RFC pilots had a high mortality rate, estimated at one in four,[48] equivalent to that of Front-line infantrymen, and that a squadron could expect one man a week to be killed,[49] but these losses related to combat over the Front. A newly arrived squadron would not have been made operational until several weeks of war-zone training had been completed, during which pilots were only flying behind the lines. No. 57 did not reach its fighting base of Fienvillers until late January 1917, and did not fly on an operation until 25 March.[50] The RFC had a much higher casualty rate than their opponents, because of superior German tactics and professionalism, and their often better equipment and aircraft. By 1917 the aeroplane flown by No. 57 Squadron (the FE2d) was obsolete and outclassed by enemy machines, but they did not sustain their first losses until the following month, when two planes were shot down by enemy aircraft of the 'Flying Circus' of the German ace von Richthofen (the 'Red Baron') on 2 April.[51] A further five were lost on 6 April. The Squadron flew reconnaissance missions and offensive patrols during the Battle of Arras, which began on 19 April 1917, and two of its planes were shot down on Friday, 13 April.[52] Two more of its FE2ds were lost on 27 April, and another three on 30 April. Some of the aircrew survived wounded or were captured after crash-landing behind enemy lines.[53] The RFC deployed 25 squadrons, flying 365 aircraft, in the Battle of Arras, and lost 245 planes (mostly two-seaters) to the Germans' 66. Some 211 RFC aircrew were killed, and 108 were taken prisoner. Afterwards, April 1917 was known as 'Bloody April' in the RFC, but No. 57 Squadron's casualties were greater in the summer and autumn of 1918.[54]

No. 76 was a Home Defence squadron, and so was not sent to France when it became operational in the summer of 1917 as a night-fighter unit. At 3am on the night of 21/22 August, seven of its fighters were sent in search of six Zeppelins which had crossed the North Sea coast. Flying at night was a new activity and not without difficulties. One aircraft suffered engine trouble soon after taking off, and made an emergency landing short of the flare-path at Shipton, when it was written off, though the pilot was not injured. Another crashed on landing on its return to Copmanthorpe, injuring the pilot, and three others landed away from the aerodrome, one making a forced landing at Flamborough Head.[55] The squadron was called upon to intercept intruding air-ships again on the night of 19/20 October, and its aircraft made two sorties, their last of the war.[56] Although never locating the Zeppelins – which did not attack York – on these occasions, it is likely that the presence of the squadron at readiness to defend them did much to reassure local people.

No. 57 Squadron never returned to Copmanthorpe, and No. 76 left and was disbanded at Tadcaster on 6 June 1919. The aerodrome initially remained as an airfield, and for a short time was part of the national civil aviation network, following the Air Ministry announcement in April 1919 on the resumption of civilian passenger flights. The ban on civil flying imposed during the Great War was to be lifted on 1 May 1919, and the aerial routes to be open to the public were revealed. At the Armistice, there were 337 aerodromes and landing grounds in Great Britain (including the one at Copmanthorpe): 116 of these were requisitioned for cultivation, and 100 for the new RAF, while 120 (including Copmanthorpe) were to be made available for civil aviation. The suggested air route from London to Edinburgh involved a stop at Copmanthorpe (after Doncaster, and before Catterick). The flight included twelve aerodromes.[57] It is not known how many civil aircraft used Copmanthorpe aerodrome, nor for how long the facility was open to them before the land was sold for redevelopment.

Notes

1 Any further information about the men named would be welcomed by the author, who can be contacted via the Society at the address given at the front of the book.
2 The Commonwealth War Graves Commission 'Debt of Honour Register' (the most comprehensive and accurate record of servicemen who died in the wars); 'Soldiers Died in the Great War'; 1901 Census; local registers of births and marriages
3 Taped interview 1972–75: Miss Beedham
4 Taped interview 1972–75: Fred Reed
5 CL Obituary, newspaper cutting, date unknown
6 CL Captions to photographs held in Local History Collection
7 Robert Graves, cited in C Winter, *Death's Men, Soldiers of the Great War* Harmondsworth 1979 p 64
8 Holmes, R *Tommy, The British Soldier On The Western Front, 1914–18* London 2004 p 594
9 Carrington, C *Soldier From The Wars Returning* Pen & Sword Books Barnsley 2006, p 75
10 Winter, C op cit p 67
11 BI COP PR41 Copmanthorpe Marriage Register 1845–1978
12 Commonwealth War Graves Commission 'Debt of Honour Register', which lists four 'G H Briggs' and 31 'G Briggs', but only one with an address anywhere near the village
13 www.yorkandthegreatwar.com. & 'The King's Book of Fallen Heroes' York Minster
14 Taped interview 1972–75: Fred Reed
15 Beckett, I F W, *The First World War: Sources in the UK National Archives* London, 2002 p 150
16 There are different estimates of the casualty rate. Niall Ferguson gives tables in *The Pity of War*, London 1998, p 298ff. Winter (p 204) states that 10% of what he calls 'fighting soldiers' died in the Great War, compared to 4.5% in the Second World War

17 Winter, C op cit p 236

18 The Long, Long Trail website (http://www.1914–1918.net/) – *Brothers Died in the Great War*; Holmes, R *The Western Front* London 2001 p 6

19 Lindsay, O & Harris, J *Hostage to Fortune; The Battle for Hong Kong, 1941–1945* Stroud 2007

20 YCRL YO352–042 Newspaper collection, local government Vol 20 p 45

21 Mr Harold Smith (b.1920) pers comm to MM 2008

22 BI Copmanthorpe Parish Registers op cit

23 Ibid

24 Register of the Bishopthorpe company of the Home Guard, kindly made available by Mrs Margaret Smith, whose father, Sgt Charles Dixon Cox, administered the unit

25 Taped interview 1972–75: Mr and Mrs King

26 BI Copmanthorpe Parish Registers op cit

27 Register of Bishopthorpe Home Guard op cit

28 Wright, T *Knights Templar, the Copmanthorpe Squadrons of the RFC* York 1991

29 *York Evening Press*, 20, 21, 22 January 1915

30 *York Evening Press*, 26 January 1915

31 Wright, T op cit

32 CL Taped interview *c* 1970

33 Wright, T op cit. Wright gives the casualties as being 40 killed, but this seems too high

34 Wright, T op cit

35 CL Taped interview

36 Wright, T op cit

37 Johnson, J *The Copmanthorpe Story* Copmanthorpe 1995

38 Ibid

39 CL Transport in Copmanthorpe in the 20s, 30s, and earlier. Unidentified monograph in Folder 2

40 Rapier, B *White Rose Base* York 1980

41 Winter, D *The First of the few, fighter pilots of the First World War* Harmondsworth 1983 p 63

42 Wright, T op cit

43 BI COP PR41 Copmanthorpe Marriage Register 1845–1978

44 Johnson, J op cit

45 Ibid

46 Wright, T op cit; Neither name appears in the Commonwealth War Graves Commission list of individuals killed in the War

47 Johnson, J op cit, p 55

48 Giradet, J M, Jacques, A & Letho Duclos, J *Somewhere on the Western Front, Arras 1914–1918* Arras 2007

49 Winter, D op cit

50 Wright, T op cit

51 Giradet *et al*, op cit

52 Giradet *et al*, op cit

53 Wright, T op cit

54 *A History of Bomber Command* www.raf.mod.uk

55 *Aircraft Accidents in Yorkshire* www.allenby.info

56 Wright, T op cit

57 *The Times* Friday 25 April 1919

CHAPTER ELEVEN

Transport

From Carrier to Haulier – the Hudson Family Business

ELAINE MARSHALL AND MARJORIE HARRISON

Before the advent of the railways, carriers provided a valuable service to village communities in and around York. They transported both goods and people on a regular basis to specified points, often inns, where passengers and goods could be dropped off and picked up. Local directories show many carriers plying their trade in the 19th century.

Around Copmanthorpe, carriers who conveyed provisions and other goods locally to and from the village and the Pack Horse Inn, Micklegate included the following: 1823, William Whincup; 1855 and 1861, J Dickinson; and 1876, Thomas Moyens (also a market gardener). Carrying was often a secondary occupation, boosting income from the land and other work.

The Hudson family, long resident in Copmanthorpe, emerged as carriers in the later 19th century, with John Hudson recorded in 1893 and Harry Hudson in 1909.[1] The family continued in the business until well into the 20th century as is evident from information supplied by their descendants, Pat Bristowe and Tony Hudson. In the late 1800s Harry had met his future wife, Annie, whose father kept a horse and carriage in Dringhouses (at the site of the present St Leonard's Hospice) from where he drove people into York. Goods were conveyed to Jarretts' village shop in Low Green (Jarretts also had a warehouse and shop in Walmgate, York) and post was collected and delivered to and from York. Harry rented land for his horses and also farmed whilst continuing to ply his trade, using horses and wagons until early in the 1930s, when he bought his first lorry (**fig 11.1**).

11.1 Harry Hudson (centre), the village carrier, *c* 1920s (Courtesy of Pat Bristowe)

11.2 The Roadmen – a group of local men employed on road and footpath repairs, c 1930s (L to R: (?), Taffy Schumacher, (?), (?), Reg Hudson, George Levitt) (Courtesy of Pat Bristowe)

As the number of people owning motor vehicles gradually increased there was need of major road improvements and during 1938 the main road (A64) connecting York and the East Coast to Leeds and the West Riding was converted from single carriageway to dual, complete with cycle path and separate footpath along both sides.[2] Harry Hudson and his two sons, Reg and Ron, were contracted to build the road by the West Riding County Council (WRCC), with the labour supplied by council employees (**fig 11.2**) and a large number of itinerant Irish labourers. His grandson, Tony Hudson narrates:

For the construction, stone was delivered by rail to Copmanthorpe Station and led to the new road by a team of twelve horses, carts, and men and as the work progressed towards Tadcaster, the stone was delivered to Bolton Percy station. That provided an unusual sight as the horses were then turned into nearby fields for the night. Tar for the work was made at Copmanthorpe station by a firm called the Limmer and Trinidad Lake Asphalt Company and then led to the road. Steam rollers completed the construction. The work was a great boost for local people following the great depression of the 1930s.

During the railway era, Tony continued,

the Hudsons conveyed goods, coal and grain from the village stations. Initially, coal was a sideline operated by the station masters in each village and Hudsons were hired to deliver it around the area until 1947 when they took over the coal yard. Harry and his wife Annie continued with the coal and haulage for many years, together with sons Reg and Ron in Low Green [**fig 11.3**]. They also had a contract for road maintenance with the WRCC and were seen around the local villages repairing roads and footpaths, along with other council employees, including Harry Stone, Frank Dunn, Frank Thompson, Tom Dickinson, Bob Wheeler, and Wilf Hastwell. When Harry died in 1958, Reg continued to operate the business in Low Green, which became R W Hudson, his brother Ron, son Tony and nephew John working with him, and from the late 1960s along with WRCC employee Bill Pickard.

FROM COPPENTHORPE TO COPMANTHORPE

After the closure and demolition of the railway station in 1959, the Hudsons purchased it for £5; all the bricks were then cleaned by Jack Beedham and re-used. Labour-intensive seasonal work for the Hudsons involved loading sugarbeet from all the local farms when extra workers were hired to fill the lorries by hand using special pronged forks known as sippets; these had round baubles on the end of the prongs to prevent puncturing the beet. Jack Beedham, Tom North and Ernest Simpson, all workers on various Copmanthorpe farms, assisted. The loads were led to the sugarbeet factory in Poppleton Road, York, and on the return journey sugarbeet pulp was often brought back for animal food. As well as those mentioned earlier, workers included Fran and Len, the sons of Harry Stone, 'But', says Tony, 'my favourite was the ladies; in those days they helped with the seasonal work of potato picking and harvesting which was a huge job involving stooking and threshing.' Recalling other events, Tony remembered the rare treats such as sweets and fancy things his grand-father 'carried' from York to the village fêtes, and how the annual village Sunday School trips were so much fun that everyone ran to the railway station, so eager were they to get to Scarborough. Also, he remembered the steam rollers, which presented a great sight when local work was carried out in the 1950s; the steam roller would arrive complete with living van and park up; sometimes the driver had his wife with him.

In 1968 Reg sold his heavy JCB excavator to Tony, who started his own business in Station Yard, later to become Tony Hudson Plant Hire. It was sold in 1979 to Richard Collier of Copmanthorpe, becoming Collier Plant Hire, and has operated into the turn of the 21st century. Reg's death in 1981 signified the end of a long family tradition of haulage in Copmanthorpe.

11.3 Harry Hudson's fleet of lorries, including the 'Snow Queen' in the centre, at Low Green c 1975 (Courtesy of Pat Bristowe)

The Road

The road now known as the A64 features prominently in the history of Copmanthorpe. The main village once lay close to the Roman road known as the Streete (now called Top Lane in the vicinity of Copmanthorpe), but had been by-passed in the Middle Ages when a diversion was made to form what is today the route of the A64. By 1938, when the dual carriageway was built, the village had expanded considerably. As well as further development on Top Lane, several large, distinctive, and fashionable villas were erected alongside the main road, which provided instant travel to York, Leeds, the West Riding, and the Great North Road. Later, after the years of post-war austerity, more people were able to purchase motor cars, enabling them to travel further for work and leisure and after the closure of the railway station there was an increasing dependency on the motor car and bus services.

By 1969 the village had been identified as an area for substantial expansion by North Yorkshire County Council. The A64 trunk road provided easy access to Copmanthorpe and expansion in the village grew. Meanwhile traffic queues locally on the A64 became a serious problem, especially during the summer months with heavy coastal traffic. Housing development in the village mushroomed during the 1970s and 80s, bringing a further increase of motor vehicles and the associated traffic problems and dangers. Businesses also developed on the disused Acaster airfield which brought heavy goods vehicles through the village. There were bitter protests and petitions by residents, the Village Trust and the Parish Council to various bodies, including Whitehall, expressing not only the fears of increasing traffic dangers in the community but equally attempting to save and conserve the older buildings and village character. All was to no avail: more old buildings were demolished, and very little space was left undeveloped.[3]

There was a great deal of business expansion in the village itself, as is evident from the myriad advertisements in the 'Village Newsletters' at Copmanthorpe Library, dating from 1974. For the motorist there were two garages advertising during the 1970s: A C Cars, Main Street, and Coates Motors Ltd. One, opposite the Royal Oak, was sold and became a fish and chip shop; the other was at The Paddocks further down Main Street, where a garage has continued to date. It is recalled that this was the site of the village's first garage, Storey's, in the mid 1950s.[4] At one time there was a fuel station with three petrol pumps in Low Green.[5]

By the late 1960s the A64 was again in need of major improvements. For over 30 years there were many proposals, protests, battles, improvements made and safety measures carried out. These included the southern interchange flyover at Copmanthorpe linking the A64 to both directions of York's outer ring-road which opened in August 1987. After a public inquiry in June 1999 by the Highways Agency measures were taken to enhance road safety. These included the closure of the Top Lane junction with the A64, removing a well-known accident black-spot, and the construction of a link road to connect the village to York, thus totally segregating the village from the A64.[6]

The 20th century saw vast changes in the carriage of goods and people. At the beginning of the century Harry Hudson travelled at slow speed to and from York with his horse and wagon but he moved with the times, building up his fleet of lorries from the 1930s although horses were still in use when he constructed the dual carriageway in 1938. His business was partially linked to the railway but the station closed in 1959. Little did the Romans who laid the original road, or Harry Hudson who travelled along its successor by horse and cart in 1909, imagine how it would lead to the huge expansion of Copmanthorpe in the 21st century.

Copmanthorpe Bus Services

JOHN MEREDITH

The only highway access to the rural area bounded by the A64 and the Rivers Ouse and Wharfe is provided by the A64 itself. This resulted in little interest by early bus operators in providing services to the six villages involved (Acaster Malbis, Appleton Roebuck, Bishopthorpe, Bolton Percy, Colton and Copmanthorpe). This area already had a railway with stations at Bolton Percy and Copmanthorpe, hence nearly all residents were within two and a half miles of a station. When the railway opened in 1839 Bolton Percy was intended to be a transfer point for Tadcaster and Harrogate, and an inn was provided at the station for through passengers. The building still exists but the rapid expansion of the railway network soon rendered this redundant and Bolton Percy station, like Copmanthorpe, remained for purely local needs.

Buses serve the A64

Motor buses were introduced along the A64 on 10 July 1922 when J Dibb and M Warnes of Tadcaster provided four buses daily from York's tram terminus at Dringhouses to the Leeds tram terminus at Killingbeck. With the centre of Copmanthorpe under half a mile from the A64, its residents could easily use this service. The return fare for the York–Leeds journey was 4s 9d (24p). Competitors soon appeared including Corcoran Bros of Tadcaster (trading as *The Ideal*), J Bullock & Sons of Featherstone, near Pontefract, and J Burns of Boston Spa, with routes between Leeds and York and on to Scarborough and other seaside resorts.

Away from the A64, the Harrogate Road Car Company Ltd had been formed in 1906 as a local operator. They later expanded their network into other parts of the county and became the West Yorkshire Road Car Company in 1927. They then gradually bought out many smaller operators including a number working around York, as well as three of the four A64 operators, while the fourth (Bullocks) exchanged their Tadcaster–York route for a Tadcaster–Pontefract service which West Yorkshire had absorbed from Corcorans. By the mid-1930s the A64 services were co-ordinated by West Yorkshire to give hourly services from Leeds to Scarborough, Bridlington and to Hull, so giving a 20-minute frequency between Leeds and York. The Bridlington and Hull services were worked jointly with the East Yorkshire Motor Services and there were also through services to Whitby worked jointly with United Automobile Services.

Copmanthorpe's first buses

The village of Copmanthorpe had to wait until 11 August 1927 for its first motor bus service when Ovington Motors introduced an approximately hourly service from York via Bishopthorpe and Temple Lane, seven days a week. In 1930 West Yorkshire took over the operation and in 1933 their timetable quoted the route as Service 60 with fares from York of 5d single and 9d return. By 1935 this route had been linked up with other services and operated from York to Leeds via Bishopthorpe, Copmanthorpe, Tadcaster, Boston Spa and Bramham and the service number had changed to 42. With the outbreak of World War II in 1939 the route was curtailed to Leeds–Tadcaster, leaving Copmanthorpe village without a service and residents reverting to the A64 services, now reduced to a 30-minute frequency.

Meanwhile York Corporation had developed its own electric tram system after taking over the city's horse tramway in 1909. This was later extended and motor and trolleybus routes were added. However, in 1934, all the Corporation's operations were transferred to a partnership with the West Yorkshire Road Car Company, the York-West Yorkshire

Joint Undertaking. Although a few of the Corporation's services already went beyond the city boundary, it was to be several years before the Joint Undertaking served Copmanthorpe. When they did come in the 1950s, they soon became the sole operator, and this was well before Copmanthorpe became part of the York Unitary Authority.

World War II and its aftermath

The Joint Undertaking did, however, introduce a minimal service to the village in 1941 with Service 14 from Duncombe Place to the Royal Oak via Bishopthorpe and Temple Lane. There was just one outward journey (16.10) and two inwards journeys (08.30 and 16.27). In their April 1945 timetable, West Yorkshire advertised Service 90 from Rougier Street to Appleton Roebuck via Copmanthorpe and Acaster Cross Roads with six journeys each way. By 1951 the village had lost the No. 14 and was then served by two West Yorkshire services: Service 90, much as in 1945, and Service 88 from York to Wetherby via Copmanthorpe –Bilbrough– Tadcaster–Boston Spa with one journey each way.

Service 90 was finally withdrawn in 1953 leaving the villages south of the A64 to be served by G E Sykes and Son of Appleton Roebuck with four buses daily from Queen's Staith to Bolton Percy via Bishopthorpe– Acaster Malbis–Appleton Roebuck–Colton, but not Copmanthorpe; Sykes continued to operate this service until 1999.

Service 88 was augmented and survived for many years although subsequently it was gradually cut back, firstly to Tadcaster and later to Askham Richard. When the writer regularly travelled on it in the 1970s its extension beyond Copmanthorpe seemed to be for the benefit of Askham Richard prison whereby a few 'trusties' were allowed to visit York. By this time the route had become No. 15 or 15A and then 87, but services to Askham Richard via Copmanthorpe were withdrawn in the early 1980s and the No. 87 was thenceforth restricted to the villages north of the A64 on its journeys between York and Tadcaster.

After York-West Yorkshire's brief initial foray with Service 14, they returned to the village in the mid 1950s with Service 15: York Rougier Street–Bishopthorpe–Temple Lane–Copmanthorpe, and this was to form the backbone of the Copmanthorpe service up to 1996, providing a roughly hourly service, Monday–Saturday, and in some timetables, a very sparse Sunday service. The route appears to have initially terminated in the centre of the village but it was soon extended with a circuit of Horseman Lane, Hallcroft Lane, Manor Heath and School Lane. This served new housing then being built in this area and later, in the 1960s, it was a short walk for residents of the new developments to the north of Hallcroft Lane. During the 1970s the village saw much greater house building in the area between Top Lane and the railway with much of the development having a single road access from Top Lane opposite the Fox and Hounds. To serve this development the No. 15 was diverted in 1981 from Hallcroft Lane to Top Lane and it terminated with an anti-clockwise circuit of Merchant Way and Flaxman Croft, the principal roads on this new estate.

In contrast to the changes within the village, the A64 services continued with a pattern very similar to that in 1939 but with a frequency decreased from 20 minutes to 30 minutes. Through services to Scarborough (43), Bridlington (44 & 45) and Hull (46) were maintained but through services to Whitby (91) ceased in 1970.

Major changes since 1990

A period of relative stability lasted until the late 1980s when three factors combined to cause major changes to the bus services:

1)   Privatisation of the national and municipal bus operators;

2)   Population growth of the village;

3)   Upgrading of the A64.

Privatisation was a protracted and piecemeal affair and resulted in an upheaval of services. The York-West Yorkshire Joint Undertaking's services were acquired by a number of small operators and although the basic route through the village was maintained, many aspects of the service such as fleet names, liveries, route numbers and the routings beyond the village were subject to changes. Operators included Reynard Bus, Target Travel and Rider York (**fig 11. 4**) but as in many other parts of the country, the initial private operators were taken over by a few major groups which led to monopoly operation in particular areas. In York's case it was Firstgroup PLC who set up First York as a subsidiary and they encompassed virtually all the local services within the York Unitary Authority's area – a much larger area than the former City Council's domain – including Copmanthorpe. First York's domination continues today, apart from some services, mainly in the south-east of the city, which have been transferred to another major group, Transdev, and others to York Pullman.

Although the many detailed changes to the village services can be overlooked, one outcome is of far greater importance. Since the outset of its bus services the village has been connected to York via Temple Lane, Acaster Cross Roads and Bishopthorpe. With a small village which between the two wars had mainly expanded southwards along Temple Lane, this circuitous route made sense but the later population explosion (from 600 in 1947 to 4139 in 1991) was almost entirely north of the railway, so more direct access to York was now demanded. This was achieved in 1991 with complementary loop services, both via Dringhouses, one outward via Tadcaster Road and returning via Temple Lane, Bishopthorpe and Sim Balk Lane, and the other in the opposite direction. A greater change came in 1997 when the basic Copmanthorpe service (which had been renumbered from 15 to 13 in 1996) ceased to serve Temple Lane and Bishopthorpe altogether. The service was then routed via Tadcaster Road in both directions and, after serving Merchant Way and Flaxman Croft on the outward journeys only, terminated at Station Road, making a clockwise circuit of St Giles Way and Main Street. The aggrieved residents of Temple Lane were provided with a sparse subsidised service from York via Copmanthorpe and terminating at Acaster Malbis. This continued until 2009 as Service 21, operated by *Door to Door* and with just three buses each way on Tuesdays, Thursdays and Fridays only. There was also a Monday–Saturday service of some half a dozen buses from Askham Bar to Tadcaster via Bishopthorpe, Acaster Malbis, Appleton Roebuck, Colton and Bolton Percy, trading as *Connexions* C1, but this did not serve Temple Lane. In April 2009 the No. 21 and C1 were withdrawn and replaced by a new No. 21 Monday to Saturday service at approximately two-hourly intervals from York to Bolton Percy serving the same villages as the C1 and operated by Harrogate Coach Travel. This left Temple Lane without any buses after over 80 years of almost continuous service.[7]

After some initial shortcomings, First York's No. 13 service has been a success story for Copmanthorpe residents, with regular services every day and on evenings except Sundays but the evening services were withdrawn in April 2009. This loss has been mitigated however by Coastliner routing their Monday–Saturday evening services to include

11.4   Rider York services on Main Street, 5 May 1995, the 50th anniversary of VE Day
(© John Meredith)

the '13' circuit of Copmanthorpe village from Horseman Lane via St Giles Way and Main Street. This amendment applies to buses from both York and Leeds.

Yorkshire Coastliner

A major change was made to the A64 bus services in the mid-1980s as a direct result of the upgrading of this trunk road. With the bypassing of Tadcaster, York and Malton, the provision of improved carriageways, and the elimination of many of the flat junctions, the volume and speed of traffic has increased so much so that it is unsafe for pedestrians to cross the road. Hence boarding and alighting passengers, half of whom would be expected to cross the road, have been put at a disadvantage and in fact Copmanthorpe has now been 'fenced off' from the A64, so denying any access for pedestrians. But this situation has been turned to advantage as the buses have been diverted via Manor Heath, Hallcroft Lane and Top Lane and the new stops provided are much more convenient for the village.

Since privatisation the A64 services have been operated by a new company under the fleet name of Yorkshire Coastliner, although this name was actually coined by the West Yorkshire Road Car Co. a few years earlier. The service is generally successful and popular although the small operator which initially secured it has now sold out to a larger group, Transdev. The Coastliner operation had suffered from having just one depot, at Malton, and hence with the lengthy routes involved, the vehicles covered much dead (ie they were not in service) mileage and unbalanced (more buses in one direction than the other) working resulted. This is particularly noticeable at Copmanthorpe in the early morning and evening. Weekday services operate at 30-minute intervals (less on Sundays) between Leeds and Malton where they divide to serve Pickering and Whitby (840), Scarborough (843), and Filey and Bridlington (845). Since 2009 all buses on these coastal services have been modern, well-appointed double deckers. However, with the facility now available to operate from Transdev's York depot, an additional half-hourly service of single-deck buses (844) was introduced in 2009. This extends from York (Heworth) to Leeds and operates on weekdays only and follows the same route as the other Coastliner services. Not to be outdone, First York has also introduced a half-hourly York–Tadcaster–Leeds service (X64) but this does not serve Copmanthorpe.

The introduction of nationwide senior citizen free bus passes in 2008 has increased patronage on many routes whilst there are others that are very lightly loaded. The 2009 massive changes to Copmanthorpe's buses reflect this situation and it seems inevitable that further changes will soon be made.

Acknowledgement

I am indebted to John Wright of Bishopthorpe whose knowledge of the bus services, coupled with his extensive personal collection of timetables, has proved invaluable in writing this account.

Copmanthorpe Station and its train services

GRAHAM COLLETT AND MARTIN HIGGINSON

York's first railway

York's first railway – the York and North Midland Railway (Y&NMR) – was built with the aim of connecting York to both Leeds and London by way of junctions with the Leeds and Selby Railway (L&SR) at South Milford and the North Midland Railway at Altofts (one mile north of Normanton).[8] The first section from York to South Milford was opened on Thursday, 30 May 1839 with stations at Copmanthorpe, Bolton Percy, Ulleskelf, Church Fenton and Sherburn (**fig 11.5**).[9]

The first train of the day left York at 07.00 and the fare from York to Leeds was 5s 0d (25p), First Class, 4s 0d (20p), Second, and 3s 0d (15p), Third. Travellers were informed that 'an omnibus will meet the trains at the Bolton Percy Station, to convey passengers to and from Tadcaster, Thorp Arch, &c.' The initial service consisted of five trains each way on weekdays (two in the morning, two in the afternoon and one in the evening) and two on Sundays (a morning and an evening train).[10]

The Y&NMR subsequently extended its line to Burton Salmon on 11 May 1840 and to Pontefract and Altofts on 1 July 1840. On 26 June 1846, the Y&NMR obtained authorisation for a direct line from York to Leeds. The route chosen was from the company's line at Copmanthorpe to join its Church Fenton to Harrogate branch (authorised in 1845 and opened on 20 July 1848[11]) immediately north of Tadcaster station. After running south along the branch for a mile or so, it was proposed to strike off near Stutton to join the L&SR at Cross Gates.[12]

YORK AND NORTH MIDLAND RAILWAY.

The Directors have the satisfaction to inform the Public, that on and after

THURSDAY, THE 30TH DAY OF MAY INST.,

THEIR LINE OF RAILWAY,

From the Terminus at York to the Junction with the Leeds and Selby Railway, near South Milford,

WILL BE OPENED FOR THE CONVEYANCE of PASSENGERS and PARCELS, CATTLE, COALS, LIME, and other Merchandise: thereby forming an uninterrupted Railway communication between York and Leeds, and York and Selby, and the several intermediate Places.

It is arranged by the Directors of the respective Railways, that the following shall be the Times for the Departure of the Trains from each place, viz. :—

TRAINS—From YORK to LEEDS.
From YORK to SELBY, and
From LEEDS to YORK,
Will start every Day, (except Sunday,)

At 7 o'Clock	... ...	MORNING,
10	Do.	Do.
1	... ...	AFTERNOON,
Half-past 3	... ...	Do.
7	... ...	EVENING.

SUNDAY TRAINS—At 8 MORNING.
6 EVENING.

TRAINS—From SELBY to YORK,
Will start every Day, (except Sunday,)

At 20 minutes past	7	MORNING,
20 Do.	10	Do.
20 Do.	1	AFTERNOON,
50 Do.	3	Do.
20 Do.	7	EVENING.

SUNDAY TRAINS—At 8 in the MORNING, and 6 in the EVENING.

Each Train will take up and set down Passengers at the following Places, where the Companies have Stations, viz.:—

COPMANTHORPE,
BOLTON PERCY,
ULLESKELF,
CHURCH FENTON,
SHERBURN,
JUNCTION NEAR SOUTH MILFORD,
MICKLEFIELD,
GARFORTH.

FARES OF PASSENGERS.

	First Class.	Second Class.	Third Class.
From YORK to LEEDS ...	5s. 0d.	4s. 0d.	3s. 0d.
From YORK to SELBY ...	2s. 6d.	2s. 0d.	1s. 6d.

And in proportion for the intermediate Distances.

N.B. These Fares include every charge, none of the Company's servants being allowed to receive any Fee or Gratuity whatever.

The Directors have made the requisite arrangements with the Coach Proprietors at York and Leeds and the Packet Owners at Selby, in order that Passengers arriving by the Railway Trains at any of those places, may be forwarded from thence to all parts of the Kingdom. Places may be taken at any of the Company's Stations, and at the following Offices, viz. :—

TAVERN COACH OFFICE, St. Helen's Square, YORK.

BLACK SWAN COACH OFFICE, Coneystreet, YORK.

ROYAL HOTEL, BULL and MOUTH, ROSE and CROWN, and GOLDEN LION, Briggate, LEEDS.

An Omnibus will meet the Trains at the Bolton Percy Station, to convey Passengers to and from Tadcaster, Thorp Arch, &c.

Places by Railway and Coach may be taken at York for Manchester, Liverpool. Birmingham, and London, and also for London by way of Chesterfield and Derby, and for any intermediate place on these routes.

Merchandise, Cattle, Grain, &c., will be charged as follows :

FROM YORK TO LEEDS.

	s.	d.
Bales, Trusses, Cases, Canvass, Candles, Stationery, and Manufactured Goods in general, per ton	10	10
Music in Cases, per cwt.	1	0
Furniture, per cwt.	0	9
Spirits, Wine, and Vinegar, per ton ...	10	10
Cement, Chalk, Colours, Dyewoods, Drugs, Copper, Tin, Brass, Hemp, Flax, Hair, Hides, Mats, Rags, Oil, Paint, Soap, Tallow, Sugar, Spetches, per ton	9	2
Wool, per ton	8	4
Iron, Stone, Timber, Lead, per ton ...	5	10
Ale and Porter, per barrel	1	6
Flour, per sack	1	0
Grain, per quarter	1	3
Cattle, per head	7	6
Sheep, each	0	9
Pigs, each	1	0
Calves, each	1	0
Carriages, 4 wheels, each	20	0
Ditto, 2 wheels, each	15	0

By Order,

GEORGE BAKER, Secretary.

Downfall of the 'Railway King'

However, the downfall of George Hudson (Chairman of the Y&NMR, also known as the 'Railway King') and the poor financial position of the Y&NMR caused the suspension of construction work on the direct line in 1849, by which time a magnificent stone viaduct over the River Wharfe at Tadcaster had been constructed. In 1883, a line was laid across the viaduct to serve a mill on the east bank of the Wharfe and this remained available for use until 1959, when it was deleted from the official instructions. The disused viaduct survives to this day.[13] The Y&NMR became a constituent of the North Eastern Railway (NER) which was formed on 31 July 1854.

Great Northern Railway reaches York

By the late 1840s, York had already become an important railway centre. At this time, numerous lines to the north were being promoted, some via York and some via Leeds. The earliest of these went via York, which became a focal point for other lines being promoted by George Hudson at that time. However, the route to London was still very slow and circuitous, via Derby and Rugby to Euston.

The Great Northern Railway (GNR) was incorporated on 26 June 1846. A direct line was authorised from London to York via Grantham, Retford and Doncaster with a loop from Peterborough to Bawtry via Boston and Lincoln. George Hudson, having fought the GNR bill, then offered use of the Y&NM railway via Burton Salmon, connecting with the Lancashire & Yorkshire Railway via Knottingley and Askern, to the GNR as a ready-made link between York and Doncaster. The company accepted on 29 November 1850 and the Y&NMR could now run through to Doncaster. Copmanthorpe was thus served by two railway companies – the Y&NMR (NER from 1854) and the GNR.[14]

New route to London

The NER obtained authorisation on 23 March 1864 for a new route from Chaloners Whin Junction (two miles south of York and close to the present Askham Bar Park & Ride site) to join the Hull & Selby line at Barlby and then a second line from a point immediately south of Selby station to join the GNR at Owston (later Shaftholme) Junction north of Doncaster. These lines were opened on 2 January 1871.[15] Copmanthorpe was thus no longer served by direct trains to London as these were then routed via Selby. It remained off the main line to the Capital until the Selby diversion line was opened in 1983 (see below).

Direct route to Leeds opens

On 13 May 1864 (modified 5 July 1865) the NER obtained approval for a cut-off from Church Fenton to Micklefield and an extension west from the Marsh Lane terminus of the L&SR to a new station (joint with London & North Western Railway) adjacent to the Midland Railway station in the centre of Leeds. The line from York to Leeds New station via Church Fenton and Micklefield was opened on 1 April 1869.[16]

Train services up to 1900

In the 1850s, trains called at Copmanthorpe only three times a day in each direction (twice on Sundays): *Bradshaw's* March 1850 guide showed up (southbound) stopping trains to Leeds and Normanton at 07.23 and 15.18, and to Leeds at 18.38, with equivalent down services at 08.35, 13.35 and 19.30. The morning trains offered First, Second and Fourth class, the others First, Second and Third. Single fares to York were First Class 1/- (5p), Second 9d (3.75p), Third 6d (2.5p) and Fourth 4d (1.6p). It would appear that holders of Fourth Class returns to York had to stay overnight, although Market Tickets (fare unspecified) were available on the 08.35 for return the same day.[17]

By 1863, then under the auspices of the North Eastern Railway, train services had expanded to thirteen up and nineteen down (three each way on Sundays), serving a variety of destinations. In the up direction these included London King's Cross by the 07.38 'Parliamentary' train (a train stopping at all stations and offering a fare of no more than 1d (0.4p) a mile, as required under Gladstone's Cheap Trains Act 1844), arriving at 15.30, a journey time of almost eight hours; and trains at 10.08, 12.13 and 16.23, which stopped at Copmanthorpe 'on request for First Class passengers for King's Cross only'. The three Normanton and/or Leeds trains continued to run at similar times to those of 1850. By this date there were also four trains that took the circuitous route to Harrogate via Church Fenton and Wetherby: 07.59, 10.34, 15.55 and 17.39. Two further trains called on request, at 13.00 for First Class passengers to Leeds and Hull and at 17.30 for Selby and Hull. Fourth Class had disappeared by this date.[18]

By 1887, the number of trains calling at Copmanthorpe remained the same in the up direction (thirteen) as in 1863, but had decreased to sixteen in the down direction. The number of trains calling by request only had been reduced, and through trains to Harrogate had been reduced drastically to just one. The through King's Cross trains had been replaced by locals to Doncaster (some of which were operated by the Great Northern Railway), apart from two request calls by down services only. There was one through Midland Railway train, at 17.23, to Rotherham and Sheffield via Pontefract Baghill, but three, spaced throughout the day at 09.22, 13.48 and 19.05, in the opposite direction.[19]

Weekday train services at Copmanthorpe again reached their previous peak at the end of the nineteenth century, with thirteen up and nineteen down trains calling Monday–Saturday in 1898, although there were only two trains each way on Sundays, one in the early morning, the other mid evening. In the down direction (ie northbound), trains to York, although irregularly spaced, averaged approximately one per hour from the first departure at 08.05 to the last at 20.57, but there were two 2-hour gaps, mid morning and late afternoon, in the up (southbound) direction.[20] While an impressive number of destinations could be reached by through services, the timetables to and from each were far from frequent.

Railway travel

The early days of railway travel were pretty spartan by modern-day standards. In 1839 there were First, Second and Third class coaches: First Class had three compartments, each holding six people, which were fitted with lamps at night; Second Class had four compartments, each holding ten people, and was open-sided but with closed ends; Third Class was completely open and probably looked like a toast rack with doors – in bad weather it must have been very uncomfortable indeed. Blizzards or rain

11.6 Plans for new station buildings at Copmanthorpe, Ulleskelf and Bolton Percy, 1903 (Reproduced by permission of the National Archives; Re527/633); inset: Copmanthorpe Station after closure in 1959 (Sanderson Collection, Copmanthorpe Library; York Library Service)

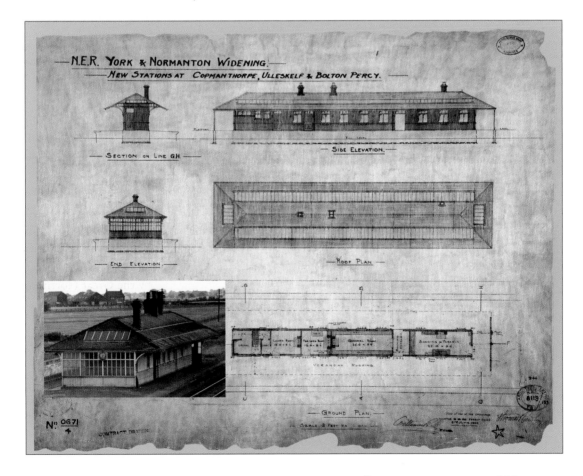

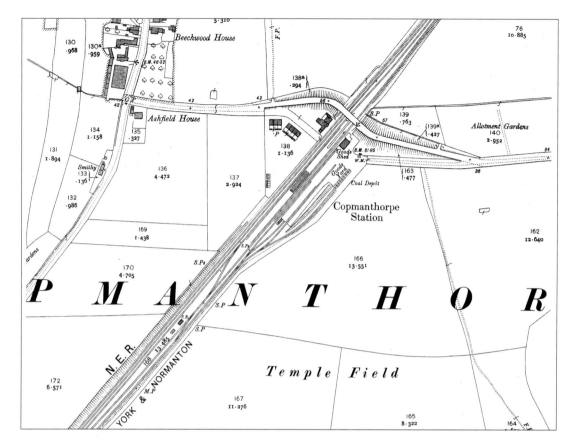

storms would have turned a simple train journey into something of an expedition, but fortunately standards improved considerably in the next few decades.[21]

Increasing capacity, new stations and signal boxes

The section of line from Church Fenton to Chaloners Whin was converted from double to quadruple track under Acts obtained in 1900 and 1901. The work took place between 1900 and 1904 and new stations and signal boxes were built at Copmanthorpe, Bolton Percy, Ulleskelf and Church Fenton (**fig 11.6**).[22] In addition, until 1948 there was an intermediate box at Colton – located near the 1983 Colton Junction for the then new East Coast Main Line (ECML) 'Selby Diversion' (see below). The original station buildings at Copmanthorpe were adjacent to the line at the end of Station Road where there was a level crossing (**fig 11.7**). The platforms extended north-east from the crossing towards York. These were superseded by new buildings on an island platform situated between the new 'Normanton' lines which had been added to the south of the original 'Leeds' lines.[23] The earlier building became the station master's house (see below). At the same time, the level crossing was replaced by a bridge.

Post-war resignalling

Plans for resignalling the line had been drawn up by the London and North Eastern Railway (LNER) prior to World War II and the base for the new Copmanthorpe signal box was laid in 1939. The route-relay interlocking signalling system at York was to be the largest of its kind in the world. After suspension of the project because of the war, work finally began in 1949. The work was undertaken by the Signal Engineer's Department at York and the Westinghouse Brake and Signal Co. A new signal box (to replace the 1904 Copmanthorpe box west of the station; **fig 11.8**) was built on the north-west side of the line adjacent to Moor Lane level crossing, approximately half a mile south-west of the station, and was opened on 12 November 1950 (**fig 11.9**). It was built as the 'fringe box' working to the new York power signal box, allowing intermediate signal boxes between Copmanthorpe and York to be closed.[24] Frank Dean – a Railway Signalling & Telecommunications (S&T) worker – recalls that: 'In my days in S&T maintenance in the early 1950s I often used to come to the old mechanical gates at Copmanthorpe. They often needed repair due to the mud in and around cranks used to swing the gates. The

11.8   The original Copmanthorpe signal box, photographed in 1937; opened 12 June 1904, closed 12 November 1950
(Ken Appleby Collection)

11.9   Copmanthorpe 'new' signal box; opened 12 November 1950, closed 13 March 1983
(© R F Dean)

new signal box controlled the gates. I have a feeling that, prior to the new Signal Box, the gates were hand operated from the gate house.'[25]

Station layout and staffing

The new station building was on the single island platform on the southerly pair of lines (the 'Normanton lines'); the two northerly 'fast' lines (the 'Leeds lines') bypassed the station.[26] The intermediate bridge support – demolished during the raising of the bridge decking for electrification – was used to store items such as paraffin for the station lamps. It provided the support for the top end of a ramp which led down onto the platform (**fig 11.10**). There was a door to the road which could be locked at night. After the station closed, this entrance was bricked up and the ramp removed. At the turn of the 20th century the station was staffed by two porters, two clerks and a station master. By the 1930s this had changed to three porters, one clerk and the station master. The signal box, which lay to the west of the station, was staffed by three signalmen, and in addition there were three gatekeepers and four platelayers. The goods yard and coal depot were on the south side of the line. NER plans show that in 1907 goods facilities comprised four sidings, one ending in a warehouse, two serving horse and general loading docks and the fourth leading to coal handling cells. There was also a weighbridge capable of weighing consignments of up to 10 tons.[27]

All the buildings have now gone except the one currently used by Collier Plant Hire, which still retains its canopy over the side entrance. Originally, this was one of two buildings used for the storage of cattle feedstuffs. Goods coming in by rail were delivered by an articulated Bedford flatbed truck two or three times a week which operated from the goods yard. Anything that arrived by rail, including live day-old chicks from Spinks of Easingwold, was delivered by this vehicle.[28]

11.10 The ramp that led down from Station Road on to the platform (Sanderson Collection, Copmanthorpe Library; York Library Service)

From Coppenthorpe to Copmanthorpe

11.11 The original
station buildings,
c 1920s
(Reproduced
by permission
of the North
Eastern Railway
Association)

The Station Master

The station-master's house was situated on the north side of the line, west of the road (**fig 11.11**). As described above, it originally housed the station booking office and waiting room as well as living accommodation; it still stands today, converted to a private house. Beyond it were two groups of NER cottages behind which were a pump, garden plots, piggeries and a cess pool. Maybe station and goods yard staff and signalmen lived in these cottages, or perhaps other railway workers such as permanent way lengthmen.[29]

The station master in those days had a special place in the community – apart from the vicar he was probably the best-known person in the village. A sideline enjoyed by many NER area station masters was the sale of coal. They were in a slightly privileged position compared to other coal merchants as they were able to stack the fuel on railway property and thus avoid the cost of storage.[30] Some had other, unofficial, sidelines to their normal duties: at one time, the Copmanthorpe station master (Mr Duggleby) – who lived in the Station House – used to do haircuts for 6d (2½p).

Goods traffic

During World War I, Copmanthorpe Wood was felled and the wood was taken by wagon to the station.[31] Later, the 1923 and 1925 LNER goods working timetables show one Class D 09.30 York–Normanton pick-up freight calling each day from 09.45 to 10.10, after which it made similar calls at Bolton Percy, Ulleskelf, Church Fenton, Sherburn-in-Elmet and Milford Junction.[32]

The coal and coke was stored in eight large cells which were placed under a raised siding, allowing the load to be deposited into the cells below, the product dropping through gaps in between the sleepers.[33] Supply was maintained by regular visits of railway coal wagons. One of the porters used to help the farmers with their different loads of potatoes, corn etc. In early summer the hay trains of over twenty wagons would come out from York; the hay was loaded and taken to Leeman Road Goods Yard, where the railway's goods delivery horses were kept.[34]

Regular visitors to the goods yard were personnel from the WWII RAF station at Acaster Airfield. A lorry would transport unwanted bombs from the airfield and a crane loaded them on to goods wagons which took them away. In those days, nobody worried about the safety of such things![35]

Pre-World War I train services

The years leading up to World War I are sometimes described as the golden age of the railways, but for Copmanthorpe the peak had already passed. Services had been reduced to ten up and nine down each weekday, mainly to or from Normanton or Leeds, with Doncaster, Sheffield and Rotherham (down only) and Harrogate (up only) served once/twice a day and no direct trains to Selby or Hull.[36]

Mr and Mrs King, who moved to Copmanthorpe before World War I, recalled travelling to York each week for the market for 7d (3p) return. However, the absence of a train to York before 8am and the very limited bus service to come back made the journey difficult: 'You could get the tram [from York] to Dringhouses and then we walked'. The trains took about ten minutes from Copmanthorpe to York and finished quite early: 'We could always get a seat and the last train out of York was 8pm'.[37]

By 1922, the last year of the NER's independent existence, services were reduced to six up and eight down trains each weekday: three each to Leeds and Normanton in the up direction and in the down direction, two from Normanton, three from Sheffield and three from Leeds, with long intervals between trains in the middle of the day. Trains to/from Doncaster had ceased with World War I. The 1923 and 1925 Working Timetables show some LNER and London Midland & Scottish Railway (LMS) down trains stopping at Copmanthorpe, by now only four minutes before York, for ticket collection.[38]

In the 1920s and '30s the Sunday School would go to Scarborough for their annual day out. They caught the train at Copmanthorpe station but there wasn't a convenient train calling at Copmanthorpe on the way back, so Mr Bean and Mr Temple would send two wagons, each hauled by two horses, to meet the group at York station and take them home.[39]

By 1938 the level of service had risen slightly to seven up and eight down trains Monday–Friday. LMS Sheffield and Pontefract services called only in the down direction. The Sunday service remained at two trains each way. The 06.55 Normanton train conveyed a buffet car but this was a matter of railway operating convenience as the carriages' next job was a long-distance service, rather than to serve the needs of hungry or thirsty Copmanthorpe passengers.[40]

The inter-war period and after

During the inter-war period the NER's successor – the LNER – introduced petrol railcars (shown in the LNER timetable as 'Rail Motor Bus one class only') on several routes as a means of reducing train operating costs and of meeting newly arising bus competition. Copmanthorpe benefited from a York–Church Fenton and back service at lunchtime and an evening peak York–Copmanthorpe and return commuter shuttle. The LNER timetable also identified the facilities available at Copmanthorpe where horses, carriages and motor cars could be loaded, and stated that: 'contact is made by Omnibus Services operated by Companies associated with the LNE Railway Company. Information as to Omnibus Services can be obtained from local Station Masters or from the Omnibus Companies'.[41]

During World War II the train service increased slightly, although Sunday trains all but disappeared, with none in 1940 and a single summer-only service to and from Leeds in 1943.[42]

An initially similar, but then gradually reducing pattern of services continued after the war, but with no Sunday trains. In 1955 there were only five up and three down trains, one more each way on Saturdays, to and from Leeds, Sheffield or Normanton. On Monday–Friday the last train towards York ran at 11.06 in the morning (15.10 on Saturdays). The 17.22 to Leeds was the last up train. The final timetable before Copmanthorpe station closed to passengers at the beginning of 1959 shows just three up trains, to Leeds at 13.15 and 17.20 and to Sheffield at 16.23; and three down, the last of which called at 10.55 in the morning. Although there was an extra train each way on Saturdays, this skeleton service was clearly highly unattractive, offering only very limited options suitable for commuting or leisure/shopping to York and precluding commuting to Leeds. Indeed only on Saturdays could Leeds be reached in time for any day-return travel opportunities.[43] At least the journey to York was quick with pleasant views. The St Giles housing estate was green fields, with a large freestanding panel featuring two men carrying a scaffolding board advertising Hall's Distemper![44]

Closure

Railway passenger services to Copmanthorpe and Bolton Percy were withdrawn from 5 January 1959 following a previous closure attempt and a public enquiry. Ulleskelf station was allowed to remain open on the grounds that there was no suitable alternative transport available.[45] Copmanthorpe station was probably never very busy: the NER calculated that it served a catchment population of about 1200 people in the first two decades of the 20th century. While some 300–400 people lived in Copmanthorpe, the others who were considered likely to use the station were spread between Acaster Malbis, Askham Bryan, Askham Richard, Bilbrough and Colton, at distances of two to three miles from the station; it is little wonder that they would have transferred their allegiance to buses as soon as the opportunity arose. Goods handling facilities outlasted the passenger service and were finally withdrawn in 1964.[46]

Copmanthorpe rejoins the Main Line!

In the late 1970s, the momentous decision was taken to reroute the East Coast Main Line (ECML) to allow the mining of the large coal reserves of the Selby Coalfield which lay beneath it. This decision reflects the huge value that was placed on the coal reserves by the Labour government of the day; ironically only a year after the diversion opened in 1983, the longest miners' strike in recent history began, from which the industry never recovered. The Selby Coalfield closed barely twenty years after it was opened. The new route diverged from the York to Church Fenton line at Colton Junction, midway between Copmanthorpe and Bolton Percy, and followed a new alignment via Hambleton before rejoining the existing route at a new junction at Temple Hirst. The previous route was abandoned between the Chaloners Whin and Barlby North junctions and became the popular cycle track. Copmanthorpe was back on the main line, just as it had been prior to 1870.

The signal boxes at Copmanthorpe and Bolton Percy were closed on 13 March 1983 when signalling control of the line through Copmanthorpe was taken over by a new panel in York signal box which had been installed to control the ECML Selby Diversion.[47] The new route was electrified in the late 1980s at 25kV a.c. overhead as part of the ECML electrification scheme.

Moor Lane level crossing

As part of the new ECML arrangements, the level crossing at Moor Lane was closed and a new road was built on the south side of the line to allow traffic to reach the bridge over the railway to Station Road. The former

FROM COPPENTHORPE TO COPMANTHORPE

crossing keeper's cottage still stands and was for sale (offering 'all mod cons') in 1983 at £33,950![48] The late Ernie Sanderson, a retired track chargehand and son of a former crossing keeper, once lived in this cottage. He was a devoted rail enthusiast and wrote several books on the local rail scene, illustrated with his own photographs.[49] Ernie was a well-liked local character known for his range of village photographs and several of his albums are now held in the village library.

On 25 September 2006, a man died when the 14.25 Virgin Trains service from Plymouth to Edinburgh Waverley hit his car at 21.01 at the former crossing site at Moor Lane. The train derailed but remained upright and came to a stop further down the line. There were no other injuries. The car had left the road and crashed through a fence onto the railway line.[50]

The future

Since the railway opened, Copmanthope has expanded dramatically from a rural village to a major suburb of York. The population of Copmanthorpe rose by 74% between 1931 and 1961[51] and has continued to rise rapidly. In 1971 it stood at 1215[52]; by the 2001 Census it was 4262.[53] If the station had survived, it would probably now have a healthy clientele of commuters, shoppers and leisure travellers to Leeds, Sheffield and York. A site for a new station has been protected by City of York Council, but there are no immediate plans to progress this. A 1999 report put the cost of reopening at £10 million and in 2004 the Liberal Democrat council formally rejected the idea. However, if Copmanthorpe's population continues to mushroom and road congestion to worsen, maybe one day it will reopen.[54] There is even the possibility that, if a tram-train (a light rail vehicle which can run on the mainline network) service is introduced on the Harrogate line, as has been suggested, the tram-trains could be extended to Copmanthorpe!

References

Printed sources

Awdry, C, 1990 *Encyclopaedia of British Railway Companies*
Bonavia, M R, 1982 *A History of the LNER: 1 The First Years 1923–33*
Cobb, Col M H, 2003 *The Railways of Great Britain: A Historical Atlas*
Hoole, K, 1965 *Regional History of the Railways of Great Britain: Volume 4 The North East*
Irving, R J, 1976 *The North Eastern Railway Company 1870–1914: an Economic History*

Wrottesley, J, 1979 *The Great Northern Railway: Volume 1 Origins and Development*

Wrottesley, J, 1979 *The Great Northern Railway: Volume 2 Expansion and Competition*

Press items

York Courant 30 May 1839 (York Central Library microfiche)

York ABC Rail Guide August 1837 – *Northern Echo & Yorkshire Gazette* 'The Green Guide' (John H Meredith Private Collection)

Announcement of withdrawal of passenger train facilities from Copmanthorpe – *The Railway Gazette* 12/12/1958 (NRM library)

Article on Ernie Sanderson (retired track chargehand), *York Evening Press* 27/4/1981 (held in Copmanthorpe Library files)

Article on former Crossing Keeper's Cottage being put up for sale, *York Evening Press* 23/6/1983 (held in Copmanthorpe Library files)

Press article on reopening of Copmanthorpe Station, *York Evening Press* 18/6/2004

Original source material

Extract from transcript of taped interview with Mr & Mrs King relating to period 1900 to 1914 approx (Copmanthorpe Library – transcribed by Catherine Pemberton)

Recollections of Frank Dean (former Signal & Telecommunications worker in the Copmanthorpe area) 1939 to 1983 – extracts from letter of 29/2/08 and accompanying photographs (Graham Collett Private Collection)

Copmanthorpe Station Signalling Diagram 30/10/06 (drawn 20/9/89 by Frank Dean) (Graham Collett Private Collection)

Secondary sources

Copmanthorpe Village History Group, 1995 *The Copmanthorpe Story* [section on Transport in Copmanthorpe in the 20s and 30s and some years earlier] (copy held in Copmanthorpe Library Book 2)

Yorkshire through time: a vision of Copmanthorpe website, consulted 26/1/2009

ABC Rail Guide (various dates between April 1859 and April 1955) – NRM Library

LNER Working Timetables 1 July 1910, 1 July 1925, 1938 – NRM Library

NER 1913 and LNER (NE Area) 1924, Traffic Statistics Office, York (held in NRM Library Ref F1B/30)

NE Region Timetables 26 September 1949 and January 1952 (held in NRM Library)

Bradshaw's Guide (various dates between March 1850 and 3 November 1958)

Copmanthorpe Passenger Services – unpublished paper by Martin Higginson January 2009

Copmanthorpe Station – unpublished paper by Adrian Pickard July 2009
Copmanthorpe Passenger Services – unpublished paper by Peter Broadbent May 2008
[Copies of the above are available in Copmanthorpe Library]

West Yorkshire Archives Service, Wakefield visited 27/5/08
The National Archives, Kew visited 1/4/09
Wikipedia website consulted 9/8/09

Recollections of Ken Appleby (former Area Manager BR Eastern Region) including photographs – (email 2/2/09 from Catrina Appleby to Graham Collett)

Authors: Graham Collett and Martin Higginson 9/8/09 (with thanks to John H Meredith, Ken Appleby, Geoff Appleby, Frank Dean, Peter Broadhead and Adrian Pickard for additional material)

Notes

1   YCA & YCRL Trades Directories and census material
2   YCRL *Yorkshire Evening Press* 16 April 1938
3   CL Various Village Trust Minutes and collection of newspaper articles, letters and items on village development during the 1970s and 1980s
4   David Forth to EM, June 2009
5   Pat Bristowe to EM June 2009
6   CL Collection of newspaper cuttings, letters and documents to and from WRCC Road Maintenance Department and Highways Agency, relating to A64 road improvements
7   The latest (2010) timetable for the No. 21 has introduced a 2-hourly service from Acaster Malbis to Copmanthorpe via Temple Lane and then on to Colton, but nothing in the opposite direction.
8   Collett, G 'Copmanthorpe Station & its Rail Services: Brief Rail History of the Area' unpublished paper March 2008
9   YCRL *York Courant* 30 May 1839
10 Ibid
11 Awdry, C *Encyclopaedia of British Railway Companies* Wellingborough 1990
12 Collett, G op cit
13 Ibid
14 Ibid
15 Ibid
16 Ibid
17 Higginson, M 'Copmanthorpe Passenger Services' unpublished paper January 2009

18 Ibid

19 Ibid

20 Ibid

21 Johnson, J *The Copmanthorpe Story* Copmanthorpe 1995

22 Appleby, K C 'Farewell Church Fenton', Signalling Records Society *Record* 93, May/June 2002

23 National Archives, Kew. Plans of Copmanthorpe Station 1904 (RAIL 527/633), York to Copmanthorpe line (RAIL 1037/240) and Copmanthorpe to Ulleskelf line (RAIL 1037/241)

24 Dean, F Extracts from letter to Graham Collett dated 29/2/08

25 Ibid

26 Pickard, A 'Copmanthorpe Station' unpublished paper July 2009

27 Higginson, M op cit

28 Pickard, A op cit

29 Higginson, M op cit

30 Johnson, J op cit

31 CL 'Transport in Copmanthorpe in the 20s and 30s and some years earlier' unidentified monograph in Folder 2

32 Higginson, M op cit

33 Pickard, A op cit

34 CL 'Transport in Copmanthorpe' op cit

35 Pickard, A op cit

36 Higginson, M op cit

37 Taped interview 1972–75: Mr & Mrs King relating to period 1900–14 approx

38 Higginson, M op cit

39 CL 'Transport in Copmanthorpe' op cit

40 Higginson, M op cit

41 Ibid

42 Ibid

43 Ibid

44 Pickard, A op cit

45 Recollections of Ken Appleby (former Area Manager BR Eastern Region) – various dates (email 2/2/09 from Catrina Appleby to Graham Collett)

46 Higginson, M op cit

47 Dean, F op cit

48 CL York Press 23/6/1983

49 CL York Press 27/4/1981

50 Wikipedia website last modified 18/6/2009

51 Johnson, J op cit

52 Ibid

53 Wikipedia website: last modified 1/7/09

54 Higginson, M op cit

CHAPTER TWELVE

Education in Copmanthorpe

WENDY WRIGHT

Early history

The early history of education in Copmanthorpe is not easy to trace. Miss Frances Frost, headmistress of the school from 1945 to 1976, who wrote about it after she retired, quotes an extract from Archbishop Herring's Visitation returns of 1743 as the earliest reference to official education in Copmanthorpe.

> There is no public or charity school, but the children are taught to read and write by a private tutor at the expense of their parents. The children are frequently catechised by the schoolmaster and myself as often as there is occasion. Signed … J Fuller, Minister of Copmanthorpe[1]

12.1 Copmanthorpe School (Sanderson Collection, Copmanthorpe Library; York Library Service)

A parish school came into existence some time later and by 1851 it is shown on the OS map occupying the site on the corner of Horseman Lane and School Lane. This may have been an insubstantial building and by 1868 work had begun on a new school on land given by Frederick Wood, the Lord of the Manor, and partly built on the site of the old parish school (**fig 12.1**). At the same time a school board was formed.[2]

The various censuses between 1841 and 1901 list the following schoolmasters and pupil teachers:

1841	John Schaak	Schoolmaster
1851	William Cartwright	Schoolmaster
1861	Mary Pulleyn	Schoolmaster's wife
	William Puckering	Pupil teacher
	Thomas Hudson	Schoolmaster
1871	Thomas Hudson	Schoolmaster
1881	Thomas Hudson	Schoolmaster
1891	Alice Johnson	Pupil teacher
1901	Thomas Harper	Schoolmaster

Other references to the school and its pupils can be found in some of the Directories of the area:

Baines (1823) makes reference to: 'A small school endowed with £4 per annum for the teaching of eight poor children', naming John Smith as the Schoolmaster and giving the village population as 281.[3]

Kelly's 1877 Directory lists Thomas Hudson as the master of a Church of England National School whilst the 1889 edition mentions a Church of England National School erected in 1869 for 65 children. It lists the average attendance as 50 pupils and names Miss E Whitehead as the schoolmistress.[4]

Bulmer's Directory of 1890 states: 'A new school was built by public subscription in 1869 at a cost of £300 it is attended by about fifty children'. Miss Emma Jane Whitehead is listed as the schoolmistress.[5]

White's 1895 York Directory states: 'A school board of five members was formed in 1891; William Carr Gypson, clerk to the board, formerly National School, erected in 1869 for 65 children, average attendance 46, Jonathon Jacques, master.'[6]

From Coppenthorpe to Copmanthorpe

An old school log book was discovered recently by Miss Rigg, the current head of Copmanthorpe Primary School. It dates from 1898 and the first entry goes a long way to explaining the lack of any earlier school records. Dated 16 May 1898 it reads: 'I, Robert Hanley, certificated teacher, last examined in the Harby Wesleyan School, Lincolnshire, state that the Revd A Willan vicar of this Copmanthorpe Parish deliberately took, after telling it to the Board, the log book away today. There were no children present when he locked the door, and we were again, locked out in the street, no reason given'. Mr Hanley's last entry dated 7 July of that year states that he had resigned his position, unsurprisingly perhaps in the circumstances.

On 3 October in that same year Mr T Harper made his first entry in the log book stating that he had taken charge of the school and was assisted by Miss Wilson. There is a continuous theme in his entries thereafter complaining of low attendance. The reasons given vary from pea picking, potato planting and potato harvesting to the annual trip to Scarborough with the Wesleyan Sunday School. Alterations to the school building delayed the reopening of school. In December of 1898 it is stated that it is almost impossible to get the rooms to a proper temperature because of the cold weather and many children were absent. On 21 May 1900, school was closed in the afternoon 'on account of the festivities in connection with the relief of Mafeking'. The annual May Day procession of the Tadcaster Breweries, the annual Copmanthorpe feast and the agricultural show were all reasons for school closures. Even a wedding in the village was listed as a reason to close the school!

The early 20th century

Work was done to improve the school but disease and illness continued to affect attendance. In early 1900 school was closed for three and a half weeks because of an influenza epidemic, and the log books also mention measles, whooping cough, diphtheria, chicken pox, ringworm and mumps as diseases which badly affected attendance levels. In 1907 a severe epidemic of scarlet fever meant that the summer holiday was extended until the end of September when six children were still in hospital and others were recovering at home.

The Conservative Government under the leadership of Arthur Balfour passed the Education Act of 1902. This act abolished 2568 local school boards and introduced 325 Local Education Authorities (LEAs) which were given power to establish new secondary and technical schools as well as to develop further the existing system of elementary schools. Copmanthorpe School now came under the authority of the West Riding County Council (WRCC).

Claude Hey took over as headmaster in January 1927 at the end of an epidemic of typhoid fever. It was also the year when the first child from Copmanthorpe, Stanley Johnson, was offered a grammar school place, after taking the County minor examination. The raising of the school leaving age to 14 increased the school numbers and in 1928 Mr Hey was responsible for 42 children aged between 8 and 14 in what would now be considered seven teaching age groups. At that time there was one uncertificated assistant for the infants and a part-time caretaker.

In 1935 the vicar, Herbert Shaw, came to the school to distribute gifts to the children of pens, pencils and bank books, each with an initial deposit of one shilling, as part of the celebration of the Silver Jubilee of King George V. The following year the school was closed for the day of the king's funeral, and later that year souvenir spoons were given to the children to mark the coronation of Edward VIII, which we now know never happened.

From 1941 the school was under the supervision of Miss Clara Gristwood. The war years were difficult for the school, the children, and families in the village. Evacuees arrived in Copmanthorpe from South Shields, Leeds and Hull, resulting in even more overcrowding at the school and extra space had to be found in the Women's Institute and the Village Hall. The school garden was turned over to food production to help with the shortages in food supplies. Teachers came and went as some joined the armed services, and supply teachers too came and went. The night of 28 April 1942 was frightening as the Luftwaffe attacked York and villagers could see the resulting fire and smoke. Few children were in school on time the following morning!

A new era

A new era began for Copmanthorpe School with the appointment of Miss Frances Frost to the post of Headmistress on 1 May 1945 (**fig 12.2**). We now know that she played a prominent role in the history of both school and village as Copmanthorpe grew from a small self-contained community with just 56 children enrolled as she began her career to the much-enlarged village we see today. By the time Miss Frost retired

in October 1976 there were 250 children enrolled, and she had overseen the
construction of not only a new school
but also a swimming pool.

The Copmanthorpe village newsletter of November 1976 contains a
wonderful tribute to Miss Frost as she
retired from the post of headmistress of
Copmanthorpe School after 31 years of
service.

12.2 Miss Frances
Frost,
Headmistress of
Copmanthorpe
School, 1945–76,
and other teachers
(L to R: Molly
Ansell, Frances
Frost, Janet Holt
and Olive Milner)

> The village owes a great debt of
> gratitude to Miss Frost for the high
> moral as well as educational stand-
> ards which she has instilled into
> two generations. The stability of her
> "school family" as it has continued to
> grow, has engendered great confidence in Miss Frost. She has been
> much loved by children, parents and staff who have responded to
> the warmth of her affectionate nature. She will be greatly missed,
> and her well-deserved retirement will allow her more time for her
> voluntary activities. She carries with her our best wishes, secure in
> the knowledge that this village owes her a very real debt of grati-
> tude. We hope she will remember with satisfaction and justification
> the words 'Well done, thou good and faithful servant'.

Miss Frost received a typewriter as a leaving present when she retired, and
then embarked on writing her own history of Copmanthorpe School. She
has kindly granted permission to quote from her work, as her own words
carry much more relevance than any interpretation we might give. She
has also agreed that her manuscript *Copmanthorpe School: Its Growth and
Development* should become part of the village archive in Copmanthorpe
library.

Her story of the school on her arrival will be difficult for today's
children and parents to comprehend – it is Dickensian in its starkness
although only just over sixty years ago in 1945. She says:

> Never shall I forget my first week at the old school. From the outside
> it looked attractive enough standing prominently on the corner,
> surrounded by fields. On the north side was a walled garden with
> two small areas of lawn, many paths around weed-ridden borders,
> and three aging apple trees. The inside was truly dismal – a cloak-

room cum cleaner's store and a stone sink with one cold water tap – leading to two classrooms divided by a half-glazed screen. This, together with the rest of the woodwork, was painted a dull dark green on top and a wrinkled brick red below. If by any chance children sitting in the vicinity leaned against the screen, clothing stuck to it! Patches of plaster were peeling from the walls, and the floor was dirty and splintered. Heating was by open fires protected by bent and rusty fireguards, flanked by equally decrepit coal scuttles – these of course empty as no heating was allowed after May 1st.

She goes on

...winter came all too soon with its attendant problems. The fire belched clouds of smoke but little heat, and the cisterns of the outside toilets froze with sickening regularity. Frosty mornings invariably started by boiling kettles of water on our one electric ring to thaw out the offending and often offensive toilets. Each Friday entailed kneeling in the icy playground digging down to the stop tap and water meter to obtain the water consumption figures demanded by 'the Office'.

12.3 Copmanthorpe School in 1961. Miss Frost, Mrs Ansell and Mrs Milner gathered with the children under the apple tree in the garden of the old school (© *York Evening Press*)

Slowly, but persistently, she worked to improve both the physical building and the school curriculum. She was one of the first headteachers to fight for peripatetic music teachers to provide instrumental music instruction in the junior schools. In 1948 as wartime restrictions were eased the old four-seater desks were replaced by dual desks and individual chairs. Miss Frost notes that 'we had new fireguards, extra books and bookshelves to put them in, and we utilised the redundant blackout curtains to make PE shorts for the girls'. She describes Copmanthorpe that year as 'still a rural village. Horseman Lane was devoid of houses and on the pond in the centre where Horseman Drive now begins we watched moorhens nesting. The large pond behind Top Lane provided a plentiful supply of frog and toad spawn and the connecting stream often served as the English Channel when we brightened history lessons by dramatising Roman and Norman invasions.'

Coronation Year (1953) was celebrated by the children dressed in fancy dress and parading through the village following the Pied Piper. In the field opposite the school they danced around the maypole plaiting the ribbons as they went, and also bought (with money raised in the village for a permanent memorial) and planted the avenue of cherry trees we still enjoy today on Horseman Lane.

The 29 April 1968 brought the opening of the new school. Miss Frost remembers:

> The new school for which we had worked and waited so long was finally a reality with undreamed of space: a large hall doubling as a well-equipped gymnasium, a dining room and kitchen, five classrooms each with its own integral entry, cloakroom, sinks and storeroom. The administrative wing was complete with office, medical room, staff room, and more storage and staff cloakrooms.

It must have felt like a palace!

However, the building of new houses continued apace and in 1969 the old school had to be brought back into use for three classes as the village continued to expand. It was also the year when a special celebration was held for the centenary of the old school. Miss Frost describes the old school building as:

> transformed into a veritable museum, with displays of old documents, photographs, books, furniture, and relics from houses and farms to show the development of equipment and transport through the century, plus a model of the old village painstakingly made in handwork classes. All this was described and explained

by Willis Dykes and other older residents with delight and enthusiasm. In the new school we mounted a village survey, each room showing a different aspect of life from one hundred years ago. Children were attired in Victorian costume, and the sun shone, so outside we held displays of country and maypole dancing and drill lessons – then and now arranged by Mr Bonham. The brass band and orchestra provided music and to underline the development in the hundred years' progress, the formal opening of the swimming pool was performed by Mr Scott, senior PE Advisor for the WRCC who had given us so much help and advice in its provision. At 4pm present pupils served tea to 32 'vintage' pupils still resident in the village, and the meal ended with a celebration cake baked and suitably iced by the kitchen staff to the accompaniment of a selection of favourite songs from our youngest pupils. The exhibition stayed open until evening to give those at work an opportunity to put the clock back also, and the day ended with a lusty rendering of Auld Lang Syne at 9pm.

How wonderful if we could re-visit that special celebration today!

Miss Frost describes the school children being involved in village history again on 17 March 1970 when the old 'Manor House' was demolished. One of the large corner construction posts was rescued by Mr Bonham's class who used rollers and pulleys in medieval fashion to transport it to the school grounds and re-erect it near the main entrance where it still stands today (see **fig 3.4a**). She also describes the children inviting older residents of the village to school in February 1971 to help them understand the new decimal currency. The children used their plastic coins and played at shopkeepers for the afternoon.

In January 1972 the new Infants school opened under the direction of Mrs Molly Ansell who had worked with Miss Frost since 1961; and with this the old school, which had been put back into service as pupil numbers continued to swell, was no longer needed. The old school building sat empty for over twenty years, before finally being demolished in 1992 to be replaced by the Medical Centre. The only part of it to be retained was the porch entrance. The circular window provides a remembrance and an echo of the large two-faced clock that was a feature of the school building, with one clock face inside and one outside.

Mrs Ansell, who wrote the final chapter in Miss Frost's book, describes the celebration of Queen Elizabeth's Silver Jubilee. A white envelope embossed with a silver crest and with COPMANTHORPE SCHOOL 1977 printed in royal blue on the flap and Silver Jubilee stamp on the first

FROM COPPENTHORPE TO COPMANTHORPE

day of issue was posted to each child. She also remembers that the older infants were taken to Castle Howard to see replicas of the Royal Regalia including the Coronation crown (St Edward's) and the Queen's Imperial crown.

Mrs Ansell concludes her portion of the book with a personal footnote:

> Copmanthorpe was a small village which expanded very rapidly. I had seen the number of pupils in the school rise from 70 in 1961 to well over 400 when I left. Having lived in the village throughout and seen my own daughter pass through the school I tried to foster links between the community and the school, continuing the happy tradition already established. I was always very much aware of my responsibility to the people of Copmanthorpe for leading the education of the young children, not only on the academic subjects but also in moral and spiritual values to equip them for life in the widest sense. It has been a privilege to work with excellent hard-working staff, supportive parents and lovely children. As I retire from the scene the first computers are being offered to us so a new era will begin. I shall always have affection for the school and will watch its future progress with great interest.

Copmanthorpe School today

Today the school is a flourishing modern educational environment with 316 pupils under the direction of Miss Judith Rigg, who was appointed head in 2002. One of her first missions was to combine the Infant and Junior sections of the school into one under her leadership. Now the two buildings are linked both physically and educationally and provide an excellent education for the children of today. The current school prospectus states 'the vision is to create a warm, welcoming and stimulating environment for all children. We aim to ensure that children enjoy school and develop a love of learning and through partnership with parents and community we will help children reach their potential academically, socially and emotionally'. This all sounds remarkably similar to Mrs Ansell's aims 50 years ago, and no doubt those of Miss Frost some 65 years ago.

The latest Ofsted report states the Copmanthorpe Primary School 'provides an outstanding education for all its pupils because it is exceptionally well led and managed ... It is too modest in its assessment of how good it is, illustrating its desire to be better still … Pupils really enjoy coming to school as shown by above average levels of attendance. Teaching is good in every class and an exceptionally playful approach is fully appreciated by pupils who regard lessons as fun'. This is no doubt why several newer members of our village community tell us they moved into the village simply because of the excellent reputation of Copmanthorpe Primary School.

There is now a wonderful new garden area with flourishing vegetables growing in raised beds. According to an article in *The Press* the children collected unused and broken jewellery for sale in order to fund this new enterprise. It is reminiscent of the gardens at the old school which were used for food production during difficult times in the past, only today it educates a supermarket-fed generation about where food really comes from.

The history of the village is still a part of the curriculum for Years Three to Six. We wish Miss Rigg, her staff and all the students of Copmanthorpe, current and future, great success in their educational endeavours as they forge their own part in the ongoing history of Copmanthorpe.

Notes

1   Frost, F 'Copmanthorpe School: its growth and development' MS held in Copmanthorpe Library
2   CL File 'Documents and correspondence from the lord of the manor'
3   YCRL Baines, W *History, directory & gazetteer of the County of York* 1823 p 142
4   YCRL *Kelly's Post Office directory of the West Riding* 1877 p 255; 1889 p 284
5   YCRL Bulmer, T *History & directory of North Yorkshire* 1890 p 872
6   YCRL White, W *Directory of York* 1895 p 366

CHAPTER THIRTEEN

Recreation and leisure

MIKE ROGERS

WITH CONTRIBUTIONS FROM ELAINE MARSHALL,
MARTIN PICKARD AND NIGEL WHITE

RECREATION AND LEISURE PURSUITS ARE important aspects
of life in a rural village, so this chapter considers the subject in
its wider sense to provide some insights into recreation in the
village from the later 19th century to more recent times. Early evidence is
obviously limited, but the focus sharpens as sources become more abundant and selection then becomes an issue.

In the earlier days, opportunities for leisure were of a simple kind.
Villagers recollecting their past on tape in 1972[1] refer to board games
and time spent reading, in particular. Beyond homespun entertainment,
children could look forward to a village party at Christmas, while adults
indulged in carol-singing, with the proceeds being shared and sometimes
spent at the pub. Church, chapel, public houses and even schools provided
additional foci for social activities, while summer distractions included the
village show and the Ascension Day Feast. Villagers recall several shows
before 1914 with sports, competitions, side-shows and even a display by local
huntsmen and their hounds. The fortunes of the show fluctuated according
to patronage and support, plus problems caused by tensions between
participating families. Visiting York was also an option for more entertainment, using the train, by walking to the tram terminus at Dringhouses or,
later, catching the bus which initially ran on market days only. Evenings
in town were less practical, however, as return services were not available
after 8pm. Another local outing was to Bishopthorpe, where day visitors
appeared from Copmanthorpe, attracted by the river and also perhaps by
the generous number of public houses on the main street.[2]

For men there were sporting options: cricket had become an established
sport by the 1870s, the *York Herald*[3] reporting a home match between the

13.1 Architect's sketch of the new YMCA building, 1920. Signed 'E. Ridsdale Tate' (Sanderson Collection, Copmanthorpe Library; York Library Service)

village team and Bishopthorpe, which the visitors won comfortably, as also a later fixture against York Railway Plant in 1876. However, a month later the village could not lose, as the match was between Copmanthorpe Parishioners (Married and Single), the latter winning by one run. The club fared better in some of the later matches recorded in the paper and in 1890 it entered the York and District Challenge Cup (established *c* 1890). Sport later became a mainstay of village recreation, and the main developments are outlined below.

A branch of the YMCA (Young Men's Christian Association) was established in the village in 1921, occupying purpose-built premises in School Lane constructed with the volunteer help of villagers (**figs 13.1 & 13.2**). The opening ceremony was performed by Princess Helena Victoria, using a silver-gilt key presented to her by Gladys Jarvis, the reigning May Queen.[4] There was no female equivalent for this club until the establishment in later years of the Youth Club, complemented by the Scouts, Guides and associated groups.

13.2 The volunteers who built the YMCA, 1921 (Sanderson Collection, Copmanthorpe Library; York Library Service)

FROM COPPENTHORPE TO COPMANTHORPE

The Village Newsletter (first distributed in 1970) provides a strong testimony to the wide range of leisure opportunities for a changing and rapidly growing community. The sections which follow are intended to illustrate some of the main developments, especially those for which abundant sources are available, while not neglecting the others.

The Women's Institute

The Copmanthorpe branch held its inaugural meeting on 11 December 1924, with 38 members and Mrs Florence Wilstrop as president. While initially using the YMCA, the branch soon resolved to build its own hall, allowing it to expand its activities and lose its dependence on hired premises. The work was undertaken by Mr W Reed (a local builder) and cost £900, the project receiving substantial support in the form of a loan (fully repaid within four years) given by Mrs Edward Shaw of Welburn Hall, then president of the Yorkshire Federation.

The hall was opened by its chief benefactor on 10 June 1928, and photos of the ceremony clearly show the pride of those involved, with Mrs Shaw and the president seated supported by the committee, all in their hats and finery (**fig 13.3**).[5] The celebrations included a village fair with stalls and side-shows plus various dancing displays; amongst these was

13.3 The opening of the WI Hall, June 1928 (Reproduced by permission of Copmanthorpe WI)

13.4 The Duke of
Kent's visit to
the WI, June
1939
(Reproduced by
permission of
Copmanthorpe
WI)

the traditional plaiting the maypole as well as 'eurythmetics' (as quaintly described by the *Yorkshire Post*).[6]

From the outset, the WI provided leisure, social and educational opportunities for women on a scale they had not hitherto known. A current member writing of this period stresses the role of 'the more affluent ladies, or those higher up in parish circles' in using their education to organise activities from which all could benefit.[7] Monthly meetings were held on Thursday and once essential business was done, a speaker usually addressed the group. Other sessions were devoted to handicrafts, good-housekeeping and country-skills (appropriate for a village group). The diversity is well-illustrated by the Programme for 1939.[8] In June of that year the Duke of Kent, on a short visit to the county, visited Copmanthorpe WI (**fig 13.4**). 'He saw something of what was being done by the Women's Institute movement to brighten the social life of village women, with many of whom he talked as they made "thrift rugs" from old pieces of cloth.'[9]

There were wider beneficiaries from the WI, although in the provision of some activities a family connection with the group was essential. From the early days members were involved in drama, ranging from pageants for members to more serious enterprises such as entry into WI drama competitions at regional level. It was from this beginning that the Copmanthorpe Players developed (see below). The WI also encouraged sport among its members, notably tennis and badminton, and the social calendar was enhanced by dances, parties, outings and whist-drives. On more than one occasion, accounts include payments for multiple sets of playing-cards.

Activities during World War II (1939–45) were adapted to the demands of the time, the hall being used as 'an Evacuation and First Aid centre', with a sub-committee organising the latter and utilising members' own skills and experience.[10] This trend continued during the austerity of the post-war years when the programme featured practical as opposed to leisure activities, like Operation Produce which included a canning school and pig club (for would-be home-grown bacon producers), plus sessions devoted to make-do-and-mend.[11]

From the 1950s activities reflected a growing affluence and wider horizons. TV parties (£1 per person) were organised for fund raising, short holiday trips abroad were promoted in the 1960s,[12] and members volunteered to talk of their own holiday experiences in far-away places. In 1974 the organisation celebrated its Golden Jubilee with a range of special events, including a flower show at St Giles church.[13]

The influence of the group is well summed up by the president speaking at the 60th Anniversary Dinner (1984) when she paid tribute to the early members and also to the hall: 'Under its roof we have all been educated and entertained, we have dined and danced and held every kind of sale ...We continue to enjoy our monthly meetings ... not only for a good speaker but as an opportunity for making and strengthening friendships.'[14] The tradition continues today.

The Yorkshire Countrywomen's Association

The YCA was formed in 1983 as a breakaway group from the national WI. The organisation still aimed to represent the interests of countrywomen but was to be run on more relaxed lines. Affiliation to the new

13.5 Copmanthorpe YCA celebrates its tenth birthday in 1995 (L to R: Joan Elwess, Jean Williams, Sally Fawcett, Ann Coatsworth, Betty Wood, Edna Thurwell, Lora Wing, Margaret Horsley, Kathleen Hesp, Margaret Edwards, and Chris MacCleod) (© Harold Wood)

organisation varied from village to village – neighbouring Acaster Malbis was one of the first YCA groups, but in Copmanthorpe, the WI held sway. The Copmanthorpe group was formed in 1985, two years after the launch of the movement, and is affiliated to other branches through a central committee (**fig 13.5**). The members meet once a month at the Recreation Centre, usually for a talk or demonstration. The programme includes two annual features: a summer outing by coach and a tombola stall at the village carnival. On a wider scale members take part in events for the entire county (which are generally held in York), including Gardeners Days, Handicraft Shows and Antiques Evenings.[15]

Copmanthorpe Players

Dramatics came to the village with the WI, the Players developing under its wing in the 1920s and retaining this link for over 50 years, a fact which was recognised in the group's name (Copmanthorpe WI Players). The complexity of the situation was recognised by the group's committee even as late as the 1970s;[16] however, towards the end of that decade the Players finally attained autonomy, while continuing to play in the WI Hall. Although this allowed people with no connection to the WI to join, the group lost its special status and with it advantages such as rent-free usage of the hall.

Photographs belonging to Henry Thomlinson, one of the longest-serving members of the group, record dramatic activities dating back to the earliest days: several show tableaux (both religious and secular, produced at St Giles and also the WI Hall), while another is of the cast of a now-forgotten play entitled *Moggeridge's Cow*. By the 1930s, regular productions were taking place: two per year plus entries in WI and British Drama League festivals. A typical example is Arnold Ridley's *The Ghost Train* staged in 1934.

Henry, who first appeared in the early tableaux, also remembers the Players in their heyday after 1945. After his debut in Lesley Storm's *Tony Draws a Horse* (1947), he played many roles up to 1975, his final perform-ances being in Patrick Hamilton's *Gaslight*. His recollections, plus archive and photographic material from the WI and the Players themselves, attest to the high production values of the group.[17] The hall, its stage and other facilities were put to good advantage, and serviceable lighting equipment was acquired, as well as wooden platforms to accommodate the audience at the rear of the hall. Scenery, costumes and props were generally made

13.6 Copmanthorpe Players' production of *Flarepath*, with Henry Thomlinson on right, *c* 1950s (Courtesy of Henry Thomlinson)

by the actors, and other members worked as back-stage crew. In 1955 the group won the WI Yorkshire Federation Drama Festival with their production of *The Red Velvet Goat*, while four years later they competed in the Yorkshire Drama Festival at Scarborough, adjudicated by Stephen Joseph, with *The Sign of the Prophet Jonah*.[18] Some productions were ambitious by any amateur standards (for example Shakespeare's *Midsummer Night's Dream* and George Farquhar's *The Beaux Stratagem*) but the normal repertoire generally centred on comedies and thrillers, in order to achieve a wider appeal (**fig 13.6**).

Two local people in particular enhanced the group's reputation. Dorothy Scott, RDA-trained and chairman of the Players in the post-war years was, as Henry Thomlinson says, 'a driving force from the group's origins'. Her training and experience as a drama teacher for the WI helped to enable the group to undertake the ambitious programme mentioned above, while her contacts at large helped to attract audiences from well beyond the village. From the mid-1970s the Players also benefited from the participation of Peter Gordon (York-born, village resident and Senior Lecturer at Leeds Polytechnic), more especially as a playwright. He came to be regarded as a resident author, and the group performed a number of his plays including the world première of *Third Week of August* (1993) and *Wild Card*, a psychological thriller (1995).

Committee minutes of the 1970s and 1980s indicate both highs and lows in the group's fortunes, with the occasional crisis brought about by shortages of actors (usually male) and lack of support for back-stage activities. Sadly, numbers dwindled and the group finally dissolved in 2006.[19]

Public houses

ELAINE MARSHALL

It would seem that ale has always been a source of leisure in Copmanthorpe! Since 1646, when the Alehouse Registers of Licensees began, Copmanthorpe has had its share of them.[20] The registers did not name the alehouses but did record the licensees' names. Thus, in that first year in Copmanthorpe's alehouse history, John Hobson, Thomas Howton, Richard Laburne and Thomas Fenton were all named. However, two of them may not have been licensees but bondsmen who deposited sums of money as a surety; this was shown to be the case from 1662 onwards when the registers record the bondsmen separately. Quite where they were conducting their business is not clear, however, as the earliest records for actual public houses only date back to the early 19th century.

The village has been endowed with two public houses for many years, the Royal Oak having been a public house since 1822 (**fig 13.7**), when John Morley was recorded as licensee.[21] In 1823 he is also recorded as the blacksmith, and during the 19th and early 20th centuries there was an adjacent forge. The earliest reference to the building itself is 1793[22] when it was a dwelling house owned by John Benson. In 1830 it was sold to John Cattle, who then sold it to John Hotham in 1834. The Royal

13.7   The Royal Oak public house, early 20th century (one of the group is a member of the Hudson family) (Courtesy of Pat Bristowe)

Oak Friendly Society was the earliest recorded activity in 1872, with 40 members and Thomas Hudson as Secretary.[23] The Oak was clearly a popular destination for outings from York around the turn of the 20th century: a photograph from 1906 shows at least eight gigs or carriages parked outside; the horses were presumably being fed and watered at the back.[24] The property was sold again in 1921 to Tadcaster Tower Brewery which in turn became part of Bass Group. On the Copmanthorpe oral history tapes of the early 1970s, elderly Mr & Mrs King recalled tenants 'Puckering and Jack Jennings at the Royal Oak and Ben Buckle as blacksmith before the First World War'. Also that:

> Horses were kept at the pub stables; they belonged to the Army, called remounts. Had 'em all over England like that; would keep 'em until there was a boat load and send 'em over to France during the First World War. There were mounting steps outside, stone steps to go up to t' granary. Mr Jennings sold Sharp's flour and Indian corn.

The stables no doubt provided steady business for the blacksmith who occupied the single-storey structure at the southern end of the range of buildings, adjacent to the green.

An article in the local press in 1947 reported on a winter's morning outside the Royal Oak when villagers assembled on the green to watch the meet of the York and Ainsty (South) Hunt.[25] 'Some farmers and their wives were members', said Miss Thompson, who lived nearby. Licensees remembered by locals include Ronnie Cuss (Cussy) and family who also ran a taxi service, Barbara Roe and family who introduced pie and pea suppers at darts matches, and Alf and Ruth Sleightholme.[26] Amongst the entertainment there were domino and darts teams, including a ladies' team, New Year's Eve parties and occasional fancy dress events. Also many seaside coach trips were organised. On one occasion the old Bedford bus supplied by Sykes from Appleton Roebuck struggled so much up Garrowby Hill near Driffield that the men had to walk up. On return journeys a pub stop was always made before reaching Copmanthorpe.[27]

The Fox and Hounds has had a more chequered history, operating under several different names since the early 19th century (**fig 13.8**). As detailed in chapter 7 in this book, the property was first shown on published maps as Copmanthorpe House in 1832; by 1849 it was the Queen's Arms Inn and in 1893 the Fox and Hounds, but some villagers have also known this establishment as the Ginger Beer House. Miss Beedham, one of the elderly residents recorded on the oral history tapes, recalled it being the

13.8 The original Fox
and Hounds
building on Top
Lane, c 1960s
(Sanderson
Collection,
Copmanthorpe
Library; York
Library Service)

Ginger Beer House which was mainly frequented by men; the fact that
it had a savings club for when a doctor was needed provided the perfect
excuse for regular visits![28] However, other villagers recall being told that
people walked up Tinker Lane to the Ginger Beer House pub next to
Askham Bryan Windmill (both of which have long since disappeared).[29]
There was, in fact, a 'Beer House' recorded at Copmanthorpe in White's
Directory of 1837 when Thomas Bell was named as licensee, and in
White's Directory of 1895 when William Newcombe was listed.[30] The
location is not given but since both the Oak and the Fox and Hounds
are known to have been operating at the time of these Directories, we
are left with the question, where was the Beer House? The establishment may have been under the Temperance Movement during much
of the 19th century, with strict licensing laws governing opening hours
and liquor sales. Some 451 Beer Houses were licensed in York in 1830,
and in the same year, there were no fewer than 448 Money Clubs held in
public houses;[31] this concords with Miss Beedham's later recollections of
a savings club at the Ginger Beer House. Licensees recalled by villagers
at The Fox and Hounds have included Mr and Mrs Jarratt and daughter
Muriel, who were there when ale was still poured from jugs, and Fred
and Hilda Turpin who became landlord and landlady in 1964, when
they arrived with their family Marilyn, Sue and Malcolm, together with
Hilda's mother, Gertrude Bradley.[32] Ale was supplied by John Smith's
Brewery, Tadcaster, where Fred was a joiner, which involved Hilda and
her mother running the pub. Sue remembers the pub's nick-name was the
Old Ginger Beer House. The original building which they moved into

was situated right on the edge of the A64 at the junction with Top Lane, directly opposite Pike Hills Golf Course. Mr Turpin named the small lounge bar the 19th Hole!

At the end of the decade, a new building for the pub was erected in the extensive grounds of the old pub, set further back and higher up from the main road and creating a now essential car park. On its completion the Turpins moved into the new Fox and Hounds and the old building was demolished. Both Marilyn and Sue were married from the pub, Sue marrying a Copmanthorpe lad, Arthur Conyers; their reception was held in the pub. Fred and Hilda retired in 1973, and by 1975 it had become a Falstaff Eating House, part of John Smith's Catering Division, with managers Graham and Debora Wilson, reflecting a change in pub traditions and heralding future trends.[33] Being situated on the main road which brought traffic from the west to York and the East Coast, the Fox and Hounds was, during the 20th century, an attractive and convenient stopping place for coaches taking trippers on excursions. Many would stop at the pub on the way for breakfast and return for an evening meal. It is recalled that whilst Micky Dunn was landlord, who was renowned for providing good meals, there were regulars who had allotments opposite the pub. They provided a convenient source of vegetables to ensure Micky never ran out! Licensees since have included Mark Heath, Colin Bower, Phil Hirst, and Richard Cowling. Over the years the pub has been host to various clubs and societies, including Copmanthorpe Golf Society and Copmanthorpe Football Club. Trophies and memorabilia were kept on display, and regular meetings, social events and charity fund-raising events held. Darts, dominoes, karaoke and discos were popular. During the 1980s local bands played, including Monkey Nuts and Bogus Brothers. The pub also fielded a Tug of War team to compete with the Royal Oak on Carnival days.[34]

More recently both public houses have belonged to Enterprise Inns; with various alterations and refurbishments, and facilities such as pool and meals, not to mention the ever-popular quiz evenings, the pubs continue to provide the modern village with facilities for leisure and entertainment.

Village dances
ELAINE MARSHALL

Ballroom dancing, both old time and modern, was a popular form of leisure and social activity in the York area through much of the 20th century. Dances, organised as fund-raising events by various clubs and

Copmanthorpe Badminton Club

invite you to the

Annual St. Valentine's Dance

to be held in the

WOMEN'S INSTITUTE HALL

On Saturday, February 16th, 1957

FANCY DRESS (optional)

Spot Prizes

Buffet

Prizes for prettiest and most original costumes

Dancing 8 p.m. to midnight to

John Wilkes' Hi-Fi Record Rhythm

13.9 Poster for a Valentine's Day Dance, February 1957 (Courtesy of Henry Thomlinson)

societies, were held in turn at local villages including Bishopthorpe, Copmanthorpe, Appleton Roebuck, Bilborough and Askham Richard, as well as in York (**fig 13.9**). The village had two venues: the Women's Institute Hall and the Youth Club. Dancing was to the music of local bands and two recalled are Stott's from Acaster Malbis[35] and the Bluettes. Larger bands played at venues in York, including the Assembly Rooms, the De Grey Rooms, the Drill Hall, Terry's Restaurant, and various clubs, some of the dances being grand 'balls'.

During the early 1950s, weekly lessons for modern ballroom dancing were held in Copmanthorpe Youth Club on Wednesday evenings. The tutors were Ken and Vera Broughton and the music was supplied by gramophone records.[36] Summer and winter, many young teenagers cycled from the outlying villages to gather together to learn the popular method of exercise. Only the severest weather prevented their attendance and they would cycle along country lanes, as well as the exposed A64, even in gales, the lads and lasses laughing and shrieking as they were blown about on their bikes; fortunately there were few cars to worry about! The fun of getting there, meeting 'kids from Cop, Bish, and so on' was the driving force that carried them along, not to mention the thrill of learning a new dance and being asked to dance, 'especially if it was someone you had fancied'! Then, having become a little proficient, attendance was made at the proper dances held on Friday or Saturday evenings. On Saturdays, to comply with the law, dancing stopped strictly by midnight. More sophisticated schools of dancing were held in York, including The Court School of Dancing and Mary Mac's.

Even though bicycle or motor bike was the mode of transport for many (**fig 13.10**), dressing up was part of the occasion and classical dresses of brightly coloured satin brocade, taffeta and georgette were popular. 'Fashion' took off in the mid 1950s, no doubt popularised by glamorous singing and dancing film-stars like Doris Day, Tammy Wynette, and Cyd Charisse. They had a large influence on the young-sters, who saved hard to acquire some glamorous attire, many of them by earning money fruit picking at the West Riding Agricultural College at Askham Bryan and potato picking at local farms. Teenage girls trav-elled by bus to Leeds to the new chain stores springing up; stores such as C&A sold many more new fashions than could be found in York, at affordable prices. Classical dresses were replaced by colourful floral printed cotton dresses and skirts, and gypsy-style blouses with coloured trims on neck and sleeves, worn with black flared skirts trimmed with brightly coloured braid and held out by stiff net petticoats; a revolution in dress sense! Even the young lads' traditional suits became replaced by 'off the peg' fashionable casual wear.

The effort was worthwhile, however, for these village dances were the origins of a great number of courtships, and ultimately long-lasting marriages of many couples.

13.10 Village lads on their motorbikes, *c* 1950s (L to R: Brian Craggs, Albert Craggs, Dennis Parker, Alwyn King, Micky Tree and Anthony Kneeshaw) (Courtesy of Pat Bristowe)

Shows and carnivals

It seems Copmanthorpe has a long tradition of shows and carnivals and many of the recollections recorded in the 1970s (Oral History cassette tapes 1972) talk of these early communal leisure activities – notably shows and the May Day celebrations (**fig 13.11**). Shows came to be held annually from at least before World War I, and an account of the opening of the YMCA notes that the ceremony was performed by the May Queen. The tradition continues today with the May Day fair on Low Green.

The Carnival, inaugurated in 1968, brought together a wide range of attractions and created a major new community interest, as well as providing an invaluable fund-raising opportunity to help finance the Recreation Ground. The latter became the venue of the Carnival from 1975 (see below). Annual themes have included The Circus (1983), The Olympics (1984) and Showbiz (1989), with often more than a dozen floats decorated appropriately (**fig 13.12**). The event has regularly featured bands, displays, dances and a wide range of competitive sports (**fig 13.13**). Visiting attractions have included a sky-diving team, motor-cycling display, gymnastics, fire appliances, and two armoured personnel carriers provided by Fulford barracks. Perhaps the most unusual display item was part of a Deltic diesel-electric locomotive brought in on a low-loader, the cab being accessible to curious bystanders.

13.11 Maypole
 Dancing on the
 village green,
 c 1920s
 (Sanderson
 Collection,
 Copmanthorpe
 Library; York
 Library Service)

From Coppenthorpe to Copmanthorpe

Other summer attractions have included the Horticultural Show and Best-kept Garden award, the former providing a competitive element for village allotment holders.

Although these annual events remain on the calendar, they are generally leaner than formerly, reflecting the social changes of the later 20th century with more diversified interests, diffidence about traditional activities and, in the case of the carnival, the new prominence of health and safety issues. The title Carnival Queen was changed to Carnival Princess (to reflect a more appropriate title for the prevalent age-range), and the tradition finally ended in 2007. With less emphasis on procession and ceremonial, the event was partially revitalised by focusing on the musical aspect, more especially through a link between Minster FM and Global York, a youthful and enthusiastic group based in the city (**fig 13.14**).[37]

13.12 The Copmanthorpe Ramblers float at Carnival 1986 (© Harold Wood)

13.13 Copmanthorpe Carnival Parade: a visiting band from Lancashire, *c* 1980 (Sanderson Collection, Copmanthorpe Library; York Library Service)

13.14 Carnival 2009: music now forms a major part of this annual event (© Mike Rogers)

Copmanthorpe and District Recreation Centre

MIKE ROGERS WITH MARTIN PICKARD

In the early days, football and cricket were played on farmers' fields, but as the village expanded in the post-war years, demand grew for a dedicated site, properly levelled and drained, which would cater for these and other sports, especially tennis and bowls. Also envisaged were a children's playground, changing rooms and social amenities.

In 1968 a committee was formed under the leadership of Reg Keen to realise this project. The Committee included District councillor Norman McLeod, Philip Turner, a partner in Price Waterhouse Accountants, as treasurer, Raymond Fox, a partner in a firm of local solicitors, as legal adviser, and Roy Thompson, Ian Scothern and Norman Anderson amongst others.

Fund-raising was a priority and the first major event was a carnival held in Mrs Bean's field in Temple Lane in June 1968. Although it was a modest affair with just one float donated by a coal merchant, it provided a focus for voluntary effort. This initiative was then supplemented by activities such as coffee mornings, sponsored walks, Christmas dances and fairs, plus events organised by the Scouts and Guides.

The project was formalised at a public meeting on 11 May 1970 which approved a constitution creating a registered charity, the objectives of which were to create and maintain 'a centre for public recreation' and 'to foster good fellowship among the inhabitants of Copmanthorpe and District'. In view of costs, this could not be done all at once, and so the story is one of gradual development with the plans being supported by the Village Trust and accepted by the Council.

After fund-raising, the next priority was finding a site. The Committee approached all the local farmers without success. However, eventually, Alf Wiseman of Ivy House Farm sought permission to develop all his land between Main Street and the railway line for residential purposes, despite the fact that only part of the area had been designated for this purpose. Reg Keen and Norman McLeod approached Mr Wiseman and offered to assist his planning application if he would donate a site for the proposed Recreation Centre. A deal was done and as a result planning permission was granted for both aspects of the scheme. The first intention was to locate the Centre near Main Street; however, in the event, this was changed to the area near the railway, while the remainder went to Manston Developments for housing (which would now be chiefly situated away from the noisy mainline). While the land swap benefited the future residents, it posed an obstacle to the sports scheme in that the land was often waterlogged.

On 29 June 1973 Mrs Elspeth Mary Wiseman, Alf Wiseman's widow, transferred approximately 7 acres (just under 3ha) to the Trustees of the Recreation Centre. And so, in early 1974, after six years of fund raising and with grants from the Sports Council and Selby District Council, Ogdens of Otley began the task of levelling the site, constructing the car park (which was a requirement of the Sports Council grant), and installing land drains. When En Tout Cas, the tennis court contractors complained about the quality of the hardcore base, a team of volunteers led by Harold Wood sieved the material by hand, carrying out this task during February 1975, chiefly after nightfall with the team stoically enduring dust, cold and biting winds.

A second-hand contractor's site hut was acquired to provide changing rooms and a meeting room, while another (obtained from Acaster Malbis) provided headquarters for the Scouts and Guides. Two sets of swings and a Jungle Jim climbing frame were purchased to form the nucleus of a children's playground. On 5 July 1975, Carnival Day, the Centre was formally opened by Councillor Jack Birch, the Lord Mayor of York (**fig 13.15**). (The latter was a surprising choice considering that Copmanthorpe was then situated within the boundary of Selby District Council!) A year later the Recreation Centre was dedicated by Archbishop Stuart Blanch (22 May 1976).

Once the project was up and running, Mr Keen turned his efforts to establishing a social centre. At the same time the work of fundraising continued in earnest. Carnivals continued to provide valuable income, but in the end the money came from several sources. Over a four-year period, Reg negotiated with a number of breweries, so that in 1980 the Recreation Centre was able to acquire a purpose-built club house at a cost of £35,000 paid for with a loan of £28,000 (at a special low rate of 3%) from Tetley's Brewery, a grant from Selby District Council of £3500 and the balance from the Centre's own accumulated cash.

Although various types of building (including a Portakbin variant) were at first envisaged, the committee opted for a brick-built structure with a tiled roof. The new premises were to have a seating capacity of 60 with catering facilities suitable for public functions like wedding receptions and folk concerts. Once the preliminaries (design, planning procedures and tendering) were complete, building began in October 1979 and the Centre was ready for the official opening on 25 June 1980. At the Annual General Meeting in 1980 a new constitution was adopted so that the Centre could obtain registration as a registered members club. In the 21 years that the Club was run as part of the Recreation Centre, it

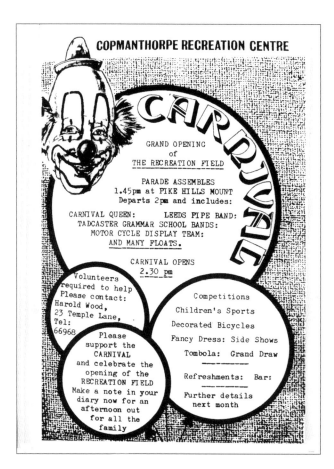

COPMANTHORPE RECREATION CENTRE

CARNIVAL

GRAND OPENING
of
THE RECREATION FIELD

PARADE ASSEMBLES
1.45pm at PIKE HILLS MOUNT
Departs 2pm and includes:

CARNIVAL QUEEN: LEEDS PIPE BAND:
TADCASTER GRAMMAR SCHOOL BANDS:
MOTOR CYCLE DISPLAY TEAM:
AND MANY FLOATS.

CARNIVAL OPENS
2.30 pm

Volunteers
required to help
Please contact:
Harold Wood,
23 Temple Lane,
Tel:
66968

Competitions
Children's Sports
Decorated Bicycles
Fancy Dress: Side Shows
Tombola: Grand Draw
————
Refreshments: Bar:
————
Further details
next month

Please
support the
CARNIVAL
and celebrate the
opening of the
RECREATION FIELD
Make a note in your
diary now for an
afternoon out
for all the
family

13.15 Poster for the opening of the Recreation Ground, 1975 (Courtesy of Harold Wood)

generated a substantial income for the Centre as well as paying off the loan from Tetley's brewery.

With this much achieved, Reg Keen explored the creation of a bowling green; but once again progress was delayed by a serious site problem. The main sewer for the village ran through the Recreation Centre above ground level, dividing the two tennis courts and the proposed site of the bowling green from the rest of the Centre, a location which meant there was not enough room for a full-size bowling-green and would also have restricted a further housing development on adjacent land. In the event, at the end of 1982, Manston Developments agreed to move the offending pipe to the northern edge of this area, and to level the site of the bowling-green, with a contribution from the Centre of only £5000.

Reg Keen proposed an ambitious scheme involving both the bowling-green and a sports hall with changing facilities. Architects drew up plans, but the £200,000 estimated cost made the scheme impossible at the time, one of deep economic depression. As a compromise the bowling-green was accepted within the Community Programme operated by the Manpower Services Commission (whereby the government gave financial and other support to projects which created employment). With Harold Wood as the supervisor, eight unemployed lads from the village were engaged on a part-time basis as labourers. The materials cost £11,000 and grants were obtained from the Sports Council and Selby District Council. The Community Programme contributed £30,000 and the work was carried out between March and December 1983. At the Annual General Meeting in May 1984 Reg Keen was able to declare that the Recreation Centre had realised 'the last project in the brief accepted at its inaugural meeting in 1968'.

The Sports Hall and changing rooms which Mr Keen had unsuccessfully promoted in 1982 were not realised until 1998 when Colin Mackie, the then Chairman of the Recreation Centre, used his personal experience as a commercial property developer to organise the construction of the present sports hall and changing room block at a cost of £160,000. Some £70,000 was provided by the National Lottery, £40,000 from the Foundation for Sports and the Arts, £30,000 from the sale of a building plot fronting onto Sawyers' Crescent and £10,000 was donated by the Football Club.

At the outset the Centre depended heavily on volunteers, of whom the most prominent was Harold Wood. He soon found himself working almost full time maintaining the Centre's facilities, chairing the Club committee for over 25 years and generously shouldering most of the responsibility for the maintenance of the sports field and buildings. It operated as such until 2001, when various factors changed this position: Harold could now commit less time to the Centre and there was also an insufficiency of new volunteers, plus a need to put the club on a more commercial footing. Colin Mackie's determination to achieve the latter was done by leasing off the Social Club to Tony McGale and negotiating a lease of land to Copmanthorpe Childcare for use as a nursery. The result was that more than half the Recreation Centre's income now came from commercial rents and suddenly the Centre found itself with surplus funds.

Since its opening, the Recreation Centre has become the home of all the main village sporting activities. The Football Club has around

13.16 Copmanthorpe Bowling Club: Ladies Pairs Champions 1993, Betty Wood and Eddie May with Flo Larins, Cecil Winham, (?) and Eddie Stead (© Harold Wood)

300 members (in four senior and ten junior teams with three for girls and one which is part of the Ability Counts scheme for the physically challenged). The Cricket Club has two main teams (plus juniors) who play against clubs in the York area. Tennis players were early beneficiaries of the new Centre and the Club has expanded from the early days, its members now using three courts. The bowling green, also an early project at the Centre, is now the home of a thriving club (**fig 13.16**).

Thanks to the hard work of all those previously mentioned and others, the Recreation Centre faces the 21st century in a strong position, able to maintain its existing facilities and, at the same time, work towards the provision of new projects, such as an all-weather games area and an additional tennis court.[38]

The Library

By the 1960s a mobile library was making regular visits to the village, but the campaign to provide Copmanthorpe with a permanent library took around 30 years to achieve fruition, by which time the population of the village had increased enormously. Mrs Jean Johnson, chairman of the parish council, played a central role in obtaining proper facilities, and she herself described the process as 'a long and difficult battle'. Cuttings from the *Yorkshire Evening Press* and a series of letters exchanged between Mrs Johnson and officials at County Hall, Northallerton (kept at Copmanthorpe library) provide an insight into the hard struggle to obtain this library provision which was blighted with problems regarding finance, planning and finding a suitable location. The original intention was to use the premises vacated when the junior school moved to its present site on Low Green. However, deeds associated with ownership caused negotiations to stall. In March 1983 North Yorkshire County Council agreed in principle to the parish council's scheme, which then got overwhelming support from a public meeting two years later and by 1990 the matter had become a hot local election issue. It is certain that Mrs Johnson's persistent campaign was pivotal in persuading the County Council to go ahead with the scheme, MP Michael Alison congratulating Mrs Johnson on her role in applying 'long-term lobbying and pressure' (October 1991). The authorities finally agreed to purchase a unit within the new shopping centre, and the scheme came to fruition in 1993.[39]

Activities for young people

While the YMCA was founded in 1921, a full range of social activities for young people did not develop in the village until after the end of World War II in 1945.

The Youth Club

From its origins in the 1920s, the YMCA building served as a village hall, hosting various functions including the Saturday night dances. But by the 1960s the 'unofficial youth club' operating there was faced with closure, prompting Frederick Allan, its leader, to begin a campaign to raise a loan to buy the hall. This was achieved with various grants, the restored premises being opened in April 1963. With its new lease of life, the building continued to serve its purpose until the early 1990s, when it was deemed to be worn out and described as having 'an almost raffish air, disrespectable, grimy and depressing'. This resulted in a new initiative to start serious fund-raising for a replacement building. A business plan was prepared and the management committee set out to match the £30,000 in grant money with funds raised by jumble sales, discos and other projects. 'We have all baked, raffled, catered and entertained *ad infinitum*' said one supporter. The new building was designed by Darrell Hind, a local architect, and the finishing work was undertaken by volunteers, with the fittings being returned from temporary storage in David Forth's piggery. 'How we came to love that place! Wherever could we have stored 60 stacking chairs, 2 full-size table tennis tables and many more essential items.' The new club was finally opened in July 1996.

Besides the core activities such as pool, table tennis and, more recently, computer games like Nintendo, drama has figured prominently in the Club's programme, notably under the leadership of Jean Howell, from which the club benefited for over 20 years. Her work chiefly involved the age group 11 to 18, although younger children were involved. The venues have included the club itself, the school, and also the WI Hall, with productions ranging from pantomimes to revues, light entertainment and plays written by the members themselves.[40]

Scouts

MIKE ROGERS WITH NIGEL WHITE

Copmanthorpe Scout Group was formed in 1968 by Bill John and Peter Fry. Mr John's previous experience as District Commissioner in Wembley was invaluable, and he continued in his pivotal role as Group Scout Leader for ten years until his sudden death in 1978.

Originally the Group neckerchief was to be white with a red cross to reflect the village's historical links with the Knights Templar, but when it was found these colours were already used by another Scout Group in York, Copmanthorpe settled on burgundy with a white border.

The Group has held Section meetings in almost every public hall in the village. In the first ten years activities were carried out in the WI Hall, Youth Club, Old School House and the Methodist Church. Their first 'permanent' home arrived in 1978 through the donation of a second-hand wooden contractor's hut rebuilt on Recreation Centre land. The 'Green Scout Hut' served the Group well for some years, although it was eventually replaced following a huge fund-raising effort. The new building was completed and opened officially in 1998 by Alf Sturdy, Deputy County Commissioner.

There has never been a shortage of demand from young people to join the Scout Group, although in common with many other villages, there have continually been challenges in securing sufficient leaders. The Scout Troop in particular was on the edge of closure a number of times, and indeed closed for c 10 years from 1972, during which time some of the Scouts were accommodated at Bishopthorpe Scout Troop. Eventually however new volunteers were found, and for a brief spell, the Group even had two Scout Troops (Jaguars and Cheetahs).

13.17 Copmanthorpe Scouts hosting Scouts from Japan who were attending the 2007 Scouting Centenary World Jamboree (© Nigel White)

The Cub Scout Section has usually been the largest, and for some fifteen years had two Cub Scout Packs (Eagles and Merlins). The Group opened a Beaver Scout Colony for a younger age group in 1988, followed by a second colony a year later (Wood and Riverbank). The colonies combined in 1998, again primarily through insufficient availability of leaders.

The Group is well established and recognised in the City of York and has had many successes competing with other Scout Groups and community organisations, particularly in sporting contests. The Lord Mayor of York acknowledged the Group's contribution to the community with a fascinating tour of the Mansion House in Scouting's Centenary year (2007). Also in this year, the Group hosted a contingent of Scouts from Japan who had been staying at the 21st World Scout Jamboree, at which almost every country in the world was represented (**fig 13.17**).

Over 40 years, the Scout Group has supported more than 700 young people, through the leadership and assistance of several adult volunteers. Scouting values of doing one's best and thinking of other people, whilst promoting the development of young people, continue to be relevant and demand to join is still high.[41]

Guides

The first Guide company in Copmanthorpe shares its foundation date (1968) with the Scouts. It was founded by Dorothy Thompson and had twelve members. Their original meeting place was a wooden hut behind the Methodist chapel, a building finally replaced in 1997. This enabled the Guides to return to the site of their original home after a spell at the old Scout hut. Finally they rejoined the Scouts at their new headquarters at the Recreation Centre in 1998.

At an early stage camping became an established feature of the guiding year. At first the company joined county groups, but then came to organise their own camps. Some of the earliest took place in a field near Kennel Wood, past the gamekeeper's cottage at Nun Appleton. Generally, sites were chosen within the county (Linton-on-Ouse, Helmsley and Ravenscar); however, on occasions the company visited other areas (the Hope valley in the Peak District and the Scout Centre at Gosforth Park, near Newcastle). More recently horizons have widened and destinations have included Ireland (1997), Toronto, Canada (2007) and Switzerland (2008). In 1998 there was a joint venture with the Scouts to explore the Caledonian Canal in Scotland by sail and kayak canoe. Other highlights

13.18 An informal
group of
Copmanthorpe
Guides (late
1990s)
(© Liz Laming/
Sue Elmer)

have included the World Guide Camp in the New Forest (1999) and a
centenary camp with the Scouts at Ripley Castle (2004).

During this period the organisation has catered for all age groups
from Rainbows and Brownies to Rangers. The number of packs has
varied over the years but the First Copmanthorpe Guide Company has
had a continuous history since its foundation. However, perhaps the
most significant change has been the widening of the age range with the
opening of the Rainbows (5 to 7 years) in 1989 and the Rangers (14 to
25 years) in 1997.

Although the movement's ethos has remained the same over the years
and is still embodied in the Guide promise, activities and programme
very much reflect the changing needs and expectations of girls and young
women (**fig 13.18**). Copmanthorpe Guides have responded to these new
challenges in various ways while retaining an interest in traditional and
pioneering activities like woodcraft and working for badges. (The latter
now include Computer Skills and Healthy Lifestyle.) They also continue
to play an active role in the community, outward looking and ready to
engage in projects like fund-raising (notably for the church, carnival and St
Martin's Hospice). More recently they have participated in national initia-
tives like Change the World (identifying areas of need and responding
to them) and Go for It (projects of a topical nature tailored to individual
interest).[42]

Other activities

This chapter has focused on specific activities and organisations, but these represent only part of the overall picture, villagers benefiting from numerous other social events, not least those provided by church and chapel.

The churches

The St Giles annual garden party was an important event in the church's calendar. Until the 1960s it was held in the grounds of what is now called No. 3 Main Street (the Old Vicarage), and featured the usual stalls, fancy-dress and bonny baby competitions, and, of course, teas. For a time the event was replaced by a social evening, before resuming in its old form in 1975 and continuing for a number of years at various locations including the school. In 1980 the church organised the first May Fayre to celebrate the 8th centenary of the building of St Giles, and after a gap of a few years this became an annual event with various attractions at Low Green. It is now a major feature of the social calendar. Other activities have included the Shrove Tuesday Paté and Pancake Lunch started c 1985 and the Shoppers' Break, a drop-in facility for morning refreshments at the St Giles Centre.[43]

The chapel also held an annual garden party, at one time in Paddock House and latterly in Low Green. While fund-raising (through the usual stalls and side-shows) was a priority, the event also had an important communal aspect. For the Methodists, socials in the WI hall and even pantomimes found a place in the calendar, and while times have changed, the chapel continues to host a variety of activities. In summer, a children's holiday club is shared with St Giles.[44]

Both church and chapel organised outings, which were always very popular, especially in the post-war years. Some of the most memorable were those of the Mothers' Union (with destinations as far away as Durham) and the Sunday School, when there was a general exodus of mothers and children from Copmanthorpe station for a day out, usually in Scarborough. In spite of changing leisure expectations, the Methodists' ladies outings still take place today.

Copmanthorpe Good Companions

Dating from 1963 and originally called the Vintage Club, this group was set up to provide a social outlet and support for the over-60s. The Wednesday afternoon meetings allowed the members to enjoy the occa-

13.19 Copmanthorpe Good Companions about to embark on an outing from the green in the 1960s (Courtesy of Pat Bristowe)

sion as a get-together with tea and light refreshments and a range of activities including whist, bingo, raffles and presentations by organisations like Wallace Arnold and 'a Scarborough Holidays for the Elderly Company'. As with other village societies, outings were popular, especially to places like Hornsea Pottery and Harrogate Flower Show with local trips to Rowntrees and seasonally to the pantomime (**fig 13.19**). (Non-attenders were sometimes given a cash subsidy in lieu of participation.)

However, what sets this group apart is its well-focused support for members coping with retirement, ill-health, bereavement and other problems brought about by advancing years. Members' birthdays were marked with a card and present, a custom repeated at Christmas (when a 10/- note [50p] was sometimes enclosed). Sick members were visited, especially in hospital, and flowers were sent as required. Committee minutes also refer to liaison with the parish clergy and there was special concern for home visits and letters of condolence. On a practical note, the club organised a chiropody service (extended to non-members in 1973), which survived for many years but before eventually being discontinued. To facilitate attendance at meetings transport was made available through the village Good Neighbours Scheme.

While raising funds for charities like the Yorkshire Evening Press Toy Fund, the group also needed to give serious attention to raising money to support its own activities, hence numerous raffles, jumble sales and Christmas fairs.

In spite of all of these efforts and the initiative of a lively committee (whose meetings at Gordon and Doreen Woodcock's house were also the occasion of much appreciated hospitality), by the early 70s the club was struggling for membership. While early meetings could record an attendance of up to 50, ten years later there were too few to allow the club to remain open during the summer. This trend prompted a number of strategies to redress the situation: the reduction of the age threshold to 50 (1972), a lowering of subs, and appeals for membership in the Newsletter. Sadly, pressure on funds put an end to the customary birthday presents and flowers were limited to hospitalised members only.

In the event there was a happy outcome, leading to revitalisation. In 1976, the old committee resigned *en bloc* and a new start was made chiefly through the energetic leadership of Roy and Lilian Conyers. A decision was made to adopt the new name Copmanthorpe Good Companions and after spells at various halls, the club finally moved to the Recreation Centre where it still holds its regular meetings today.

The club's minutes record its expanding activities, for example the purchase of three significant items in 1977: a piano, projector and radiogram for use at meetings. Talks now feature in the programme, the Citizens' Advice Bureau, crime prevention, and the vicar on dialect, being typical examples. Members have been entertained at Copmanthorpe School with concerts and carols, there have been dances in the WI hall, and a team entered in the village quiz. From the outset there was a strong link with the Carnival: initially the club provided a stall but in some later years it also entered a float, notably in 1982 when its 'Britannia' entry won Third Prize.

The revitalised Good Companions celebrated their 30th anniversary in 2006. Today the club has a steady membership of about forty, although men, as ever, are only a fraction of the total! It now concentrates on its core activities, and remains an important asset to the community.

Copmanthorpe Rambling Club

This group was founded in 1974, chiefly through the initiative of Norman Anderson, its first chairman, who organised what were called Avenue Walks (taking their title from Horseman Avenue, where Norman lived). At first the members were chiefly family and friends, but news of its activities spread without much advertisement and the group quickly extended to welcome any interested villagers.

Twenty-eight people took part in the first walk at Goathland (August 1974). The Yorkshire countryside has proved to be a popular location for rambles over the years, and these came to be held on a regular basis (the third Saturday of the month). Traditionally there have been no A and B options, with members all covering the same distance; however, four times a year shorter evening walks are organised in the village neighbourhood. Special activities have included hiking weekends and annual long-distance walks (including the Lyke Wake Walk, the Beverley Twenty and the Ribble Way in Lancashire).

The group still includes a number of long-standing members, some of whose children now share the activity, while others, having left the district, return to walk with old friends.[45]

Copmanthorpe Allotment Association

In common with many villages, land was designated for allotments from an early date. The plot next to Temple Lane (between the railway and Drome Road) is actually labelled as Allotment Gardens on an OS Map as early as 1892. The association gained formal status in 1943 under rules outlined by various Small Holdings and Allotment Acts (1908–31) and implemented by the parish council. However, the real motivation came from the Dig for Victory campaign (launched very soon after the outbreak of war) to encourage citizens to transform their gardens and cultivate any suitable land for home-grown produce in the light of wartime shortages. There is still a strong demand for plots today.[46]

The way we live now

The period under review has seen considerable change. At the outset social and economic constraints meant that leisure opportunities were very limited, but during the 20th century communal activities gradually became established, as has been illustrated. All have helped to foster a sense of community, although recent changes in horizons and expectations have perhaps made recreation and leisure within the village less communally orientated again. But there are notable exceptions: the WI and similar organisations continue to flourish, as do Scouts, Guides and their affiliated groups. The pubs have re-invented themselves and the Recreation Centre remains a busy focus for sport and other activities. Our Victorian forbears could hardly have anticipated such change; and what will the future bring?

Notes

1   Copmanthorpe oral history tapes
2   Linda Haywood (Bishopthorpe History Group) to MR 2008
3   *York Herald* 1871 to 1890 (Micro-film/YRL)
4   YMCA Opening Ceremony Invitation (CL)
5   Photos of opening ceremony 1928 (Copmanthorpe WI archives)
6   WI Minute Books (from 1924/ Copmanthorpe WI archives)
7   Jary Fowler (Note on Copmanthorpe WI history: a personal view 2008)
8   Programme for 1939 (Copmanthorpe WI archives)
9   From an article in *The Times* 1999
10 Johnson, J *The Copmanthorpe Story* (2nd edition 1995) p 37
11 Committee minute 08/12/1947 (Copmanthorpe WI archives)
12 Committee minute 19/07/1965 (Copmanthorpe WI archives)
13 Programme for event 1974 (Copmanthorpe WI archives)
14 Speech at 60th Anniversary Dinner (Copmanthorpe WI archives)
15 Yorkshire Countrywomen's Association: Association prospectus 2009;
    Based on notes by Wendy Duffus 04/2009
16 Committee minute 07/07/75 (Copmanthorpe Players)
17 Henry Thomlinson to MR 19/08/08; Collection of programmes and
    production photos (Further material from WI and Copmanthorpe Players
    archives)
18 Programme for Third Yorkshire Drama Festival (Scarborough 05/1959)
19 Committee minutes (Copmanthorpe Players archives – various dates from
    1980)
20 YCA K17 York And Ainsty Alehouses Registers 1646–1769, K68:1 York &
    Ainsty Alehouses 1646, K68:2 York & Ainsty Alehouses (Recognizances)
    1646
21 YCA C17 F30A: 1822 Court of Quarter Sessions of the Peace Register 182
    p 83
22 CL Copy letter 08/03/1982 from Bass North Limited PRO to Miss N
    Cammidge, 25 Top Lane, Copmanthorpe
23 YCA Johnson & Tesseymans *Directory of the City of York* 1872 p 396
24 Murray, H *A Directory of York Pubs 1455–2003* p 152
25 YCRL Yorkshire Gazette 20/06/1947
26 Village residents: Charlie & Sue Burton, Gordon Thompson, Sue Conyers,
    David Forth to EM, 01/2009. (Mr & Mrs Sleightholme); also CL, Village
    Newsletter advertisement 12/1977
27 Village resident Gordon Thompson to EM 14/01/2009
28 Oral History tapes, early 1970s
29 Pat Bristowe (neé Hudson) and Tony Hudson to EM, 07/2009. It seems both
    memories are correct: the original Ginger Beer House was up Tinker Lane and
    later moved to the building that became the Fox and Hounds (see chapter 14)

30 YCA White, W *History, Gazetteer and Directory of West Riding of Yorkshire* 1895 p 365

31 YCRL Y178.1 Temperance

32 Sue Conyers (neé Turpin) November 2008 and David Forth, 08/01/2009, to EM

33 CL Village Newsletter March 1975 and YCRL 'Tally Ho! To This New Look Pub' *York Evening Press* (YEP) 17/06/1978

34 Peter Eady, Peter Barraclough and David Forth to EM 08/01/2009

35 Charlie Burton to EM 09/2008

36 Gordon Thompson to EM 14/012009

37 Copmanthorpe oral history tapes (*passim*); Village Trust committee minutes (from 1972); Reports in the YEP and associated titles (Cuttings held in CL Folder A to H); Harold Wood to MR 07/2008; Chris Godber to MR 05/2009

38 Village Trust committee minutes from 1972; YEP and associated titles (cuttings held in CL); Copmanthorpe and District Recreation Association Minute Books (1978–82 and 1982–98); Harold Wood, Martin Pickard and Patrick Solich to MR (07/2008 and 05/2009)

39 Johnson, J *The Copmanthorpe Story* (2nd edition 1995) p 59; Correspondence between Mrs J C Johnson, members of the North Yorkshire County Council Library staff and Mr Michael Alison MP (1991–93); YEP and associated titles (cuttings deposited in CL 1980–93); Planning documents (Selby District Council 1991)

40 The Youth Club: Joan Howell; booklet commemorating the opening of the new building 07/1996; Stuart and Christine Arnott, Ernest Howell to MR 03/ 2009

41 Scouts: Nigel White (illustrated portfolio on the history of Copmanthorpe Scout Group 1968–2008)

42 Guides: Liz Grossett, Margaret Pawsey, Joyce Miller and Dorothy Thompson to MR 02/2009 and 05/2009

43 St Giles church: based on notes by Tim Piper 05/2009

44 Methodist church: Mike and Dorothy Unwin, Jary Fowler to MR 03/2009

45 Rambling Club: Dorothy Thompson and Norman Anderson to MR 02/2009 and 05/2009

46 Allotment Association: Rules as to Allotment Gardens made by the Parish of Copmanthorpe 08/1943 (Leaflet in the possession of Mike Unwin)

CHAPTER FOURTEEN

In living memory

LENORE HILL AND RON HILL

W E HAVE BEEN VERY PRIVILEGED to talk to several Copmanthorpe folk who were generous enough to share their memories of Copmanthorpe for this chapter (**fig 14.1**). Many of them were born in the village, or moved here as young children. Their memories paint a vivid picture of life in the village throughout the twentieth century.

There were many memories of school, as inevitably it is a big part of every child's life. Some memories were happier than others, as some of the children enjoyed school and others were less enthusiastic – much like today! The teachers mentioned by name were Miss Patrick, Mr Claude Hey

14.1 Old postcard showing view of Main Street, *c* 1912

(who later moved to be the head teacher at Bishopthorpe School), Miss Gristwood, Miss Frost, Miss Milner and Mrs Hey (Claude Hey's wife). One person did feel that the children who came from the farm-workers' cottages were not helped as much by Mr Hey as the 'better off' children, as it was understood that their parents would be unlikely to be able to afford for them to go on to the grammar school [this was in the 1920s]. Some remembered that he liked to tell the children stories of his exploits in the trenches in the First World War. There were also memories of his Jowett car, and the house he had built on Top Lane, which was later demolished to make way for the new estate. Miss Gristwood lived in Main Street and used to bring her Dalmatian dog to school with her. He would lie by the fire with a pencil and paper in front of him and be told to do his lessons!

The school building (see **fig 12.1**) was heated by open fires, with the prefabricated extra classroom heated by a solid fuel stove. There were six little beds in the school, and the six youngest children would have a nap after lunch.

Milk was delivered to the school in $\frac{1}{3}$ pint bottles and given without charge to every child. In summer it could be warm which did not improve its flavour! In the winter there were times when it froze, and the frozen milk would stand an inch or more proud of the bottles with the tops blown off.

An annual visit by the dentist, who brought a treadle drill with him, and the daily spoonful of cod liver oil were not popular events! Not surprisingly however, nature walks and gardening were popular lessons, and like today, unusual events were remembered for many years: on one occasion a bullock got stuck in the pond in the field next door to the school and all the children sat on the wall to watch his rescue.

For many of the children who lived in the outlying farms it could be a long walk to school and back every day, and often jobs had to be done before and after school. One gentleman told us that he and his brothers and sisters had to creep into the loft to sleep, and had to be careful to close the trapdoor so that no-one fell out during the night! It was very cold in the winter, and too hot in the summer. One of the war-time tasks for the children was to pick the rose hips in the autumn, which were then sent off to make syrup for babies.

Summers were remembered as being warmer and sunnier than now, with outside play possible for most of the summer holidays. Winters were colder, with much more snow and ice. Snow ploughs were needed to clear the roads and drifts could be waist high. Long icicles would hang from gutters and 'Jack Frost' painted beautiful fernlike pictures on the insides of windows (no central heating then!) The snow ploughs, with other vehicles, were stored in the West Riding County Council depot, the entrance to which was in Main Street. The land was rented to the council by Henry Thomlinson, and Reg Hudson, the haulier, was involved in clearing the snow with the snowploughs every winter.

Going in to York in the 1920s was 'like going abroad'. In the days before Sykes started the bus service, people would walk to the station to catch the train. Jackson Hudson (see **fig 14.4**) remembered himself and his brothers arguing over which one of them would carry home the meat for his mother, as it felt like half a bullock. Not surprising considering it not only had to feed all the children, his parents, and three other men who worked on the farm, but it had to last all week!

As described in the chapter on Recreation and Leisure (chapter 13), there were several regular events in the village calendar. These included sports day, which predated Carnival, and was held in Main Street, with the finishing line by the Royal Oak pub (**fig 14.2**). (No problem in those days about closing the road!) There was also a fancy dress competition which took place on Low Green, at one time judged by Captain Riley who lived in Top Lane. Each year a May Queen was crowned, later superseded by the Carnival Queen.

Other memories of childhood involved playing with friends. There was no TV, computers or even, in the early days, radio (or wireless as it was called then). There were few toys or books, and those few were greatly treasured. Children did, however, have a lot of freedom to roam around the countryside, and people felt that there was a lot more wildlife to see. The pond life had special mention, with toads, frogs, sticklebacks, minnows and newts having been particularly popular.

As we have seen in the chapter on Recreation and Leisure (chapter 13), the Scouts and Guides have flourished in the village. Names that were recalled included Doreen Caunt, who after helping with the Brownies for a while became Brown Owl and continued for 29 years. Jean Hawthorne, who was her Tawny Owl, became Brown Owl of a second pack of Brownies and served for many years also. Fred Allan and Paddy Power (who was a PE teacher at St Peter's school) were involved with others in setting up and running the first youth club in the village.

The village fielded both cricket and football teams who competed against other villages, in the case of the football team in the Ainsty League. The football pitch was on a field in Horseman Lane, while the cricket pitch was behind the vicarage and extended up to the railway line and the bridge (**fig 14.3**). There were two big ponds in it, and a row of trees which

14.2 A Sports Day, forerunner to the present Carnival, showing Charlie Burton, dressed as a jockey, winning the Fancy Dress competition. To the right is Captain Riley who used to judge the competitions (nd, c 1950s) (Courtesy of Mary Driver)

FROM COPPENTHORPE TO COPMANTHORPE

were known for the cuckoo that used to perch in them to sing. In the days before the Recreation Centre was built, Mrs Allan would serve the cricket teas from a tent erected behind her house.

The Sunday School outing to Scarborough each year by train was quite a big occasion as trips out and holidays were less common in those days, and many of the adults went along as well. The last trip by train was in 1964 before the station closed. The Sunday School was run by Elsie Reed, who was very popular with the children. She lived in Hurton Villa with her brother Fred, and another sister, Edie. Fred, who served in the Machine Gun Corps in France during World War I, was the parish council chairman for many years (see **fig 14.7**). Their brother Alan, who had served in the Royal Flying Corps (see **fig 10.5**), lived in The Laurels and was the parish council chairman for many years. Their father was the Mr Reed of Reed and Allan, the decorators.

There were many memories of the dances, including the police dance held in Bishopthorpe. A lot of the young people from Copmanthorpe would attend that dance, going on their bikes, with Constable Gatenby, from Bishopthorpe, seeing them safely home afterwards. There were also recollections of old time music hall, badminton and tennis clubs and playing tennis at Mrs Blundy's house, or Mrs Johnson's (widow of Dr Johnson, who never practised in Copmanthorpe, but retired here). The Johnsons lived in the house called Broadlands which was later sold to the Raylor family (of Raylors Scaffolding). The Raylor family was very involved in amateur dramatics in the village and Eleanor Raylor also ran the Girls' Friendly Society.

Miss Lemare, who lived for a while in Ivy Cottage with a Miss Goodwin, was renowned for being very musical and conducted her own well-known orchestra. After Miss Goodwin died, Miss Lemare moved first to one of Blow's Cottages, and then to Askham Bryan.

Some families bought their first TV to watch the Coronation in 1953. Many neighbours gathered in each others homes to watch the ceremonies as few people owned their own set. There was a party on the village green for the children. The school children, under the direction of Miss Frost, were involved in planting the cherry trees in Horseman Lane which continue to flower beautifully each year.

Copmanthorpe was very much a farming village, with numerous farms in and around, so many of the memories were of the farmers, the horses, and the jobs which the children did before and after school, egg collecting being quite an important one. Some children also helped with milking, and enjoyed encouraging the calves to suckle by dipping their fingers in the milk and allowing the calves to suck them. People recall cats lining up in the milking parlour near the old Manor House waiting for Geoff Mason to direct a stream of milk across their faces: it was funny to watch them lick their paws as they wiped the milk from their fur! Less popular jobs were carrying in the sticks and coal for the fires, and carrying buckets of water from the farmhouses, as many of the cottages had no water supply.

The area where the shopping centre is now situated used to be occupied by barns, outbuildings and a fold yard belonging to Trowell House Farm. Next door to it, where the fish and chip shop and newsagents are now, was the house known as Copmanthorpe Manor. By this time it was divided into two cottages, the one nearest to the farm buildings being occupied by Miss Mary Thompson and her brother Bill, who worked for Ted

Bean at Manor Farm. After the house was demolished in the 1960s (see chapter 3), a petrol station occupied the site before it was replaced by the current shops. A second petrol station was situated in Main Street next to Copmanthorpe Motors. Harry and Geoff Dykes ran a motor repair business from a cottage at 8 Low Green and they also had a petrol pump.

There were some problems with flooding every winter near to the garage at the end of Main Street, caused by blockages in the open drainage gutters. Floods were also common in Horseman Lane and Hallcroft Lane where there was a pond. Reg Hudson would meet the school children at the flooded area in his tractor and transport them through the water so that they could get to school and home again.

Many children left school at the age of fourteen and went to work on the local farms. Jackson Hudson, who was born and brought up at Copmanthorpe Grange, had his first job in the 1930s at Woolas Hall (near Appleton Roebuck), then owned by the Green family (**fig 14.4**). He was paid seven shillings (35p) a week for the first year, which then went up to eight shillings (40p) a week in the second year. The wages were all paid at the end of the year and if the worker left before the end of the year he would not receive any pay! Hiring for farm labourers was held at Martinmas (11 November) in St Sampson's Square.

14.4 Jackson Hudson's family with other farm workers at Nova Scotia Farm, Acaster Malbis, 1914 (Courtesy of Jackson Hudson)

There was a lot of horse work in those days. Alaister Milner remembers the threshing machines and traction engines coming to the farms, and the early tractors: Marshall, Fordsons, Farmalls, and a Little Grey Fergy as Ferguson's were affectionately known. Many people in the village will remember coal being delivered by horse and cart, and the Beans' ponies, Trigger and Billy, with their milk floats. One pony knew his milk round so well that he would set off to the next house without the person delivering the milk if he thought things were taking too long! He also enjoyed the odd nibble of a rose bush or two as he passed.

Farmers (and others) would take their horses to be shod at Acaster Malbis or Askham Bryan, although in much earlier days there had been a blacksmith in Copmanthorpe, next to the Royal Oak pub, and also a smithy in Moor Lane. The blacksmith would sometimes visit the farms; Copmanthorpe Grange had its own little forge that he could use when he came.

14.5 Mary Driver (née Burton) walking cattle towards Low Green, assisted by her dog (nd, post-1945) (Courtesy of Mary Driver)

The street was always busy with horses, and gardeners were always ready with a bucket and shovel! Jack Holiday, who lived in Primrose Cottage, Main Street, was famous for his beautiful rose garden, well supplied with 'horse muck'! Sadly a garage now stands where his rose garden once was. The York and Ainsty Hunt used to meet on the village green. The cows from Manor Farm were driven along Main Street and over the railway bridge every morning and back every evening until the 1980s, providing another good source of manure for the local gardeners.

The village seemed to have two parts, 'the village' being centred on Main Street and 'the Drome' around Drome Road. The railway bridge was seen to mark the division of the two areas.

The Drome housed the Royal Flying Corps in wooden bungalows on concrete blocks, built like that as the area was prone to flooding because of the high water table. When the RFC left, people moved into the bungalows that had been used by them; four others bought plots of land and built their own – these included a Mr Collier and a Mr Colley (a tailor). Pat Bristowe remembers that when they were digging the foundations for new bungalows a huge number of boots were found – but all for one foot – no pairs! The people were known in the village as the Drome Smallholders. Later some brick houses were built, and a shop, whose owners were called Thompson; there was also a fish and chip shop at one time and Mrs Driver remembers the children singing a little rhyme, 'Jimmy Jonas, Jimmy Jonas, sells fish, don't buy it, don't buy it, it stinks when you fry it'! The hangar left by the RFC was used to store wood for the building projects. Unfortunately it burnt down one night and sadly, as it was not insured those people lost a lot of building materials. There were no mains services to that part of the village except water, the bungalows being lit by paraffin lamps.

Harry Hudson used to be involved in transporting goods and post around the villages and in and out of York. In the pursuit of his business he met Miss Annie Young who lived on Tadcaster Road in the house which later became St Leonard's Day Hospice. Her father owned horses and carriages

14.6   The Hudson family: George and Ruth (née Shipley) of Copmanthorpe Grange seated, with their children. Standing left to right are Hilda, May, Kate, Ted, Hannah and Bessie. The two boys seated with dogs are Jackson (left) and Pete (right). This photograph was taken at the Grange in the 1920s (Courtesy of Jackson Hudson)

which could be hired to transport people around the villages and town (**fig 14.6**). Harry and Annie married and lived in a cottage in Low Green. Their son, Reg, carried on the haulage and coal business and is remembered by many in the village. He was a well-known and cheerful face at the station where he collected his coal (see chapter 11).

Reg Hudson and Fred Reed were invited to a Royal Garden Party at Buckingham Palace to honour the forty years that they had each served on the parish council (**fig 14.7**).

Mr Starr, Doreen Caunt's father, used to live and work in Towton. During that time he would often have to drive cattle, by foot, from Tadcaster to York Cattle Market which was sited around the area where the Barbican Centre now stands. He was paid two shillings and sixpence (half a crown; 12½p) a week. The family moved to Copmanthorpe Grange when Doreen was two years old.

14.7   Fred Reed and his sister Elsie with Reg and Mary Hudson (right) attending a Buckingham Palace Garden Party (1960s) (Courtesy of Pat Bristowe)

The Scollet family lived in The Villa on Main Street (**fig 14.8**). One of the daughters, Molly, became a housekeeper for Bob Shaw at Croft Farm on Low Green. Her sister Kitty married Jim Burton. They farmed at Wilstrop Farm before moving to Holly House on Low Green; Holly House is still in the ownership of the family.

14.8   The Scollett and Bean families: Kitty Burton (née Scollett) stands at the back. On the seat left to right are Mrs Bean, Miss Jenny Bean and Mrs Scollett (nd, post-1945) (Courtesy of Mary Driver)

One individual who was mentioned was Miss Sonia Royle, who moved to Copmanthorpe with her mother in the early 1950s. They lived at No. 9 Church Street, Sonia remaining there until a couple of years before her death in 2006. Sonia and her family had a narrow escape in the Baedeker raid on York in April 1942. They lived at that time in Malton Way, Shipton Road, and had to take refuge in their air-raid shelter. Malton Way suffered considerable damage during the raid, because it was situated between Clifton Airfield and the main London to Edinburgh railway line, both of which were targeted by the bombers that night. Sonia joined the WAAF later in 1942, but in 1943 became one of several female drivers for Handley Page, the manufacturers of the Halifax bomber, who ran aircraft repair depots in Rawcliffe and Water Lane. She often drove to London and back in the day to collect components from the main factory in Cricklewood, and had many interesting stories to tell of coping with solitary journeys all over the country, often on bomb-damaged roads.

After the closure of Handley Page, Sonia worked for various organisations before establishing Royle's Secretarial Agency in York. She continued her interest in driving, and was quite an accomplished rally car driver.

The station was a very busy place. One of the pre-war station masters was called Charlie Tennant-Hudson, while another, Mr Duggleby, was seen as a very nice man, always smiling. The porter was called Arthur Kettley. The waiting room was always warm, with a lovely fire burning in the grate; the local 'copper' was usually to be found there, keeping himself warm! His bike would be left on the top of the bridge, unlocked, but never stolen! There was a footpath and wooden steps from the platform to the centre of the railway bridge. Many people used the station to travel to work and back and goods were brought to the village by rail. Some of the farm crops, such as sugarbeet, were transported out of the village by rail. A large amount of stone was delivered there for building the A64. At that time Reg Hudson employed as many as six men to transport the stone up to the road. Tom Richardson, the postman, would pick up the mail from the guard on the outward bound train each morning. Mr Sanderson (Ernie Sanderson's father) was in charge of the signal box and the crossing in Moor Lane. He would shout in a loud voice "Are you coming over or not? Look sharp." He would open the small gate to let the children cross on their way to and from school, or to swim in the pond (with the minnows, newts and leeches!). Another person remembered a second signalman called Mr Levitt. In 1964 the station was closed and sold to Reg Hudson for £5 on the understanding that he would demolish and remove it. This he did, using the materials to build a new home for his family at No. 2 Low Green. In order to do this, four cottages, owned by him, were demolished. They were of the same style as several other groups of cottages in the village at that time, of which only Blow's Cottages (opposite the Co-op store) now remain. Before 1904 the cottages were owned by Allans of Ivy House Farm; this farm was later sold to the Wiseman family and it was Alf Wiseman who donated the land to build the Recreation Centre.

Another interesting relic of the old station was the station clock which was bought by Ernie Sanderson (well known for his wonderful photographic record of the village), and was on the wall of his house in Moor Lane for many years.

Copmanthorpe was a small village until relatively recently. The 30mph signs delineating the built-up area were on the side of the school wall in Horseman Lane, at the bottom of the railway bridge in Station Road, just into Moor Lane, and where School Lane turns into Manor Heath. Some of the earliest 'new buildings' were the council houses in Horseman Lane and the police houses in School Lane. Sergeant Long and Constable Widdieson lived in those houses and had their own little police station and cell there.

In spite of the village's small size, there were several shops and (in keeping with the name of our village) trades people. The Post Office used to be in the shop in Church Street which is now the butcher's shop. It was kept by two sisters, the Misses Thorpe, and later by Molly Thompson (née Hobson) who was their niece. There were brass scales on the counter, and large glass jars full of sweets, which were sold to the children in twists of paper. The post office later moved to No. 10 Main Street, thought to be one of the oldest houses in the village.

Matt Thomlinson, the butcher, lived in Holly House (later occupied by the Burton family). His shop was at the front and the slaughter house was in the buildings at the back of the house. The slaughter man, who was called Willis Dykes, lived in Rose Cottage in School Lane. The business was later moved into the shop attached to the Royal Oak pub. Later again it moved to the back part of the Mace shop which became Costcutter. Matt's son, Henry, continued the business. The shop which was vacated by the butchers became Atkinson's greengrocers, and is now used as a store for the pub.

Mrs Conyers lived in a cottage in Main Street, and the newspapers were delivered from there by her son, Lionel. He was renowned for enjoying a chat, and would say 'nice day' to everyone he passed. The newsagents was later run from No. 8 Main Street (**fig 14.9**), and was owned by Mrs Bean (sister-in-law of Ted Bean who owned Manor Farm next door). The house and business were later bought by Mr and Mrs Stan Oates, and Mrs Oates ran the shop for many years.

14.9 No. 8 Main Street, at one time Mrs Oates' newsagents shop (early 20th century) (Courtesy of Mary Driver)

Mr Jarratt was the landlord of the Ginger Beer House, which at one time occupied the original Fox and Hounds building (see chapter 13). It was he who bought the old Primitive Methodist building and turned it into a grocer's shop. (That building later became the Co-op, and was then demolished when the modern Co-op was built on the site.) Mr and Mrs Temple worked in the shop, as did Mr Jarratt's son, Stanley. Sadly, Stanley Jarratt was later killed in the war. Mr Jarratt, who was also known for keeping whippets, used to walk down to the shop every day to collect the takings.

❦

Jackie and Alaister Milner discovered recently that their cottage in Main Street had also been a shop in the past. They saw some people looking at the cottage who, they discovered, were visitors from the USA. The visitors were trying to identify the cottage for neighbours of theirs who had an old photograph showing some of their ancestors standing outside it in about 1897. The cottage at that time was a shop, and items for sale can be seen in the right-hand window (**fig 14.10**). In its more recent past the cottage was owned by Mr Masterman of Ivy House Farm, and later still by Mr Raylor who bought it for his gardener to live in.

14.10 No. 18 Main Street: Christopher and Isabella Woodward with their daughter Alice Anderson. At this time (*c* 1897) the cottage was also a shop – note the display in the right-hand window (Courtesy of Alaister and Jackie Milner)

❦

When the Wesleyan Methodist chapel (see chapter 5) closed in Church Street, it became a fruit and vegetable shop for a little while, called Millers. It then became Mr and Mrs Cussan's DIY shop. It is now the store room for the new Co-op. Both Mrs Oates and Mrs Cussans were well known for being helpful to everyone, and welcoming to new people in the village.

There were three joiners in the village, all called Fred! They were Fred Forth, Fred Allan and Fred Milner. There were also three builders, Charlie Parkinson and Son, Eric Kneeshaw and Son, and Bill Storey. Mr Storey lived at the back of Paddock's House and owned garages to let and a builder's yard there. Stan Oates was the painter and decorator.

The village bus stop and the telephone box were originally sited on a small area outside the barn of Ivy House Farm but this piece of land has now been incorporated into the garden of the farmhouse. The early street lights were lit and extinguished by hand, at one time by Fred King, and later by Ron Hudson and then his nephew, Tony.

There used to be farm buildings followed by a row of cottages belonging to Wilstrop Farm which ran from Main Street to Back Lane. The alley they were situated in was called Washing Tub Alley. Another unusual name which has disappeared is Doctor Lane, which was situated roughly where Yorkfield Lane is now, and ran from Yorkfield House to the railway line. Snipe, which are ground-nesting birds, used to nest in that area.

Some things don't change – Mr Oates remembers that a mistle thrush used to sing in the trees of the vicarage garden, and one still sings there today. Similarly, swifts still nest in the eaves of the old post office in Main Street.

There were many memories of the Second World War. It was felt by most that rationing was slightly less of a problem here than for those who lived in the towns, since there was more opportunity for people to produce food for themselves, and to 'trade' with one another, swapping excess vegetables or eggs, or even meat if a pig had been slaughtered.

There was a local Home Guard which used to drill in the yard at Yedmondale, on Low Green, every Sunday morning. The Captain of the local Home Guard was called Mr Wood. He had three daughters, the youngest of which, Daphne, became secretary to the Archbishop of York while another, Ruth, sadly died of cancer as a teenager. The brick building on the cricket field which was used by the Home Guard was later used to store the cricket equipment. Quite a few of the men who worked on the farms were members of the Home Guard, as farming was a reserved occupation [ie the men were not called up for National Service].

Mrs Daniel, who moved into the right-hand side of the ancient building known as the old Manor House with her family in 1933, remembers the school children being taken across the road to some trenches which had been dug in Masons' field. They were drilled regularly, and had to practise donning their gas masks and lining up in the 'holes'. The children did not really understand what it was all about, and Mrs Daniels doesn't remember the trenches ever being used for any purpose.

Mrs Daniel also witnessed the mid-air collision of two bombers one Saturday morning. She and her sister were on their way to the railway station with their mother when they heard a grinding noise and looked up to see the planes begin to fall. Her mother yelled "come to mother" and she threw the two children to the ground underneath her. Fortunately both planes missed the village: one fell in the fields behind Moor Lane, and the other nearer to the A64, but fourteen young men died that day. As their train pulled out of the village the girls and their mother could see two black columns of smoke rising into the air.

Another memory is of German and Italian prisoners of war working on the farms. The Italians seemed young and wanted to say 'hello' but the Germans were less friendly and had big patches sewn onto their clothes. Mrs Daniels states that 'they dug a big ditch near the woods, and ruined our bramble patch for years!'

There used to be a derelict old cottage opposite where the Co-op shop is now which was used by the fire and emergency services to practise rescuing people from the upper floor. They left it in an even more dilapidated state and it was demolished after the war.

Fred Allan (of Reed and Allan) was, at one time in his military service, involved in repairing and making seaworthy some of the 'little boats' used in the Dunkirk rescue.

People watched in horror on the night that York was bombed. The fires could be seen from Copmanthorpe, and Michael Unwin's father, who was part of the Royal Observer Corp, was on duty in York on that night.

In common with most of the country, there was a street party to celebrate the end of the war.

At one time, the vicar and church wardens would meet before Christmas to decide how to disperse money left in several small charitable funds to be given to the poor of the parish. Michael Unwin was part of that group in the days when Mr Fowler was the vicar. Initially the help would be given in kind, commonly bags of coal, flour and sugar; later people were given the cash to use as they wished. The amounts were small, and eventually this charitable activity ended. He remembered that the little group would meet in a small room in the vicarage which was always very cold!

Our contributors have seen many changes in the village, some more welcome than others. It has been sad to see some of the vandalism and littering and noisy, aggressive behaviour but most people still find the village a friendly and busy little community and value all the activities and the way that the two churches work together so well. The increased population has been more than most people would have liked, but has probably enabled Copmanthorpe to keep the variety of shops and services which we enjoy and which many villages have lost.

We are grateful to the following people who have contributed their memories to make this chapter possible.

Mrs Betty Allan

Mrs Pat Bristowe (née Hudson)

Miss Joan Burton

Mrs Doreen Caunt

Mrs Patricia Daniel (née Everard)

Mrs Mary Driver (née Burton)

Miss Frances Frost

Mr Jackson Hudson

Mr William Kendall

Mr Alaister Milner and Mrs Jackie Milner

Mr Stan Oates

Mrs Betty Royle

Mr Michael Unwin and Mrs Dorothy Unwin

Appendix: Field Names

DAVID BREWER

Introduction

There are over 100 different names used to describe the fields, groups of fields, and divisions of fields in the parish of Copmanthorpe. In addition there are nearly 100 variations of these names. Some go back to the very earliest documents which are associated with the Knights Templar. Others are much more recent, appearing for the first time in the Tithe Award of 1840, although they may have existed long before that date. Although many of these names do survive and are in use to this day, the trend has been for fields to become known mainly by their acreage. The first sign of this was in the Tithe Award where Fifteen Acres is the first quantitative name for a field.

When trying to decide why an area or field was given a particular name it has been invaluable to be able to identify most of the locations, either directly from maps such as that of 1722, or indirectly from the large volume of wills and other documents. These have confirmed that field names in this area have survived for centuries with little more than variations in spelling, such as Phillip Ruddings which goes back to Phillip Ryddynges in 1308. Some of the spelling variations probably reflect the fact that most of the documents would have been written by non-residents of Copmanthorpe such as solicitors, surveyors, land agents, or their clerks. These 'foreigners' may well have struggled to understand what an uneducated resident was saying, especially as the local would be speaking in their own version of Yorkshire dialect, but the local may have been the only source for some of these names. This was the strategy adopted by the Ordnance Survey, who compiled 'Name Books' for every county; these books gave details of all the names for local features which had been given to the surveyors by local residents. Sadly the Name Books for England were destroyed during World War II. Some names have been quite difficult to trace backwards, and it would not have been possible without knowledge of the locations referred to. One example is Cogg Garths: to interpret the meaning of this one needs to know that dovecotes were originally located in this area.

It is perhaps necessary to point out that although the meanings given are educated guesses based on the substantial amount of information available, some are more reliable than others; in some cases more than one meaning may be interpreted from any one name, and all or none of them may actually be 'correct'. Generally, the older the reference material the more likely it is that the meaning deduced for a name is credible. A basic rule seems to be that if in doubt, the field name is probably derived from a personal name and at least 30 of the field names are believed to be in this category.

A debt of gratitude must be expressed to Paul Cavill from the Institute for Name-Studies in the School of English Studies at the University of Nottingham, for his advice and guidance during the compilation of this list of possible meanings for field and associated names.

Copmanthorpe parish: Field Names and their possible meanings

Abbreviations

ME	Middle English
OE	Old English
OFr	Old French
ON	Old Norse
O Scand	Old Scandinavian
pn	personal name

Balke 1640; OE balca or ON balkr = partition; unploughed area, usually between ridges or furlongs

Bell's Closes 1811; *pn* eg Thomas Bell 1811

Blakewood 1558; OE blaec = black or bleak; land covered with gorse or heath was called black land to distinguish it from cultivated land

Bolton Close 1722; *pn* ?

Bond Hill 1647; ON bondi = peasant, but free; variations include **Bondell Flatt** 1678, **Bondale** 1746; **Bundles** and **Bundles Ash** 1840

Bottoms 1712; OE botm = valley, usually with a stream

Brecks 1722; OE braec = brake or thicket, strip of uncultivated land; var
Bricks 1811 & 1840

Brocket Wood 1548; OE brocc = badger; the -et might signify 'place
characterised by badgers'; may also mean deer. This Wood is adjacent to Phillip Ruddings but is now in Appleton Roebuck parish; var
Brockit Wood 1640

Broome Close 1643; OE brom = a coarse shrub; this term included
gorse, heather, holly and butcher's broom and is the origin of the
common name, broom, for *planta genista*. This was also the origin of
Plantagenet as the family name of the English Kings from Henry II
as their emblem was broom

Burchhous Flatt 1722; could be exactly as it sounds, or possibly means
'the place where birch brooms were made'

Butts 1811; ME butte = end-pieces of the open field; it could also have
been the area set aside for archery practice. Butts was an area in York
Field identifiable by Butts Drain in the 1843 Enclosure Award

Buxtyhurst 1640; ON buskr = bushy + OE hyrst = copse/wood; var
Buckstyhirst 1678, **Buskey Hirsts** 1722; **Bushey Hirsts** 1813,
Busky Husks 1840

BySteades 1722; by the steading (farmstead) from OE stede = place; var
Barsteads Flatt 1811

Campy Croft 1840; *pn* eg Francis Campey in 1807

Carr 1664; OE ker from Norse kjarr = marsh, low lying ground

Cat Tail 1840; identified as a long thin field, but it could also refer to
timothy grass, *Phleum pratense*, which was also known as cat's tail

Cawkers Furlong 1664; ships were 'caulked' using oakum, the coarse
woody fibres (tow) separated from flax and hemp which were both
grown here; var **Coaker Flatt** 1746, **Cokers** 1746

Chare Ends 1643; this was the turning point at the end of the
flatt/furlong

Close 1558; ME from OFr clos, ultimately from Latin clausum =
enclosure

Close of Mr Laycock 1664; *pn*

Cock Garths 1664; this may be a progression from Dovecoate Garth.
Some of the dovecotes are known to have been in this particular area.
Dove + OE cot = a small shelter for livestock especially pigeons, so
Dovecot Garths, shortened to Cot Garths, to Cock Garths and even-
tually to **Cogg Garths** in 1722

Colton Hagg Intack 1640; ME Hag is probably from ON hogg = clearing, but is also associated with moor or peat bog. This land was taken in (see **Intacks**) from High and Low West Fields adjacent to Colton Hagg in the next parish called Colton.

Copper Nooke Furlong 1664; may derive from the village name *or* could refer to the colour of the soil

Crabb Tree Flatts 1643; Crab apple trees no doubt grew there – a common tree in hedges

Croft 1626; an enclosed field usually attached to a house and worked by the occupier; note, it is not the house itself

Crookergate 1643; ME crok from ON krokr = crook or bend + ON gata = road. This name occurs in both High and Low West Fields and the division between them in 1722 is decidedly crooked so the access road between them would fit this description

Crosse Land Furlong 1664; not all furlongs were arranged in the same direction; var **Crossland Flatt** 1722

Damsell Gate Furlong 1664; Damsel can imply association with the Blessed Virgin Mary which is appropriate as at least part of this furlong was owned by the church for a significant period. This becomes **Damsell Gate Flatt** in 1678 and is **Damsell Flatt** in 1746

Dogge Closes 1678; may be an indication of very poor land *or* could indicate land full of couch-grass which was known as dog-grass or dog-tails. It was called this because *triticum canimum* was (and still is!) eaten by dogs to cause vomiting. Possibly *pn*

Doughty Close 1840; *pn* eg Robert Doughty 1606

Dovecoate Garth 1664; two dovecotes are known to have existed – see **Cock Garth**

Dunfield Nooke Close 1651; OE dun = dull greyish brown colour, or it could mean horse. In context it seems to develop into **Dowfits** 1722 and 1840

Earthwayte 1651; ON 'ar = by the river + ON thveit = clearing; var **Earthyts** 1662, **Earthwaite** 1664, **Earthwayts** 1664, **Earthwaits** 1712, **Harwit** 1716, **Earfitts** 1722, **Earthwaits** 1746, **Earfitts** 1811

Elve Wood 1840; where else would elves be!

Eshelby Close 1840; *pn* eg Edward Exelby 1840

Fawcet's Croft 1840; *pn* eg Anne Fawcett 1840

Feild 1640; **High** (Upper 1643) and **Low** (Lower 1643) **West Feild**, **York Feild** and **Temple Feild** (note the spelling of feild) are the Open fields of Copmanthorpe. Derives from OE feld = large tract of open country, as opposed to woodland

Fentons Close 1640; *pn* eg William Fenton 1560; var **Fentons Cow Pasture** 1678, **Fenton Close** 1722, but reverts to **Fenton Pasture** 1811

Field Close 1722; close taken from one of the fields

Fifteen Acres 1840; was this the beginning of the end for proper names for individual fields?

Fisher Close 1840; *pn* eg William Fisher 1722

Flatt 1664; from ON flatr. This was a group of strips in the open fields and is interchangeable with furlong in the records for Copmanthorpe

Fosse Close 1626; enclosure near the Foss. OE foss = ditch

Foss Crouke Close 1640; a curve/bend in the Foss – see Crookergate; var **Fosse Crooke** 1678

Fousegale 1643; see **Foxgales**

Foxgales 1664; in 1664 this area is shown as **Foulskills** alias **Foxgales**, and may have been previously referred to as **Fousegale** in 1643 and becomes **Fuskills** in 1813. Of the many possible explanations the most likely is that it was actually a personal name. Georgius Foxgale, sadler, and Antonius Foxgale, innholder, are admitted to the Freedom of York around 1600

Frying Close 1722; this was a wet part of **Earthwaytes** so the ing could indicate it was liable to inundation (see **Little Yng Close**), but the fry is less certain. The shape of the original field does resemble a frying pan which may explain why it becomes **Frying Pan Close** in 1779, then **Frying Pan** in 1840

Furlong 1664; OE furh = furrow + lang = long. Originally thought to be the distance a team of oxen could pull a plough without a rest. As this depended on so many variables it was not a reliable length, but it eventually became what we now know as one eighth of a mile. However, it was also a measure of area, again originally related to what the team of oxen could achieve. By the time of this written record Flatt and Furlong are interchangeable in Copmanthorpe, with both just meaning a group of strips in the open field

Fuskills 1813; see **Foxgales**

Gares 1678; OE gara = triangular plot of ground. In this context it was the irregular part of the plot remaining when the main rectangle of the plot had been worked

Garth 1643; ON garthr = yard or enclosure associated with a dwelling, developing into the word garden

Gil Crofts 1664; O Scand gil = land in, near or containing a narrow valley *or* in this area it could be a personal name but no Gills are known to have lived in Copmanthorpe

Great Snapes 1640; OE snaep = marshy land; var **Great & Little Snapes** 1678, **Snape Close** 1722, **Snipe Lease** 1722 (see Temple Lease), **Snake Style** 1779 (see **Wormhills**), **Snipe Lees** 1840

Greyne Gaites 1558; OE grene = green, notably a green piece of land + O Scand gata = road or street. The old green lanes did have associated grazing rights so this may refer to that. The term Gate progressed in this context to mean general grazing rights usually on common land

Hall Croftes 1626; the Crofts associated with the Hall, although by this date the Hall is believed to be in another location. However, it is also possible that the name is derived from OE halh = nook, corner or fragment of land. At one time High West Field would have extended nearly to the original Town Street, but as garths and crofts were taken from this open field, this piece of land eventually became a detached corner of High West Field, hence halh

Hall Intacke 1651; quoted as the Intack behind the Hall. This field was located in the area to the east of today's Ivy House Farm

Hargeryes Furlong 1664; personal name relating to Margaret or Marjorie?

Hassiker 1643; OE hassuc = coarse grass or sedge such as occurs in boggy ground *or* it could be a combination of OE haes = brush-wood + either ME ker (marshy land) or ME aecer (plot of land); var **Hassock Flatt** 1664, **Hasacres** 1722, **Hassakers** 1746, **Hasicar Flatt** 1811, **Hasacre Flatt** 1813

Haver Croft 1678; ON hafri = oats

Hawkills 1722; hill where hawks may be flown

High West Field – *see* **Field**

High Close 1722; this was the highest enclosure to the south of Low West Field; var **Eye Close** 1840

High Croft 1722; refers to the position, being near the highest point in the parish

Hill 1647; OE hyll = raised area of land. Most of the area around Copmanthorpe is very flat, so any undulation would qualify as a hill!

Hollyn Hill 1840; OE holegn = holly, an important source of winter fodder; the higher leaves are not so prickly so it was collected and fed to the animals at a time when there was very little fresh food for them

Houlsworth Close 1640; *pn* from the tenant in 1640 Mr Hawkswourth?

Hullay Close 1840; *pn* Widd Hullay 1796

Hulley Croft 1840; *pn* Mary Hulley 1840, a descendant of widow Hullay?

Intacks 1651; ON intack = land taken in (from the open field) and enclosed; var **Great Intake** 1678

John Close 1840; *pn* – there have been many Johns. This area previously part of Orthwaite

Kirkby Farm 1712; *pn* eg Matthew & Thomas Kerkby 1678; var **Kirkby Close** 1840

Lamb Croft 1840; *pn* John Lamb 1808

Leayes 1664; see **Temple Leayes**

Lightfoot Close 1643; *pn*

Little Yng Close 1558; ON eng = meadow/pasture especially by a stream and subject to inundation; becomes Ings; var **Town Ings** 1712, **Far Town Ings** 1722

Long Croft 1626; descriptive – it is long and narrow

Long Land Flatt 1813; presumably descriptive, but not the same plot as above

Low Briggs 1722; OE brycg = bridge, or stream crossing; this is near the Foss in the area where the footpath crosses the Foss to Bishopthorpe

Low West Field – *see* **Feild**

Lyne Barker's Furlong 1664; *pn*

Matthew Close 1643; *pn* – there have been many Matthews

Milne Reding 1678; ME milne = Mill + reding = cleared land; var **Mill Rudings** 1722, **Mill Ruddings** 1811

Mill Hill Flatt 1722; presumed to be the area in York Field where a windmill stood

Moor (East & West) 1640; OE mor = waste/barren land, tending to be wet; var **Moore Close** 1643

Nooke 1651; ME noke = land in a secluded corner

Orthwayte 1651; the Or is a regular development from ON 'ar = by the river, so Orthwayte and **Earthwayte** (see earlier) both mean clearing by the river, but have developed slightly differently perhaps to avoid confusion (see separate locations on the 1722 map); var **Orthwaite Carr** 1664, **Orth-waites** 1678, **Orthwaites** 1678, **Orfitts** 1722, **Orfits** 1840

Oxmoure Close 1584; oxen were the main draught animal

Park 1308; originally this was a legal term designating land held by royal grant for hunting or as a pleasure ground and would have been enclosed, unlike open forest

Pasture Laine 1640; could be the lane to the pasture (**Fenton Pasture** in this case), but as it is let out separately it is perhaps the lane itself that is the pasture – see **Greyne Gaites**; var **Pasture Lane** 1815 and becomes **Smithers Close** 1840

Petty Close 1722; ME petty = small (from French petit) but in 1722 these two closes were not particularly small! Could be a personal name; var **Petty Pasture** 1840 describes the same fields

Phillip Ryddynges 1308; Phillip may have been a member of the Fauconberg family who owned land in the area; (Philip de Faukenberg, Charter Roll of 1252). Ryddynge is from OE Rydyng = cleared land; var **Phillip Redings** 1678, **Phillip Rudings** 1722, **Phillip Ruddings** 1811

Pinder Close 1722; OE pundere = land allocated to the keeper of the parish pound (to house stray animals)

Puck Close 1840; probably a (fanciful) misunderstanding by an outsider of how the locals pronounced **Park Close** as that is what it had previously been called (see **Elve Wood** also in 1840)

Randall Snape 1647; *pn* + OE snaep = marshy land (as it no doubt was, being next to the Foss)

Rose Park 1640; Rose may come from the important local family called Ros, and could even be named after Roese Ros from the 12th century. It may also indicate the presence of wild roses. It is in the area thought to be referred to in 1308 as the **Park** (see earlier). In 1678 part of this is enclosed and called **Rose Park Intake**, which becomes **Park Close** in 1722 and **Puck Close** in 1840

Sandhill 1647; as it sounds?

Sandwith 1558; Sand + with, from ON vithr = wood. This referred to land held in the area between Bilbrough and Healaugh which is the location of the lost village of Sandwith

Sedgepitts 1722; sedge is a common grass type of wet areas. The 'pits' may have been natural or it is possible that they were created to encourage sedge growth for thatching; var **Segpits** 1813

Shaghe 1308; thought to be from OE sceaga = land near or containing a copse

Short Moor Gripps 1643; ME grip from OE gryp = open furrow or drainage ditch, so literally the short drainage ditches on the Moor. The word Grip is still used on the North York Moors, but now

From Coppenthorpe to Copmanthorpe

usually refers to the drainage channels at right angles to country lanes; var **Short Moor Grip Furlongs** 1722

Smithers Close 1840; associated with the blacksmith. In 1840 this field is adjacent to Copmanthorpe Lodge so it is possible that there was a smithy there for the farm

Spring Close 1678; in OE spring could either mean the source of a stream, or a plantation. Either could apply in this case as it is next to Copmanthorpe Wood; var **Spring Ruding** 1640

Stinting 1813; from stint as in restrict; a stinting was an individual's share of common meadow

Stony Land Over Furlong 1664; literally the far furlong on the stony land; becomes **Stone Flat** in 1746

Streetgate Flatt 1746; the 'street' in this case was the York to Tadcaster Turnpike road – the gate was across the end of what is now Top Lane, the Flatt was in Yorkfield to the south of the Street Gate

Stumpcross Flatt 1678; ME stump and OE cros are both associated with boundary stones. In this case Stumpcross Flatt is near to the point where the boundaries of five parishes meet, which also coincides with the 3-mile milestone from York; becomes **Bondhill flat**

Temple Field – *see* **Feild**

Temple Lease 1640; Temple from the Knights Templar connection with Copmanthorpe + OE laes for pasture or meadow; var **Temple Leayes** 1664, Temple **Lees** 1678, **Temple Lees** and **Lease** 1722

The Gale 1643; Bog myrtle, locally known as Gale from OE gagel, would have been common in the wet areas of Temple Field where this was located. Gale Beer was a popular local brew! Var **Gale Lane** 1664

The Paddock 1643; a small field or enclosure

Towler Tofte Furlong 1664; Towler, probably the surname of the tenant, is thought to derive from OE tollere = toll collector, which could be relevant here as it is in York Field which is next to the York to Tadcaster Turnpike road. This idea is further supported by the fact that the name changes to **Towler Tofts** 1722, **Toll Tofts** 1811, then back to **Towler Tofts Furlong** in 1813. Toft is from Old Scandinavian 'topt' meaning ground attached to a house, so does this indicate that the collector of tolls also had his homestead there? If so this is the very first mention of any dwelling outside the confines of the village

Townend Flatts 1722; the Flatts at the end of the township

Tyth Meadow 1651; approx one tenth of this particular plot, **Hall Intacke**, was owned by the Church at this date

Upper Sike 1643; ON sik = stream or drainage channel, which then gave its name to meadow land beside a stream, which it was

West Dikes 1722; a Flatt in Temple Field, presumably near the west dike

Whin Bed 1815; whin = gorse + OE bedd = an area of ground where flowers/plants are grown. Gorse, as well as growing wild, was actually cultivated and had many uses, such as winter fodder/fuel/dye/chimney brushes

Wibargarth 1626; *pn ?* + Garth

Wood Bridge Flatt 1722; in Temple Field, presumably near the bridge to the wood which may have gone over Wood Dike

Wood Dikes 1643; a Flatt in Temple Field presumably near Wood Dike, with the wood being just to the south of Temple Field; var Woodyke Flatt 1746

Wood End 1722; at the end of Hagg Wood

Wood Nook 1722; this is in a very secluded corner (see Nooke) near Hagg Wood

Wood Riddinge 1626; clearing near the wood

Wormhills 1640; OE wyrm = snake (adder, slow-worm and grass-snake may all have been present) + hills. It is also possible that it could refer to the wyrm or dragon of folklore, the Nunington Worm being one of the most notorious! This idea is supported by the shape of the 'hill' in this area which may have been thought of as the Dragon's lair; it would have been a notable feature before hedges had been planted

Wrenkers 1643; *pn?* ON vrengill = something bent + kjarr = marsh, so marsh on a bend which in this case may be a bend in the road between High and Low West Field as it is mentioned in the same context as **Crookergate** (see earlier) which may be the name of this road

York Field – *see* **Feild**

Yorkside Closes 1811; to the west side of York Field